Unsung Stories of Black Wome

CH01431886

"This book is based on archival material, interviews, and poetry from members of Manchester's Abasindi Black Women's Cooperative. The authors—activists and academics, Adele Jones and Diana Watt are both simultaneously architects of, and witnesses to, this piece of history. Their authenticity has equipped them to deliver a highly informed, well-referenced, compassionate, and novel perspective on the lives and impact of their sisters. The book's 8 chapters are well sequenced and cover a wide range of concepts, all of which skilfully explore the juncture of feminism and anti-racism from both a global and local perspective. This book speaks to everyone and is as well placed in libraries and classrooms as on coffee tables. You don't just read '*Unsung Stories*', you savour it. You will want to dip in and out as the mood takes you—be it to fuel your activism, free your soul, calm your spirit or just soak up the beautiful images of the women and families making history".

—Professor Carol Baxter, *Hon Professor, Imperial College London, UK*

"The book is excellent and very much needed today, especially in light of the ways in which a number of human rights are being shaken and stripped away by a racist, anti-immigrant, and anti-Black political climate. It provides an historical insight into Black women's activism in the UK particularly, in the North of England which is often erased in discussions of Black British (women's) history. It records and celebrates how Black women fought to create a space for community engagement, a space to be seen and loved in a hostile, politically, and socially challenging environment. This book serves as a guiding light for future Black activists in the UK, to help them continue the fight against oppressions in all their various forms, in a sustainable and cooperative way".

—Dr Opemiposi Adegbulu, *Lecturer in Law, Robert Kennedy College, Switzerland*

"This vital collection of reflections, analysis, and interviews around the work and history of Abasindi rescues the Black British experience from both its male and London-centred distortions. In so doing it celebrates and contextualises the important work of so many Black women in Manchester both as artists and activists while broadening our understanding of what resistance can look like and who is driving it".

—Professor Gary Andrew Younge, *Award-winning author, broadcaster,*
and Professor of Sociology, The University of Manchester, UK

"This book is a gem and a joy to read. It makes a crucial contribution to the filling of a yawning gap in literature on the intellectual and political history of Black women in Britain by making visible the valuable contribution of organisations such as Abasindi in supporting women of colour and their families through racial aggression, poverty, and institutional hostility. It should be recommended reading for all educators at every level—by excavating the history of Abasindi and its women, the authors simultaneously highlight and address the epistemic injustice that pervades knowledge production—and thus undermines justice in practice—in Britain and around the world".

—Professor Iyiola Solanke, *Jacques Delors Chair in European Law, University of Oxford, UK*

"This book is an invaluable and long overdue contribution to the history of Black feminist activism in the UK. Based on archival material, interviews, and poetry from members of Manchester's Abasindi Black Women's Cooperative, and analysing contemporary issues that impact Black women, their families and communities, it is a timely and necessary contribution to the UK's Black feminist archive".

—Shirley Anne Tate, *Associate Professor in Race and Culture, and Director, Centre for Ethnicity and Racism Studies, University of Leeds, UK*

"This book has made visible the often-hidden history of Black women's activism and grassroots organising against injustice and oppression. It offers detailed and grounded testimonies from Black women involved in a range of struggles and brings together gender politics and anti-racism activism to deepen our understandings of the key role that they have played, and continue to play, in shaping the history of Black people in Britain. This is an inspiring, powerful, and uplifting book that pays tribute to the courage and strength of Black women and is a welcome addition to the literature on Black people's historical legacies".

—Professor Claudia Bernard, *Goldsmiths, University of London, UK*

"This book is a praisesong for the women who founded, organised, and developed the Abasindi Women's Cooperative. It is also a coherent and forceful critique of a society and economic system that seek to undermine Black lives and deny our self-actualisation. Adele Jones and Diana Watts have cogently shown how the Abasindi women employed the personal and political in a radical liberatory stance. They also reveal the similarity of Black experience in White-dominated societies in terms of economic disadvantage, the racialisation of poverty, the alarming drop-out rate of Black high school students, the criminalisation of young Black men, and the placement of Black children in care. The book thus has an international appeal and can be used in comparative studies of the Black experience. This book is powerful. I wholeheartedly recommend it".

—Professor Afua Cooper, *James Robinson Johnston Endowed Chair in Black Canadian Studies, Dalhousie University, Canada*

Adele Jones • Diana Watt

Unsung Stories of Black Women's Activism in the UK

Spirits of Resistance and Resilience

Second Edition

Springer

Adele Jones
Department of Behavioural Sciences
The University of Huddersfield
Huddersfield, UK

Diana Watt
Louise Da-Cocodia Education Trust
Manchester, UK

ISBN 978-3-031-64200-5   ISBN 978-3-031-64201-2   (eBook)
https://doi.org/10.1007/978-3-031-64201-2

1st edition: © Authors 2015

This Springer imprint is published by the registered company Springer Nature Switzerland AG
The registered company address is: Gewerbestrasse 11, 6330 Cham, Switzerland

If disposing of this product, please recycle the paper.

The cover photograph is taken from a vigil organised by the Abasindi Black Women's Cooperative (see Chap. 1) held in commemoration of the Black young people who lost their lives in a fire at a birthday party in New Cross, London. The blaze, on 18 January 1981, killed thirteen young people; twenty-seven people were injured, and one survivor committed suicide two years later. The inquest into the deaths recorded an open verdict, but many Black people were of the view that the fire was caused by a racially motivated arson attack and this tragic event is often referred to as the New Cross Massacre. Darcus Howe described the fire as 'the blaze we cannot forget … [and which] marks an intergenerational alliance to expose racism, injustices and the plight of Black Britons' (2011) (see Chap. 7 for more on this). https://woodsmokeblog.files.wordpress. com/2017/10/1981-bufp-new-cross-massacre.pdf. The photograph features Black women activists (from left to right) Abina Likoya, Joy Smith, and Shirley Inniss. Abina— singer, musician, and artist was an anchor for the Abasindi Black Women's Cooperative (the source of this book) for over thirty years, Joy was an Abasindi member and Shirley Inniss was one of the organisation's founders.

It is vital that Black women sing their stories into existence otherwise history will treat us as if we are the backcloth for someone else's design. This book asserts that the Black woman is 'plot' not 'plot-space' and as we sing our activism into the history books, we hope that social justice activists around the world will add their own harmonies.

Preface

This book was first published by Trentham Books, Institute of Education, University College London in 2015, under the title 'Catching Hell and Doing Well: Black Women in the UK—the Abasindi Cooperative'.

Discourses on race and gender inequality have changed in the years since the book was first published and this new edition has been updated to reflect some of these changes. ***Unsung Stories of Black Women's Activism in the UK: Spirits of Resistance and Resilience*** still draws its primary sources from the work of the Abasindi Black Women's Cooperative (see Chap. 1) but also includes new material that weaves hidden histories with contemporary realities. For example, we discuss the UK's Windrush Scandal and the marginalisation of Black women in migration stories; we explore the call for slavery reparations, given new impetus by the #BlackLivesMatter movement and we do this by forefronting the experiences of the enslaved woman (see Chap. 4). In our chapter on body politics (Chap. 5) we set our experiences as Black British women within an international context and discuss the analogies between two Black South African women: Saartjie Baartman and Caster Semenya who were both subjected to dehumanising treatment because their bodies did not conform to hegemonic views of womanhood. These women's experiences are separated by two hundred years and yet the parallels provide a stark reminder of the continued pervasiveness of race and gender discrimination. Semenya's case also reminds us of the importance of celebrating Black women's resilience and achievements. An outstanding athlete (required to undergo degrading invasive tests and take testosterone-reducing medication in order to compete with other women), Semenya's successful legal challenge against the world's governing athletics organisation in the European Court of Human Rights (July 2023) vindicates her contention that she had been discriminated against. This landmark victory is not only important for Semenya but benefits others too, since it requires sports bodies to respect the human rights and dignity of all competitors. In Chap. 7, we deepen our analysis of Black women's experiences of violence in the wake of the #MeToo movement. Founded by survivor and Black woman activist Tarana Burke, the movement's hashtag exploded on social media in 2017 leading to a global awakening to the 'magnitude of sexual violence' (https://metoomvmt.org/). The #MeToo movement released the power of survivors' voices and has arguably been the most impactful campaign against sexual violence the world has seen. Despite this, many women remain effectively silenced because of structural discrimination. Highlighting UK immigration policy and practice as an example, we discuss the ways in which the State restricts access to justice and services for Black women migrants and refugees who are abuse survivors.

Like the hydra, race and gender oppression are multi-headed and a single book cannot address all its forms. We acknowledge that there are gaps and omissions. For instance, we do not have a chapter on health inequalities even though improving access to better health care was central to many of our campaigns as evidenced by the fact that Abasindi women were instrumental in the establishment of the Manchester Sickle Cell and Thalassaemia Centre and the African Caribbean Mental Health Services. We might have also included a chapter on housing, as Abasindi had a visible presence in protests against urban regeneration plans that threatened homes and businesses in the Black community. Notable here is that Elouise Edwards, one of Abasindi's central figures, was a founding member of the Arawak Walton Housing Association—the largest independent Black and minority ethnic housing association in North West England. We could have included chapters on the intersection of disability, race, and gender or on the impact on Black families of women's imprisonment (Black women are disproportionately represented in the prison population) since we worked with women who faced all these challenges. While all these issues are important however, we decided to confine our writing to those aspects of Abasindi's activism in which the organisation had most expertise and experience. Firmly situated within a specific historical location, the new edition also reflects experiences and contributions from the younger generation of Black women activists in the UK and is therefore as much future oriented as it is focused on the past.

It is easy to overlook those who have worked to elevate British society. It is especially easy to overlook them if they are Black and, if they are Black women, you may not see them at all for their stories are often hidden and there is no network of 'old boys' to back-slap claims into facts or fist-bump truths into recognition. Black British women often ask the question, 'where am I' in your accounts of history? The response is usually one of muted embarrassment or concocted rationale. It is simply not good enough. When Black women are rendered invisible in accounts of social life in which they were not only present but made significant contribution, this is the literary equivalent of wielding a slave-master's whip to subjugate and silence. But of course, as this book testifies, Black women will not be silenced and as our activism proves, we cannot be subjugated. 'Unsung Stories' does not claim to be representative of *all* Black British women but the approach taken to the research that underpins the book is one of inclusivity. Our response to the question 'where am I' would simply be 'look here, we think you will see aspects of yourself'. And to the White women, and men too, who are interested in the intersections of race and gender oppression, please consider this book a series of conversations that also include you.

Huddersfield, UK   Adele Jones
Manchester, UK   Diana Watt

Acknowledgements

Although this book was written by the two authors named on the front cover, it represents a collective endeavour of the women of the Abasindi Black Women's Cooperative. Not only have we drawn on archive material and the memories of Abasindi members, families, and friends, but we have also been gifted with photographs, interviews, and poetry that have brought the book to life. Beyond publication, there is no debt of gratitude to repay though, since each contribution reflects an individual commitment to see the work and achievements of this vital organisation documented for posterity—sisters and brothers, we hope we have done you proud. Alongside our historical analysis, we have woven in discussion of some of the contemporary issues affecting Black women and their families and as we can all testify, racial and gender equality are still distant goals. Additionally, the current political and economic climate has set back many of the gains of Black and working-class communities in Britain and it is our hope that this book will inspire the new generation of activists to take us forward again.

We acknowledge the women of Abasindi, past and present and the friends and family members who have contributed to the material for this book; please accept our apologies if we have overlooked you: Nkosi, Dkizo, Yinka, Zinzi, Thembi, Ashley, Abubakarr, Paul, Olajomke, Melanie, Yvonne, SuAndi, Shirley May, Cath, Abina, Pauline, Shirley, Abiola, Miselo, Moiwale, Kaya, Liz, Francia, Magdalene, Joy, Evadney, Lorraine, Tara, Sam, Caroline, Maria, Louise, Ester, Chalana, Olajumoke, Patricia, Emense, Mumba, Estree, Gina, Lorna, Alima, Malaika, Norma, Paula, Beverley, Doreen, Mary Murphy, Deene, Mama Elouise Edwards, Mama Lindiwe Tsele, Mama Cynthia Gordon, Mama Julie Asumu, Dudu, Popgee, Doretta, Coco, Rose,

Mary, Sibongeli, Betty, Pat, Amina, Barbara, Madge, Charmaine, Merle, Bernadette, Tinu, Christine, Tina, Sandra, Laverne, Sharon, Brenda, Talla, Viveen, Saidat, Ruffina, Dorothy, Carol, Luna, Veronica, Ruth, Marcia, Judy, Ken, Keisha.

Contents

recognition of her work with vulnerable women and children. On the matter of the award, she comments:

"The title of this award is symbolic of much we have railed against, but as Black women, we also fight against being made invisible and it is important that our contributions to society are recognised. That the only national form of recognition available reifies an imperial history that has done Black people so wrong is an anomaly we must fight to change – another battle for another time".

Diana Watt   PhD is a former Senior Lecturer in Youth & Community Work studies at Manchester Metropolitan University and Associate Lecturer with the Open University. Her PhD research was on three generations of mothering practices among Jamaican heritage women in the UK. Diana is one of the founders of the Abasindi Black Women's Cooperative and her political work with the organisation is what inspired her personal and professional development in the field of education and community work. An academic activist at a time when a key concern was how teachers—'predominantly white, monolingual, female and middle class' (Hick et al., 2011, p. 6) could be enabled to be more culturally competent in teaching an increasingly diverse pupil population, Diana was one of the UK researchers on a National Teaching Fellowship Project on diversity and achievement among non-traditional students. This resulted in the publication of *Promoting Cohesion, Challenging Expectations: Educating the Teachers of Tomorrow for Race Equality and Diversity in 21st Century Schools* (Hick et al., 2011) which she co-authored. Diana was also a recipient of the Public Engagement Fellowship scheme at Manchester Metropolitan University; this provided an important opportunity for her and her colleagues to address some of the concerns in relation to the experiences of African-Caribbean heritage school pupils and led to the Manchester Conference for Black Parents, Children, and Young People. The conference included contributions from Black academics and activists from across the country and was credited with creating impetus for change in Manchester and providing a lasting reference point for improving educational outcomes among

Black children more widely. Diana's publications include book chapters and essays on mentoring and the early development of Youth Work in the Black community. She is a Trustee of the Louise Da-Cocodia Education Trust, one of the civil society organisations that sprang out of the Abasindi Cooperative and which provides relevant and accessible education, employment, and enterprise services, in particular to people of African and Caribbean heritage.

List of Figures

1

We are Descendants of the Windrush Generation

Abstract There is a dearth of literature on Black women's activism in the UK and indeed, on the contribution of Black British women more widely to tackling social injustice. This book aims to fill this gap and extends the feminist mantra 'the personal is political' by showing how the personal can shape the political through collectivist action. In drawing on personal and professional testimonies grounded in over three decades of community activism and scholarly analysis, the authors weave together the story of the Abasindi Cooperative, a British-based Black woman's organisation famed for its progressive and far-reaching social justice programmes. Founded by descendants of Britain's 'Windrush Generation' (The Windrush Generation refers to subjects of the British Empire who travelled to the UK from Africa and the Caribbean between the late 40s and 1971—often at the invitation of the British government—and who in recent years have been confronted with expulsion and illegal deportation (Windrush generation: Who are they and why are they facing problems? - BBC News). Abasindi and the women who were its lifeblood simultaneously navigated the politics of race, gender and class and initiated a practical form of intersectionality even before Kimberlé Crenshaw's coining of the term gained currency within feminist scholarship (Crenshaw, 2023). Detailed and grounded testimonies from Abasindi women deepen understandings of discrimination and exclusion and highlight the key role Black women have played in confronting these issues and in shaping the history of Black people in Britain. Alongside Black women's agency and the politics of representation, the book takes in colonialism, apartheid, the transatlantic slave trade and, reparation and thus extends its reach beyond British shores to the global arena.

© The Author(s), under exclusive license to Springer Nature Switzerland AG 2024 1
A. Jones, D. Watt, *Unsung Stories of Black Women's Activism in the UK*,
https://doi.org/10.1007/978-3-031-64201-2_1

Keywords Black women • Social injustice • Feminism • Intersectionality • Colonialism • Windrush

Introduction

> When we speak we are afraid our voices
>   will not be heard and when we don't speak
>   we are still afraid, so we might as well speak.
>   (Audre Lorde, 1995)

Established in 1980 and functioning for over three decades, the Abasindi Black Women's Cooperative was the 'village' community centre (Fig. 1.1) in the heart of urban Manchester.

Through its progressive activism, the organisation challenged many facets of racism and gender oppression and facilitated the progression of Black women, children, and youth. The Abasindi women were not only social justice activists, but they were also creative social entrepreneurs and developed numerous initiatives: a Saturday school, a summer school, creche, hair braiding, craft workshops, African dance and drumming groups, cultural exchange programmes, immigration, and political campaigns and, they ran a shop

Fig. 1.1 Abasindi was housed in an old Church Building in Moss Side, Manchester

selling African and Caribbean art. Their activism focused on improving education for Black children and women, challenging the everyday criminalization of Black youth, improving political representation, and preventing the deportation of Black women and their families who had migrated to Britain. Abasindi also supported survivors of domestic violence and agitated to increase Black women's access to refuges and other support services. The organisation sought primarily to advance opportunities for Black women and children but its doors were open to everyone.

It is important to declare from the outset that while Abasindi was undoubtedly a collective of formidable women, we were not superwomen. The Black woman as indomitable, with shoulders so broad she can carry the weight of her family, community, and face whatever comes her way, is a myth that does not serve us well. It provides those who should be providing us with services and resources the excuse not to do so and it assumes we can put up with anything—we cannot, we will not. Black women have no need of further myths, even positive ones. We were the Black women we provided support to—we were survivors of child sexual abuse; victims of domestic violence; our sons were locked up in prisons or put away in special education units; we had grown up in care, or had lost children to the care system, or worked within the care system; we had family members who were facing deportation; we lived in poverty and awful housing conditions or we lived well; we struggled for meaningful employment that matched our talents and we faced race and sex discrimination in the workplace; we misused alcohol and whatever else we could find to escape our lives; we were disabled, or we were not; we were straight, we were gay—maybe both; we were mothers or we were not but we were all mothered; we got too sick and we died too young; we fought and we cried; we laughed and we loved; we were some of these women some of the time or we were not—we were **all** Black women. That our collective sisterhood enabled us to rise above our personal challenges is testament to the spirits of resistance and resilience this book is about—we dedicate this book to all Black women and especially to those who died too young. One Black activist who inspired the early work of the Cooperative and who died too young was Olive Morris (Fig. 1.2), a Jamaican-born activist who settled initially in London.

Olive Morris is credited with catalysing the UK's Black Women's Movement during the 1970s and co-founding the Organisation of Women of African and Asian Descent. In 1975 Olive Morris moved to Manchester to pursue a degree in Social Sciences and together with Kath Locke and other women, established the Manchester Black Women's Co-op which later became the Abasindi Cooperative. Olive is celebrated by Black women across the country and though she achieved much, her life was cut tragically short. She died at spawned twenty-five Nobel prize winners, among them Sir William Arthur Lewis, a Saint Lucian economist who in 1947, became the country's first Black lecturer when he was appointed to the University of Manchester. Manchester University is where the atom was split for the first time and where the first computer was created. The city was also the home of Alan Turing, a mathematician famous for cracking Nazi codes during the second World War. Persecuted for being homosexual, Turing is now regarded as one the most innovative thinkers of the twentieth century and his wartime achievements are credited with shortening the war by two years, saving an estimated fourteen million lives. In 2022, Manchester University was ranked among the top ten universities in the world for societal impact. Of note, the award-winning writer and broadcaster Lemn Sissay, was Chancellor of Manchester University for seven years (2015–2022). This is of consequence to our story for two reasons. Firstly, Lemn's appointment to the highest position in one of the best universities in the country when set against a background in care which robbed him of the opportunity to achieve academically is as incredible as it is improbable. Secondly, Lemn Sissay is a long-time ally of Abasindi and has worked closely with one of its members, Adele Jones on initiatives to improve opportunities for Black young people in care and for young care leavers more generally. For example, Adele and Lemn were successful in establishing a scholarship for doctoral study specifically for young people that had been in care. *The Lemn Sissay Scholarship* initiated by the University of Huddersfield in 2010, was the first scholarship in the UK designed specifically to offer a care leaver the funds and support to undertake a PhD. Lemn also has an artistic connection to the organisation - it was the Abasindi Cooperative that provided Lemn, then a fledgling poet of seventeen years, with his first opportunity to perform in public (see Chap. 3).

Other prominent Black citizens of Manchester include Kath Locke, Louise Da Cocodia and Elouise Edwards, three of the most influential community activists of the Windrush Generation who collectively, are responsible for numerous initiatives tackling social inequality among the city's most vulnerable groups (see Chap. 2).

This diverse, multi-cultural city has drawn immigrants from around the world and like most British cities contains pockets of deprivation riven with social and racial inequalities. But Manchester holds a unique place in the history of race and gender relations for other reasons too. Of significance for the struggles of Black and working-class people for example, is the fact that Manchester is the city where the Industrial Revolution was born. Manchester is where the first inner-city railway was built and where the country's first working canal and the world's first steam-driven mill were developed. Boyed by these industrial infrastructure developments, Manchester became the largest producer of cotton in the world. However, it is through the production of cotton that the city's ignominious place in sustaining the trans-Atlantic slave trade is revealed. Since 2020, against a backdrop characterised by the '#Black Lives Matter' (BLM) movement, the killing of George Floyd at the hands of a Minneapolis police officer and the UK's 'largest ever race equality protests' which were inspired by these events, Britain's institutions have been called upon to examine their role in slavery (Wolfe-Robinson, 2023, p. 3). One such institution is the Guardian Newspaper. Founded in Manchester over two hundred years ago by liberal reformers after the 1819 Peterloo massacre,[1] the Guardian Newspaper has established a national reputation for its journalistic standards and is one of Britain's leading quality newspapers. An examination into the Newspaper's past however, showed that the capital through which it was founded, and which provided Manchester's wealth was derived from slavery's shameful history, the legacy of which continues to impact the present (Olusoga 2023). It is widely known that a great deal of Britain's prosperity during the nineteenth century came from the processing of cotton produced by enslaved people. A lesser known fact, however, is that Manchester, referred to as 'Cottonopolis', was the centre of that industry (Olusoga, 2023). Olusoga states 'much of the cotton that was spun, woven, dyed, processed, and traded in Manchester was produced by the almost 2 million enslaved Africans who lived, worked, and suffered on cotton plantations in the southern United States' (Olusoga, 2023, p. 7). Manchester today is undoubtedly a great city but as Stallard (2023, p. 17) points out, its greatness has been built from the 'produce of enslaved labour and profits from the slavery trade and plantation agriculture… [leaving] local and global legacies we are still only beginning to understand'. The extent of the wealth Manchester and the rest of Britain gained from the enslavement of African people may never fully be known. Neither is it possible to calculate the costs of the racial and economic inequality that gave birth to slavery and which slavery's legacy has continued to spawn (Olusoga, 2023). Olusoga contends that the racial stereotypes used to justify the slave trade outlasted slavery and 'infected our culture, our language, and to an extent, our subconscious' (Olusoga, 2023, p. 9). The women of the Abasindi Cooperative would concur, and the communities supported by the

---

[1] The Peterloo Massacre refers to a working class protest held at St Peter's Fields in Manchester in August 1819 in which the army, sent in to disperse the crowd, killed eleven people and injured 400 others. The people had been calling for political reform; in response, the government increased tax on newspapers so that working-class people could not afford to read them. (https://www.bbc.co.uk/bitesize/guides/z6c6cqt/revision/2).

organisation would testify to the continuation of racial and economic inequality even if they are not fully cognisant of its origins.

The second reason that Manchester stands apart from other cities is that it is the birthplace of Emmaline Pankhurst (1858–1928), the political activist who first pinned the city to the mast of radical feminism. The suffrage movement she founded in Britain helped women to win the right to vote and she was named by *Time Magazine* as one of the hundred most important people of the twentieth century: 'she shook society into a new pattern from which there could be no going back' (Time Magazine, 1999). Emmeline Pankhurst was born in Moss Side, and it was in Moss Side, less than a mile away from Pankhurst's house that the Abasindi Black Women's Cooperative was established. Abasindi women recognised the contribution Pankhurst made to women's emancipation however, we were also aware of Black women's invisibility in the historical accounts of the British suffrage movement and preferred to take our inspiration from the Black women suffragettes of the United States of America: Sojourner Truth, Frances Ellen Watkins Harper, Ida B. Wells, Mary Church Terrell and Sarah Parker Remond (Smith, 2020). Grounded in the abolitionist cause, these women laid the foundation for our own activism more than a century later. Despite the marginalisation of Black women in the suffrage movement, Pankhurst and Abasindi were aligned in two important respects: both were concerned about the circumstances of poor women and their children, and both were committed to women's rights of autonomy. Emmeline was horrified by the terrible conditions unmarried women and their children faced in Manchester's workhouses and worked tirelessly to bring about improvements. And at a time when unmarried women were socially marginalised and considered a societal scourge, Pankhurst agitated to ensure the right to vote would be extended to them as well as to women who were married (Pankhurst, 2015—first published in 1914). Some 70-plus years later, the women supported by the Abasindi Black Women's Cooperative were also among the most economically deprived and socially marginalised in the city. Moss Side, a gateway for the Windrush Generation[2] experienced repeated slum clearances between the 1960s and 1990s which exacerbated deprivation and through which 'whole communities were relocated, and large tracts of housing stock were demolished' (Brown & Cunningham, 2016, p. 23). With inadequate compensation to purchase new

---

[2] The Windrush Generation refers to subjects of the British Empire who migrated to the UK from Africa and the Caribbean between the late 40s and 1971—often at the invitation of the British government—and who in recent years have been confronted with expulsion and illegal deportation (Windrush generation: Who are they and why are they facing problems? - BBC News).

homes, Black families were dispersed, and many others were forced into the dependency and the economic disenfranchisement of house rental.

> One of the most striking legacies of the three decades of redevelopment that remade Moss Side from the late 1960s was the rapid movement of the Caribbean population into public housing. While these trends were paralleled elsewhere in Britain …, the scale of the clearances in south Manchester gave them a particular inflection. Despite limited access to public housing before 1968, within a decade it was estimated that 59 percent of the Caribbean population of Manchester were in council housing compared to a national average of 45 percent for this ethnic group across the country as a whole (Brown & Cunningham, 2016, p. 23)

The de-industrialisation programme brought in by the Thatcher government led to a rapid decline in manufacturing and this was felt particularly keenly in northern cities, including Manchester. Underscored by pre-existing systemic inequalities and the decimation of communities through the urban regeneration programmes described by Brown and Cunningham (2016), Black people were disproportionately impacted, and unemployment rose to record heights. Jacobs (2022) suggests that during the 1980s 'Urban deprivation saw unemployment in Moss Side reach a staggering 80%, leaving those of school age with few prospects and their elders devalued by their experience of employment' (Jacobs, 2022).

If Emmeline Pankhurst's militancy was developed, as she claimed, by observing the conditions faced by the impoverished women she came across, then the political education of Abasindi women was fomented through witnessing the injustices that Black women and their families were subjected to in the 970s and 80s. Pankhurst's direct action included violent confrontation and the destruction and burning of property to achieve her aims and in this regard the two organisations could not have been more different. Abasindi believed in confronting those with power, but never with violence and having been witness to the destruction of homes and communities, were more concerned with the preservation and repurposing of property. It was *this* principle that influenced the decision of the organisation to squat in an unused building in Moss Side. But there *was* a second point of alignment—Pankhurst was a strong proponent of women's autonomy and she established the Women's Social and Political Union (WSPU), an organisation that was open only to women. The Abasindi Black Women's Cooperative was also only open to women (although we worked closely with those men and White women's groups that shared our aims). To ensure our political autonomy was never compromised Abasindi rejected external funding and sustained itself through its income-generation activities.

The third reason Manchester is particularly important to our story is that the city was host to the 1945 Pan-African Congress; perhaps the most notable of all Pan-African congresses. Attended by future African leaders together with esteemed Pan-Africanists from the USA such as WEB Du Bois and Amy Jacques Garvey and financed by Guyanese-born Ras T. Makonnen, this meeting is considered a defining point in African history (Bakare, 2023). Why Manchester was selected for this historical event is discussed in Chap. 2, but with its focus on severing colonial ties, there can be little doubt that the Congress catalysed and cemented the growing clamour across the continent for independence from colonial rule. Kwame Nkrumah, revolutionary Ghanaian politician attended the meeting. An ardent promoter of Pan-Africanism and considered one of the movement's intellectual thinkers, Nkrumah led his county to independence and in 1957 became Ghana's first Prime Minister and later, its first President. The Kenyan statesperson Jomo Kenyatta was also at the Manchester Congress and like his compatriot Nkrumah, he also led his country to independence (in 1963) and following in Nkrumah's wake, he *too,* became its first prime minister and later its first president. Amy Jacques Garvey (married for a time to Marcus Garvey) was a key organiser of the Congress and chaired the first session on freedom from British colonial rule—it is highly probable that it was in *this* session that Nkrumah and Kenyatta were able to flesh out their political strategies for achieving independence. Amy was one of only two women present at the Congress and she was very vocal about what she saw as the marginalisation of women: "Very much has been said about the negro (*sic*) but for some reason very little had been said about the Black woman" (Foster & Francis, 2020). Taking place thirty-five years before Abasindi was born, most of our members were too young to understand the significance of the 1945 Manchester Congress. Nevertheless, many of us *did* acquire an appreciation of the importance of Pan-Africanism and if not enamoured by the movement's failure to address women's oppression were nevertheless influenced by its broader ideals concerning self-determination. Kath Locke, a founder of Abasindi (see Chap. 2) *did* recall the 1945 Congress. One of three girls born in Moss Side in Manchester to an English mother and Nigerian father, Kath's political education began at home. Her father, a supporter of Pan-Africanism himself, organised a meeting of the movement in the family home and taking advantage of the presence of African leaders in the city, invited Jomo Kenyatta and Kwame Nkrumah. Kath met both men and though she commented that "as girls our interest was not readily encouraged", she was to develop a lifelong commitment to Pan-Africanism. Recognising though, that the Pan-Africanist movement held little promise for the Black women in Britain who were demanding greater equality in education and employment, Kath's involvement was to remain largely symbolic and for the next forty years, she dedicated herself to the cause of Black women's equality. In 1980, together with other Black women, she founded the Abasindi Black Women's Cooperative.

The name Abasindi, the Zulu word for 'Survivors'—was chosen by members of the organisation as a tribute to the strength, resilience, and competence of Black women, in particular those of Africa and the African-Caribbean Diaspora that were actively involved in struggles against the dehumanizing and oppressive forces of apartheid, neo-colonialism, racism and sexism.

This book provides an historical account of the birth of the Abasindi Black Women's Cooperative (Fig. 1.4) and traces its political impact as a significant

Fig. 1.4 Early members of Abasindi Cooperative: Alima, Pauline, Rose, Yvonne, Abena, Maria, Coco, Diana and Kath

contributor and historical antecedent to contemporary social movements that tackle race, class and gender oppression in the UK.

In documenting the work and achievements of a community organisation that warrants a place in history, the book also connects the reader to the resurgence in feminist scholarship and the role of Black women in present-day community activism. Though it is primarily the work of the two named authors, the book draws on the contributions and recollections of the many Black women who were involved with Abasindi—'we move with memories':

> We move with memories
> Voices we remember
> In places we no longer recognise
> Like tides they wash over us
> So that if we stand perfectly still
> Possibly, we can hear the sea
> The benchmarks of our journeys
> Are not measured by distance
> But by the rubble of demolition
> As society moves on
> We just grow older
> Our every days of normality
> To work, school, the market
> Are made from homes
> Distanced by thousands of miles
> From this place we reside
> So that we recognise fellow passengers
> As the strangers we see daily.
> Old people
> Who once danced on their toes
> To rhapsodies of yesterday
> Now move
> Pass symbols of their longevity
> As their feet tap a nervousness to arrive
> And return home
> This is a place for moving and waiting
> Day dreaming, wondering to go or to leave
> Smiles are wide to faces seen for the first time
> And secrets are carelessly leaked to people
> Who may never meet again
> Café culture is held fast
> By the grease of English breakfast
> Served all day

As kitchen gossip turns a nosey eye
To a single lady sipping tea
Society has changed
But morals are still fashioned
As in the old days.
How many kisses welcomed
Those waiting on those to arrive
And their departures damp with sadness
Their ghosts
Are still visible in names of sweethearts
Pen knifed into metal
And the angst of love discarded
Wept its agony into wooden post scars
Yellow caps parading work men
Interrupt
The daydreams
Swinging a sledgehammer of time
Drilling away the past

Close your eyes
To hear the wild scream of a child's excitement
For adventure
Compete with the shriek of brakes burning rubber
As a choir of voices rise together
Typical, either there are none
Or they all come together
As heads in military precision
Nod towards the empty dock
Going, going gone.
'We Move with Memories', SuAndi© 2014

SuAndi (Fig. 1.5) is a freelance poet and writer and was the Director of the Black Arts Alliance, which in its time was one of the most important Black creatives networks in the UK. She has produced three anthologies of poetry and for more than 20 years has written, performed, and conducted workshops at community events in Manchester, across the UK, Europe, and the US; her poems appear in several poetry collections and her work is featured in gender and writing courses. Her numerous works include a monodrama, *The Story of M* and a libretto for the opera *Mary Seacole*. Her critical engagement with the representation and aesthetics of Black British writing has earned her international recognition especially in relation to women and race and she is a long-standing guest poet for the British Council Writers Tour. An unsung heroine

Fig. 1.5 SuAndi; poet and writer

of Black British culture, SuAndi's poetry has inspired many people. A multi-talented artist and performer, her work is underpinned by her unshakeable ideals as a human rights' cultural activist and campaigner against racial inequality. The poems that feature in this book have been dedicated by SuAndi to the memory of the Abasindi Black Women's Cooperative.

The aims and objectives of the Co-operative were to provide a social support base for Black women and to establish a community resource centre and, supplementary and cultural educational facilities for Black children and young people. Over time, the objectives of the organisation were expanded to enable collaborations with men who shared our aspirational goals. This position questioned the very basis of White, western feminism and was anathema to several women's organisation. There were inevitable costs in breaking solidarity with White women on the matter of collaborating with men and while we understood their concerns, we also recognised that we had more in common with Black men in tackling racist oppression than we did with White women. Predictably, we did encounter men who attempted to sieze control of our agenda and our strategies, but we were a formidable force and were able to sustain our position—collaboration on our terms. This approach meant that we were able to keep the whole family at the centre of our activism and we discovered the importance of our inclusive stance whenever we had to support women in confronting male violence and, in supporting male victims of police violence.

This book makes use of research, archive materials, narrative interviews, photographs, poems and theoretical analysis and through this blended method, the social issues which inspired Abasindi's action for change are explored. Clarke (2003) argues that in celebrating the achievements of women in the past, we also need to acknowledge and challenge the problems that women are faced with today—we hope we have achieved this.

As members of Abasindi, the authors follow in the tradition of many Black women writers who invoke their own lived experiences and those of other Black women and whom Omalade refers to as Griot historians. Omalade argued that the role of the Black woman Griot is unlike that of the historical role played by male Griot in West African societies and that before a language capturing the experiences of Black women in the Diaspora can be created, the Griot-historian must break "de chains" and become submerged in the waters of Black women's pain, power and potential (1994, pp. 105–106). As authors, we *were* submerged in these waters but also aimed to transcend the barriers of feminist scholarship and the constraints of academic publishing. Collins (1990, p. 15) points out that scholarly work about race and gender relations is generally not attributed to Black women hence the creation of a 'false dichotomy between scholarship and activism, between thinking and doing'. Black feminist Gail Lewis, in her talk on the differences between the US and the UK in the recognition and status of Black women's writing suggests that in Britain, Black women have been more strongly associated with activism than academia. The reasons she proffers are that more Black women in America went to university during the 1960s and '70s than in Britain and that their involvement in the Civil Rights movement gave them additional visibility (2011). Another reason may be the race and gender inequalities within British higher education settings which has had the effect of suppressing the contributions of Black women. In her research on UK professors, for instance, Rollock found that fewer than 1% of professors in the UK were Black and when both race and gender were considered together, Black women represented the smallest group, being three times less likely to be professors than White women and half as likely as Black men (2019). If Black women are not part of the academy, they cannot write as academics, and they will not be published in the academic press. Racial inequality in education is a problem right across the sector (see Chaps. 6 and 7) but at this point in our story, it is important because it raises the question: is it enough to be a women's activist without engaging with theory and is it enough to engage with theory without being an activist? This book settles the question—as activist academics the authors, Adele Jones and Diana Watt (Fig. 1.6) bridge the gap between scholarship and activism and between historical and contemporary divides. In

Fig. 1.6 Diana Watt; activist academic

drawing on our personal and professional perspectives grounded in decades of lived experience and critical thought we weave together the story of Abasindi Cooperative and in so doing reveal historical narratives of political struggle that have their resonance in the present.

Descendants of the Windrush Generation

Abasindi's membership consisted of women who were the daughters and granddaughters of the Windrush Generation and some of us were 'barrel children;' the name given to children left behind when their parents departed for

England. There were over 500 passengers on the *Empire Windrush*, the original ship commissioned by the government in 1948 to bring skilled workers from the Caribbean to help rebuild Britain after the Second World War. In lending its name to the phrase 'Windrush Generation' the term is commonly understood as encompassing those 'British subjects' from Africa and the Caribbean who migrated to Britain between the late 40s and 1970s—often at the invitation of the 'mother' country (Windrush generation: Who are they and why are they facing problems?—BBC News). In Manchester some of these early migrants were amongst those who were involved in the establishment of the West Indian Overseas Co-ordinating Committee (WIOCC), an umbrella organisation for community organisations set up to support those who arrived in Britain in that Windrush era. In his book '*Me Ago England and 'Culture',* Douglas (1985) writes of the immigrant's hopes of benefiting from the relationship with the motherland. Selvon's novel *The Lonely Londoner* however, deals with the shattering of the illusion of belonging; these West Indians did not belong and as the British government was to demonstrate decades later, they would never be viewed as belonging. Immigrants from Cyprus, Malta and Italy were often held to infringe criteria of neatness and quietness, but most were thought to live respectable family lives. Unlike these immigrant groups, West Indians were seen as failing to conform to the expectations of British society. Early signs posted in the windows of rental properties reflected this: 'No Irish, No Blacks, No Dogs.' There were also signs that stated: 'No Poles, Eastern Europeans, or Jews' but as time passed, Polish people eventually gained respect as conformist and good householders keen to improve the state of their properties. On the other hand, people from Southern Ireland were often said to be 'as bad as the darkies (*sic*).' (Patterson, 1965, pp. 178–179). An additional dynamic was that the influx of West Indian men gave vent to myths about Black hypersexuality, and the Black male was viewed as a threat to the innocence of White women. *The Daily Mirror* ran an article entitled 'Introducing to you…the boys from Jamaica – Are they stealing our women?' (Webster, 1998, p. 60). Fearing the moral corruption of a nation, the arrival of the West Indian woman was initially welcomed by British men so she could 'provide a companion for the coloured male immigrant so he will keep away from British women,' (Collins, 1957, pp. 137, 253). *The Mirror* went on to reassure its readers that the arrival of Black women would ensure that Jamaican men would no longer seek intimate relationships with White women, the inference being that they would stick to 'their own kind'. This article was a rare reference to Black women and up until the 1960s, the literature on migration focused almost solely on the experiences of men. For example, women were totally missing from Lawrence's (1974) study *Black Migrants: White Natives,* even though this was described as a study on 'Race Relations in Nottingham.' Pryce (1979, p. 300) justified the exclusion of women from his study *West Indian lifestyles* by referring to the limitations of his research methodology: 'as a male researcher, I had only limited access to women in the West Indian community for research purposes.' The marginalisation of Black women was further reinforced through a statement by Morokvasic (1983, p. 16) who described the representation of female migrants as 'an accessory of a process they are not really taking part in.' Highlighting the invisibility of Black women in experiences of migration, Pedraza (1991, p. 304) summed up the state of research as follows: 'we have yet to develop a truly gendered understanding of the causes, processes and consequences of migration.'

Early researchers such as Lawrence and Pryce might have at least, referred to the activism of Claudia Jones who did much to challenge the discrimination faced by early immigrants and created initiatives to engender social cohesion that have had long-lasting benefits. Claudia was born in Trinidad and spent many of her formative years in America. However, in 1955, her membership of the Communist party led to her arrest, imprisonment, and subsequent deportation from the US to Britain (Sherwood, 1999). Within three years of arriving in England she had launched Britain's first post-war Black newspaper, *The West Indian Gazette*. Claudia Jones later described the *Gazette* as having served 'as a catalyst, quickening the awareness socially and politically of West Indians and Afro-Asians in Britain for peace and friendship between all Commonwealth and world peoples' (Sherwood, 1999, p. 147). Donald Hinds who worked on this paper alongside Claudia Jones and was amongst London's first Black bus conductors noted that the Gazette came out at a time when 'White passengers would bounce straight up out of their seats if a coloured *(sic)* passenger was bold enough to sit next to them.' Such was the disdain that Black people were held in that some of the White passengers would rub their hands on the 'coloured' bus conductor's hair for luck. Hinds reported that following the explosion of racial disturbances in April 1958, Claudia was amongst a small group of people that went on to organise the first indoor Caribbean carnival with the intention of improving race relations—this was held at the St. Pancras Hall on 31st January 1959 (Boyce-Davies, 2011). Prior to the existing Notting Hill carnival which first took to the streets between 1959 and 1964, six indoor carnivals were held at different venues in London (http://www.irr.org.uk/news/claudia-jones-and-the-west-indian-gazette/); these were followed by carnivals in other cities with large Caribbean communities, including in Manchester. These later carnivals were less concerned with race relations than in providing a peaceful means to confront decades of marginalisation, as Gewirtz-O'Reilly (2020) argues: 'In carnival, embodied performative art occupies the street. This radical act of 'taking space' is central to the political significance of the tradition of carnival in the African Caribbean Diaspora tradition.'

During the 1960s and 1970s immigration was a key preoccupation of the British government, (as it is today) resulting in a raft of oppressive immigration laws. One of the effects of the 1962 Commonwealth Immigration Act was the splitting up of families; this was particularly the case with older children who were not considered by the State as dependents. In response, Claudia Jones was one of the community leaders who organised a mass demonstration against this Act (Carter, 1986). Claudia's death, in 1964, marked the beginning of collective action on the part of Black women and her influence inspired activism against racism, poor working conditions and sexual discrimination within the workplace. For example, African-Caribbean women workers were at the forefront of the 1971 night-cleaners' strike for better working conditions (Bryan et al., 2018). The 1962 Commonwealth Immigration Act was followed by the 1971 Immigration Act which was even more restrictive, giving only temporary residence to people arriving from Commonwealth countries. British immigration legislation has always reinforced structural gender inequalities in both explicit and implicit ways and its effects can be particularly cruel to women and children in need of protection from abuse (immigration rules often override women's and children's rights). From 1980–2000, Abasindi launched, supported, and won many anti-deportation campaigns on behalf of Black women (see Chap. 7). Despite these achievements and our close relationship with immigration lawyers and advocates, we could not have anticipated just how heartless and unjust Britain's immigration system was to become. In 2010, the UK Border Agency destroyed thousands of landing cards and for hundreds of early West Indian immigrants, these were the only official records of their lawful arrival in Britain. In 2012, Home Secretary Theresa May, revealed her 'hostile environment' policy; the government's aim being to prevent those without the right to be in the country from accessing health and social services, employment, banks, and accommodation. Because of the Border Agency's earlier actions, many of the Windrush Generation were subsequently wrongly identified as illegal immigrants and over the next five years faced eviction from their homes, the loss of jobs held often, for decades and, the refusal of medical treatment. At least sixty-three people were wrongfully deported and many more were placed in detention centres and subject to unlawful imprisonment and degrading treatment. These were people who had lived and worked in the UK for most of their lives. Facing protests from Black communities and mounting condemnation from all sectors of society, the government was forced to apologise for 'the appalling treatment of the Windrush Generation.' In 2018, the government set up a taskforce to resolve the immigration status of those affected and to issue compensation for the harm caused. In 2020, there were still over 3,700 cases to be resolved and an independent review concluded that the Home Office had shown 'inexcusable ignorance and thoughtlessness' in tightening regulations without any regard to those of the Windrush era that would be affected. Activists have fought to ensure the rights of the Windrush Generation are protected and Black women activists have sought particularly to ensure that the role of Black women is not obscured. In recognition of the 75th anniversary of the *Empire Windrush* landing on British shores, members of Abasindi together with the Louise Da-Cocodia Education Trust (another Black community organisation in Manchester) organised 'Windrush Women: The Backbone of the NHS' (Fig. 1.7). Performed in 2022 in Manchester to sell-out audiences, this dramatic re-enactment highlighted the contribution that Black women of the Windrush Generation, their daughters and granddaughters have made to the National Health Service.

The Windrush Review also recommended a review of the 'hostile environment' policy however, in 2023, the government enacted a new Immigration Act which reinforces the policy and makes Britain one of the most hostile countries in the world for immigrants. Particularly targeting asylum seekers, the Immigration Act effectively dismantles the asylum system and denies rights and protection to victims of human trafficking and modern slavery, mostly women and children.

Such repressive immigration legislation is based on racial discrimination and also perpetuates the notions of white superiority and black inferiority that link back to slavery and continue to permeate British society. This is illustrated, for example, by the response of the British government to refugees fleeing an outbreak of civil war in Sudan early in 2023 and which contrasted markedly to the treatment of refugees from the war in Ukraine. An article in the Guardian Newspaper (7 May 2023) reported:

> The Home Office has been accused of operating an "unashamedly racist" refugee system after refusing to offer people fleeing fighting in Sudan a safe and legal route to the UK, in stark contrast to the schemes offered to those escaping the war in Ukraine. With the final evacuation flight from Khartoum to the UK having left last week a lack of options from the UK government has crystallised concern that it has adopted a segregated immigration policy. No safe and legal routes have been made available to help Sudanese refugees flee and there is no sign of an announcement outlining a new scheme to deal with the fallout of the conflict. By contrast, almost 300,000 visas have been issued for Ukrainians to leave their war-torn country, including 193,900 for its homes sponsorship scheme, launched in March 2022. Another 94,900 have been granted for a fam-

Fig. 1.7   Windrush performance pamphlet

ily scheme allowing Ukrainian refugees to join relatives in the UK. Immigration experts increasingly believe the explanation for such contrasting approaches is the skin colour of those fleeing the two countries. (https://www.theguardian.com/world/2023/may/07/home-office-accused-of-being-unashamedly-racist-towards-sudanese)

So we battle like
Queens should.
Mothers called to combat,
Like the battalions of our families,
All those who did not lie down
Whilst others took possession
Of our rise and fall.
Spirited like our mother's mother
And our mother's before
We did not yield ground,
But braced ourselves for the journey
In hulls of tall ships to distant shores.
Bejewelled cargo of victors and brave women
We are the jet-Black fabulous jazz of isosceles,
We stand in all our yesterdays
Where the valiant had once stood
Where heroes now stand,
You set a path for us to ascend
To find the very best in us,
As we enter the city gates,
We are people that have battled,
Against those who would try to defeat us.
You made us strong, you gave us your voice
You left us with your songs, told us to rise,
On the dawn, and to overstand the storms,
You made us spirited,
We are Kenya, Egypt,
Senegal, Rwanda,
Mali, Libya,
Madagascar, Nigeria
Jamaica, Barbados, we are Trinidad
We are a people called to arms,
A people not afraid.
We are the jet-Black fabulous jazz of isosceles
Shirley May ©

Summary of Chapters

Chapter 2, 'Legacy of Black Women's Activism' sets out the social and political context which gave rise to the Abasindi Cooperative based on the experiences of women from the 1960s onwards and reflecting a continuation of

Black women's activism in the work of Una Marson and Amy Jacques Garvey. It describes the specific ways in which Black women seized the freedom to act and the freedom to grow as a collective. Using research, archive materials, narrative interviews, photographs, and poems, the social issues which inspired their action for change are explored.

Chapter 3, 'Cultural Expressions of Resilience' explores the involvement of Abasindi Women's Cooperative in the promotion of African/Caribbean art forms as part of a broader struggle for recognition and representation. Additionally, it examines the strategic relationship of Abasindi with other organisations sharing similar goals; for example, the organisation's involvement in the NIA Centre, the first 'cultural' space in the Northwest to focus explicitly on African and Caribbean art forms.

Chapter 4, 'Ancestral Journeys and Diasporic Connections' discusses the work of Abasindi Drumming and Dance Group in enabling Black women and young people to rediscover the value of their own culture within the African Diaspora. It was also an opportunity to develop the creativity of its members. The role of music, dance, and other forms of creative expression as a central function of community life is explored.

Chapter 5, 'Loving Body, Skin and Hair' reflects on Black women's concerns with race and representation within a broader political struggle. The chapter also discusses the ways in which Black hair and skin care became a focus of challenge to the racism of cultural neglect within a care system that distorted Black children's self-image and damaged their self-esteem. This chapter documents the importance of loving the (Black) self as integral to positive identity formation and at the political level calls for an acknowledgement of cultural diversity and respect for difference in meeting the needs of Black children in care.

Chapter 6, 'Sowing Seeds of Success', discusses the emergence of Black supplementary schools in response to Coard's report: *How the West Indian Child is made Educationally Sub-normal in the British Education System*. It goes on to look at the role of Black women in the development of Abasindi Saturday Supplementary School and that of the Louise Da-Cocodia Education Trust (a legacy organisation of Abasindi) which was established in 2008.

Chapter 7, 'The Politics of Sisterhood', is an acknowledgement of the ways in which Abasindi created its own version of feminism, crossing boundaries and building alliances as a pragmatic strategy in tackling issues of immigration and domestic violence. The chapter documents the role of Abasindi in the 1981 Moss Side uprisings against racism and the contribution of the Manchester Black Access Course developed in the wake of the riots in supporting the politicisation of Black women.

Fig. 1.9 'Ordinary' Abasindi women; achieving the extraordinary: Kath Locke, Diana Watt, and Maria Noble

Chapter 8 concludes by acknowledging and celebrating 'ordinary women' who came together within Abasindi to achieve extraordinary things (Fig. 1.9). The authors draw on their personal reflections to demonstrate ways in which the academy and professional spaces have become sites of political activism for Black women who are increasingly engaged in seizing opportunities to contribute to scholarship and the production of knowledge.

2

The Legacy of Black Women's Activism

Abstract The early experiences of Black women workers have been described as a 'long catalogue of hardship', providing the fertile soil for the growth of the activism portrayed within this book. As set out in Chap. 1, the experiences described herein are channelled through the prism of the Abasindi Black Women's Cooperative, a Manchester-based collective that drew its inspiration and resilience from these early workers, many of whom were Black women workers of the Windrush era (1940s–70s). Though the women were from Manchester, working class Black women facing similar hardships could be found in any of Britian's cities and major towns. Many of these women worked in food production and packaging while others worked in the clothing industry which was notorious for sweat-shop conditions and low wages. Within the National Health Service, Black women were employed mainly as domestic cleaners and canteen workers. Those who wished to train as nurses were often rejected or channelled away from the State Registered training towards the lower status State Enrolled qualification. It was standard practice for migrant women to be recruited at the bottom end of the occupational ladder regardless of their abilities. Up until the 1960s, the literature on migration focused primarily on the experiences of men and little therefore is known about how these women workers experienced the downgrading of their skills and how they rose above relegation, as so many of them did. Here, we rectify a history in which these women were mostly hidden and in so doing, set out our proud lineage as activists. Never myopic, Abasindi also drew inspiration from women from outside of Britain including women from South Africa who were struggling against apartheid. In this chapter we explore these influences and describe the experiences and perspectives that fired up our refusal to accept victimisation.

A. Jones, D. Watt, *Unsung Stories of Black Women's Activism in the UK*,
https://doi.org/10.1007/978-3-031-64201-2_2

Keywords Working-class • Migration • Women workers • Resilience •
Activism

Identity and Voice

Identity and finding a voice are regarded as central to women's development. In their publication, the *Heart of the Race*, Bryan et al. (2018, p. 7) stated that '…it was high time we started to record *our* version of events as Black women in Britain…we had relied for too long on the version of our story put forward by white historians and sociologists. And we had seen the women's movement follow suit, documenting 'herstory' from every angle but our own…'. As the years moved on, we, the authors of this book, have watched members of the Abasindi Cooperative become debilitated through illness or age and we have witnessed too often, the premature passing of our sisters, most often from cancer related illnesses (Black women in England are up to two times more likely to receive a late stage diagnosis for some cancers than White women—Limb, 2023). Like Bryan et al., we realised there was an imperative to preserve the incredible history and achievements of these women. Our concern was not just to make ourselves heard—we had always been distinctly and loudly audible—it was that Abasindi had an important story to tell and if *we* did not write, there would come a time when there was no one around who could. Young Black women activists, and young men too, should know that they were not birthed into activism by chance. Furthermore, British society more widely needs to recognise the grit and determination that women, such as those from the Abasindi Cooperative have put into trying to improve a country that remains inhospitable to Black people. Lewis (2005) insists that women should tell their stories in their own words and on their own terms, and identifies oral life history as an avenue through which to accomplish this. The writings of African American women further assert the right to speak out and reverse the devaluing and silencing of hundreds of years of racial and gendered subordination (Walker, 1983, p. 59). Alice Walker's writing is concerned with rescuing Black women from silence through the establishment of sisterhood and the writing of what she terms 'womanist prose.' She regards the experiences of Black women in America as a series of movements from racial and sexual oppression to a state of consciousness, thus allowing them to have some control over their lives. This evolutional process is both historical and psychological and consists of three interrelated cycles: suspension, assimilation, and emergence. For African and Caribbean women in the UK, Alexander and Dewjee (1984) suggest the use of letters, diaries, autobiographies,

Fig. 2.1 Francia Messado

testimonies, photographs, and drawings are important sources in the reclaiming of Black women's history, as in their research on the life of Mary Seacole.
Drawing from these ideas and the influences of Black women activists such as
Una Marson and Amy Jacques Garvey, this chapter sets out the social and
political context which gave rise to the Abasindi Black Women's Cooperative.
Here, Abasindi member Francia Messado (Fig. 2.1) describes what the organisation meant to her.

> My Sister used to say, "It's as if you have two families – your biological family
> and Abasindi'. In so many ways she was right! Within this global family of
> beautiful, Black, strong, astounding women they are fundamentally akin to
> sisters, aunties, mothers, grandmothers, as well as friends. Being a member of
> Abasindi has been both a privilege and an opportunity. I was invited to Abasindi
> in 1979, then being a young mother, without a sense of life direction. In
> observing and listening to the first conversations around the big wooden brown
> table, the first buzz word that still rings true for me today was *self-sufficiency*.
> Motivated by what I'd seen and heard – yes self-sufficiency was definitely in
> action at Abasindi, hence my involvement which in turn encouraged my learn-
> ing, development, and growth. A sister-member once said, 'I need Abasindi
> more than it needs me'. Upon reflection, I can concur with that sentiment, as
> Abasindi was indeed a lifeline. We communicated, expressed, laughed, cried,
> shared problems and dreams, negotiated, made decisions, and organised –
> always empowering one another in striving to make a holistic human differ-
> ence. There was so much to do and be a part of in Abasindi. Saturday school,
> Summer school, crèche, hair plaiting, sewing, cultural groups including
> Kutumba and Abasindi Pan-African Drummers and Dancers, women's and
> cultural exchanges, immigration and political campaigns, the cultural shop, the

Moss Side Arts Group, the Nia Centre, and fundraising events. Abasindi was also the village community centre in the heart of Moss Side and surrounding areas, opening its doors to everyone. Abasindi's Centre was used for Church services and other celebratory life events including parties. Over the years, the range of skills I learned assisted in my participation in a variety of roles. This included Summer school assistant, performer/workshop facilitator in dance/music, activist, chairperson, and project-coordinator. It also led to encountering many opportunities. For example, I became a singer, dancer, and drummer with the Abasindi Drummers and Dancers whose performances ranged from sounding in solidarity with immigration campaigns in the local streets of Moss Side, to performing at PANAFEST in Ghana. Abasindi has been fundamental in both my personal and professional life. All was due to the selfless, priceless exchange of shared energies with external progression of these amazing women's abilities and the results of collective achievement. Humble gratitude and love to all Abasindi women. Warriors, role models, mentors, elders and youth, near and far, on earth and in spirit. I am truly blessed to be part of such an invaluable experience. It has enlightened me and instilled confidence and positive resilience. These treasured memories have helped me to evolve, and they continue to inspire the woman that I am today.

Striving and Thriving

In his paper 'Better Mus' Come' Farrar argues that community 'is a term used by people of all ethnic groups not simply to characterize the present or to demarcate 'us' from 'them', but to evaluate the present and the past and to carry dreams, hopes, yearnings for the future'. Symbolically it stands for the yearning for a better life, as in the civil rights struggles in America where Dr Martin Luther King declared that the 'Aftermath of nonviolence is the creation of the beloved community'.

> Building the "beloved community" is both the process and the hoped-for outcome of individual and political empowerment. It is where we are going and how we will get there. It is the essence of Dr Martin Luther King Jr's dream: a caring community where race and class is transcended and social and economic justice is the rule and not the exception. (Lee, 2001, p. 1)

The building of 'beloved communities' by Black migrants in cities such as Manchester at the end of the Second World War was in part due to the rise in migration from the Caribbean islands to the North West of England. However, ever since the sixteenth century Black people have been inextricably linked to the structure of British society as both slaves and free men and women. Bryan et al. (2018, pp. 9–10) state:

> Our presence in eighteenth century England was an accepted reality. Black women and men were sold openly at auctions; the busts of 'blackamoors' emblems of the trade, commonly adorned local town halls. Black servants were common too, and our children were the inevitable appendages of slave Captains and high-society women. Freed and runaway slaves were conspicuous among London's beggars and were known as 'St Giles Blackbirds'. Though in constant fear of recapture, we lived side by side with the white working class, intermarrying with them and taking part in the life of the community.

The development of post-war migrant communities was signalled by the arrival of the Empire Windrush at Tilbury Docks on 22 June 1948. Fryer (1984, pp. 372–373) described the passengers on the Empire Windrush as 'Five Hundred pairs of Willing Hands', who then found themselves amongst those that would eventually be regarded as 'competitive intruders.' Glass and Collins wrote:

> Coloured people are feared as competitive intruders; they are thought of as promoters of crime and carriers of disease; they are resented when they are poor; they are envied when they are resourceful and thrifty. They are looked down upon; they are patronised; occasionally they are treated just like everyone else. (1960, p. 120)

Up until the 1950s, international migration was heavily dominated by men, and this is seen as critical in explaining the high level of female-headed households in many of the Caribbean islands. These women could be found living independently within a closely-knit community or as head of an extended family to include their own children as well as those of other relatives or strangers. In her discussion on women-headed units in West Africa, Ekejuiba (1995) applies the term 'hearthold-household' to describe a family unit that may exist independently or within an established household. This unit is made up of women, children, and dependants with shared responsibility for the caring and nurturing of other members of the hearthold, an ethos that Abasindi borrowed from.

> When I think of Abasindi, I conjure up a picture: the red building symbolizing the blood that unites a people. My memories, random but empowering, come flooding back in all their splendour, answering questions that have only just come to mind. Ain't I a woman?', an image, imprint in my thoughts, a picture

of a stern woman [Sojourner Truth], who demanded that in a time when she was not even observed as a human being she be recognized as a woman. The women themselves were a force to be reckoned with. They were creative and strong, as evident in their efforts to raise a family in the context of the group dynamics - there was always so much to do. As I reflect on my life as it is, I am not sure where I would find the time to do as much as the Abasindi women did and with such aplomb. From a child's eye view, women ran things, held down jobs, raised children, and did Abasindi. (Melanie Duncan).

'West Indians' and West Africans

The organisers of the 1945 Pan-African conference held at the Chorlton Town Hall stated that one of the reasons for choosing Manchester was the fact that:

Manchester had become quite a point of contact with the coloured proletariat in Britain, and we had made a name for ourselves in fighting various areas of discrimination … Manchester was an expression of a mass movement intimately identified with the under-privileged sections of the coloured colonial populations. (Fryer, 1984, pp. 347–349)

Britain's Black colonial population included the passengers on the Empire Windrush. These men, most of whom were Jamaican, had served in the British armed forces during the Second World War and viewed their journey as a return to the 'Motherland.' The brothers, Mike, and Trevor Phillips (1998, pp. 4–6), describe the event 'as a journey through the gateway of history, on the other side of which was the end of Empire and a wholesale reassessment of what it meant to be British. To the majority of those aboard, their arrival in England represented a leap into the unknown, an adventure in which no one knew what they would find'.

Euston Christian, Manchester's first Black Justice of the Peace, was amongst the passengers on the Empire Windrush who had come to England during the Second World War as a member of the Royal Air Force. After six months back in Jamaica, he returned to England on the Empire Windrush. He agreed to take up 'extended duties' with the RAF and served in the force for several years. He was amongst those, including the late Ashton Douglas (Mr. Dougy), Aubery Lawford and Pip Gore, who founded the West Indian Sports and Social Club in Moss Side. These men's love of cricket gave birth to a centre which has become one of the mainstays of Manchester's African-Caribbean community. The current work of Tom Nelson, Leon Smith and Cleveland Brady is a testament to this legacy. Even before the Windrush many of the West African sailors had settled in areas such as Cheetham Hill and Salford. From the 1940s the number of merchant seamen from the Caribbean islands and West Africa increased. Some began to move their families into Hulme, an area that provided much of the material for Friedrich Engels's study on the conditions of the working class in England.

The opportunity to survive and thrive was made possible by a range of supportive networks which included a local GP—Dr Peter Milliard and Mr. Harding, proprietor of a local hostel. These men provided cheap medical support and accommodation for Black seamen. Small businesses, shopkeepers, barbers, and night club owners were also amongst those who provided financial support to the community. Phillips (1975, p. 273) argues that 'it seems unlikely that the Black communities in any other British city would have been able to deploy the political, financial and organizational resources to host the 1945 Pan-African Congress'. The organisers of the conference also cited another reason for choosing Manchester, namely Black people's contribution to the development of the city.

> You could say that we coloured people had a right there because of the age-old connections between cotton, slavery, and the building up of cities in England. Manchester gave us ... an important opportunity to express and expose the contradictions, the fallacies and the pretentions that were at the very centre of empire. (Fryer, 1984, pp. 347–348)

The delegates at this conference included Amy Jacques Garvey who, along with her husband Marcus Garvey, co-founded the Universal Negro Improvement Association (UNIA). The conference on 15 October, began with a discussion on Britain's racial problems. Speaking as the chair of the session, Amy Garvey observed that:

> A nation without great women is a nation frolicking in peril. Let us go forward and lift the degradations which rest on the Negro woman – God's most glorious gift to civilisation. (Swaby, 2010)

On the issue of race and gender, Amy, Marcus Garvey's second wife acknowledged that Black women's experience of oppression was often distinguishable from that of Black men. She is thus seen as belonging to a legacy of Black female activists who were cognisant of the distinctive plight faced by Black women because of racial, gender, *and* class oppression—intersectionality.

gone out of business. Faced with rapidly rising house prices in other areas and continued racial discrimination, most Black householders accepted tenancy from the local authority, because compensation payments were too low to purchase an equivalent size house elsewhere.

> Our first home was in Meadow Street in Moss Side … soon after I bought my house and had tenants in my spare rooms, I lost this house under compulsory purchase order from the court. They paid less than what the house was worth, and I subsequently made a loss on it. (Roots Oral History Project, 1992, p. 8)

The proportion of Black owner occupiers fell dramatically. The total number of Black people to become council tenants rose from 291 in 1970 to 789 in 1971 but by 1975, most Black people in Moss Side and Hulme were council tenants. The attempted dispersal of Black people was short-lived as large numbers refused to be re-located on housing estates away from the city centre. Night workers living outside the area often found that little or no public transportation was available at nights. Furthermore, the local schools were also reluctant to accept Black children from the inner city (Phillips, 1975).

Further re-development in the early 1990s yet again involved the disruption and at times destruction of established community networks. The groups that were based in the old St Mary's school, re-named Moss Side People's Centre, included the Moss Side Adventure Playground, the Family Advice Centre, and the Abasindi Co-operative. The building was 're-appropriated' by the city council, these groups were evicted, and the property sold to private developers—it was later converted into a privately owned nursery. Despite these changes, the spirit of 'beloved community' remains a vibrant aspect of life in Moss Side, as evident in the 2012 celebrations of the life of Kath Locke, one of the founder members of Abasindi.

Black Women's Activism

The early experiences of Black women workers have been described as a 'long catalogue of hardship' which provided fertile soil for the growth of Black women's activism. In Manchester many of the women travelling on the 'African Queen' bus were to be found working in food production and packaging. Others worked in the clothing industry, some of it notorious for sweat shop conditions and low wages. One woman told us in an interview:

I was doing a job, it was a menial job but there were white people and although we were all doing exactly the same kind of work, they use to get more money than us, the coloured ones…most days we do exactly the same amount, they still got more money than I did. (PhD Thesis, Watt, 2002).

In the absence of capital investment, Lewis (1994) argues that the substitution of cheap labour from the Caribbean and Indian sub-continent as well as indigenous women workers represented an attempt on the part of Britain to deal with the effects of its long-term decline. Alongside this intensification of the rate of exploitation for women workers there was the added dimension of the sexual division of labour. This took place irrespective of women's racial origin and had the effect of determining the occupation into which they would be absorbed. For Black women 'the ideology of racism and the practice of racialism were to intertwine with the ideology and practice of sexism, both of which were to impact on the structural characteristics of the British economy to determine the industrial and occupational location of Black women workers. One woman went as far as to describe her experience in 1964 as a form of twentieth century 'slavery'. This was at a crisp-making factory in Manchester where she was eventually sacked for taking a stance against working in an environment which denied workers, the majority of whom were Black women, the right to go to the toilet without the permission of the White female supervisor. This was at a time when, according to Bhabha and Shutter (1994, pp. 38–39):

The only kind of work that most black women were able to find was in industries where low pay and bad conditions prevailed. These included the textile industry – both the large mills in the North West of England and the small, family-based sweated businesses in the East of London – and hospitals and other service industries where, more often than not, they worked as cleaners or orderlies.

The racialised practices of employers and some unions fed the misapprehension that Black women workers were working for 'pin money' (Lewis, 1994). It was standard practice for migrant women to be recruited at the bottom end of the occupational ladder. Thus, Black women were excluded from working in shops or offices (Webster, 1998, p. 130). This was the experience of Una Marson who migrated to England during the 1930s. Despite her educational achievements and professional credentials, in the search for office work she found herself confronted with the harsh realities of racial discrimination.

I tried to register for work as a stenographer. One agent told me that she didn't register black women because they would have to work in offices with white women. Another agent tried to find me a position and he told me though my references were excellent, firms did not want to employ a black stenographer. (Jarrett-MacCauley, 1998, p. 51)

Black Women in the National Health Service

Within the National Health Service, Black women were employed mainly as domestic cleaners and canteen workers. Those who wished to train as nurses were often rejected or channelled away from the State Registered training towards the lower status State Enrolled qualification. There was also a tendency for Black nurses from the Caribbean to be concentrated in specific areas such as geriatrics, learning disability and mental health. This was similarly the case for African doctors who were over-represented in areas of psychiatry and geriatrics. Furthermore, there was a noticeable absence of Black people in areas of physiotherapy, chiropody, speech therapy and radiotherapy. For those who came directly from the Caribbean to train as State Registered Nurses (SRN) one woman described it as a period fraught with difficulties.

I arrived in England in 1951, to pursue a course in nursing at a hospital in London. During my career as a student nurse, I came across a series of problems with nursing sisters who make you go to the sluice all day to wash waste from incontinent patients. It was very difficult then to figure out why it was always the few black nurses and Irish who got sent down to the sluice … There were other aspects of nursing duties to be done, but invariably you end up in the wretched sluice, either cleaning bed pans or washing the messy bed sheets. Freezing cold, freezing but you had to accept it, though you knew it was wrong. You would be upset but you couldn't show it. It was difficult, very difficult. (Roots Oral History Project, 1992, p. 21)

A study during the 1980s found that 61% of the qualified nursing workforce was from overseas. Within this group, Irish and Malaysians were often State Registered Nurses (SRN), ward sisters, and nursing officers while Caribbean and Filipino women were likely to be State Enrolled Nurses (SEN) or nursing auxiliaries.

I began my nursing career as a cadet nurse. At first, I did not enjoy nursing because I was pushed into doing the SEN course. During the period of my training, I realized that not only was I getting top marks but some of the other trainees were quite dumb, and I was having to help them out. After completing my training, I decided that nursing wasn't for me … Although I successfully completed my first degree in Social Administration, at the time a career change was not possible, so I returned to nursing on a part-time basis. At this stage I made the decision to upgrade my nursing qualification to that of Registered General Nurse … Having completed the RGN in 1993 within the space of six years I was on the 'g' grade. However, I was aware of the fact that many Black nurses who had successfully completed their conversion course were still on the lower 'D' grade. A few years later, I obtained a further degree in specialist nursing, and my work to date has included that of a specialist nurse counsellor. (PhD Thesis, Watt, 2002)

The children of these early migrants from the Caribbean islands had similar experiences, as in the case of the British born woman whose parents came to England in 1954. This woman's mother was amongst those who had the opportunity to train an SRN. Having worked on a voluntary basis with the elderly, she decided to train as a nurse. During the interview, she was asked whether she knew the difference between a State Registered and State Enrolled nurse. In response she told the interviewers that her mother and other women in her family were State Registered Nurses. The members of the interviewing panel responded by informing her that SENs were good bedside nurses and as such they regarded her as a suitable candidate for this category of nursing. Although extremely upset, she did not realize that this rejection was based primarily on the colour of her skin and thought that the interviewers just did not like her. She knew that some of the children had not liked her at school because whenever someone called her nigger, she would, in her own words, 'batter' them and the headmistress would respond by telling her that she had a 'chip' on her shoulder. This was not the same with the interviewing panel because they had only just met her, and she was really at a loss as to why they were so unpleasant towards her. She nevertheless remained undeterred and subsequently trained as an SRN at one of the London hospitals. As a State Registered Nurse, midwife, and health visitor with a Master's Degree in Women's Studies, she has subsequently worked in various management positions within the field of health care.

The late Louise Da-Cocodia (Fig. 2.2) was one of the early post-war migrants who came to England to train as a State Registered Nurse (SRN).

After obtaining my State Registration, I undertook midwifery training and subsequently completed the health visitor's course, then I took up a senior post in Berkshire. I came to Manchester to take up a post as Assistant Superintendent of District Nurses. In my senior post, it became apparent that some of the white nurses under my supervision didn't like receiving orders from me … There were resentments, because you'd see them sort of thinking, "and who do you think

Fig. 2.2 Louise Da-Cocodia

you are you so and so;" although there was nothing they could do about it because I had the authority. (Roots Oral History Project, 1992, p. 21).

In addition to her work with the National Health Service, not to mention the care of her two children Richard and Nisemi, Louise Da-Cocodia became the chairperson for the West Indian Organisation Co-ordinating Committee

(WIOCC) in 1984. Two years later she co-founded Cariocca Enterprises and Arawak-Walton Housing. In 1989 she was awarded an honorary Master's degree by the University of Manchester for services to nursing and the community. In 1990 she was nominated to the Manchester Magistrates Bench where she served for 14 years. Based on her activities in the field of racial justice she received the Manchester Race Award (1995) for improving race relations in the city. The same year she became a member of the General Synod of the Church of England. Four years later she was appointed Deputy Lord Lieutenant for Greater Manchester. Having first received a British Empire Medal in 1992, Louise Da-Cocodia was awarded an MBE in 2005 for her tireless service to the local community. Following a brief period of illness, she unexpectedly passed away on 13th March 2007. As one of the founder members of the Cariocca Education Trust and in acknowledgement of her work, the organisation was re-named the Louise Da-Cocodia Education Trust.

The experiences of all these women in the NHS were not unlike the position of Mary Seacole, the once forgotten and now celebrated Jamaican nurse who travelled at her own expense to the Crimea in 1855 with the sole purpose of volunteering her services as a nurse. Her offer was rejected and despite Seacole's extensive nursing skills, she was not amongst the 38 nurses selected by Florence Nightingale to accompany her to the Crimean War (Day, 1994). In 1856, William Howard Russell, an influential journalist and special correspondent of the *Times* wrote, 'I have witnessed her [Seacole's] devotion and her courage … and I trust that England will never forget the one who has nursed her sick, who sought out her wounded to aid and succour them, and who performed the last offices for some of her illustrious dead' http://www.justgiving.com/maryseacolememorial. Mary Seacole was nevertheless forgotten. So much so that in 1977, an approach by the Manchester Black Women's Mutual Aid to host the first Roots festival on 'The Life and Times of Mary Seacole' at a local secondary school was rejected on the grounds that no such person had existed. According to one of the members of the Manchester Black Women's Mutual Aid, the teachers threatened to walk out, claiming that the women in the group were just troublemakers. Following the success of this first Roots festival held at Manchester's West Indian Centre, it was decided that it should be an annual event. With the arrival of a new and supportive head teacher, for the next twelve years, the week-long Roots festival was held at the school which had initially rejected it. The themes included 'The International Year of the Child,' 'Harriet Tubman and Growing Up in Multi-Racial Britain'.

Abasindi is Born

Sudbury (1998, p. 98) argues that Black women's organizations are spaces in which Black women can create oppositional and empowering narratives of self. The Organisation for Women of African and Asian Descent (OWAAD) 1978–1982 (Fig. 2.3) was thus seen as the catalyst for the creation of a number of Black women's organizations throughout the country.

In Manchester this included the Manchester Black Women's co-operative, the Manchester Black Women's Mutual Aid, the Moss Side and Hulme Women's Action Forum, and Sojourners Refuge. The Manchester Black Women's Co-operative was initially established to create a place for women to develop office skills geared towards meeting the training and employment needs of young Black mothers. It also provided the space for young men and women to become politically involved with the development of their community, relating the liberation struggles in various countries in Africa with their own experiences of racism and class discrimination. In 1979 members of the group undertook a lengthy and critical review of the organisation and concluded that although it was situated *in* the community, the membership was not representative *of* the community. They acknowledged that while community can be a place for women's activism, it can also be a place which limits women's control and choices—the organization needed to provide space and opportunities for women's political growth and development. The late Elouise Edwards (Fig. 2.4), one of Abasindi's central figures, stated that few of us are chosen as leaders and that women's contributions are ignored or played down—Abasindi aimed to redress this.

Fig. 2.3 OWAAD (The Organisation for Women of African and Asian Descent)

Fig. 2.4 Elouise Edwards (Mama Edwards)

I was asked to write and explain what Abasindi Co-operative means to me. I am grateful for this opportunity to do so as I am just beginning to realise the depth of feelings I experience when I look back and remember the women and the things they have achieved. Some of them have since passed on and some have returned to their homelands, but I shall never forget the strength that emanated from each one of them. It was their strength and courage that enabled me to become the person I am today. So this is my attempt at describing my life-changing experience of being a member of Abasindi.

A-Action, alert leaves no stone unturned in their quest for the correct solutions
B-Born to survive
A-Accessible haven for women
S-Strong in mind and body
I-Ideology – strong views relative to the aims and objectives of Pan-Africanism
N-No nonsense, firm and resolute
D-Determined, intent on carrying through any initiatives undertaken
I-Independent – self sufficient
W-Wise Women
O-Organised, structured, and professional
M-Motivated – taking comfort from our history
E-Education -each one, teach one
N-Nurturing – enabling others to reach their full potential
S-Stability – long term focus
C-Conscious of who we are and what we are
O-Opposing threats to any woman who seek the service
O-Outstanding in thought, word, and deed
P-Patient – giving time to everyone
E-Efficient – to be the best
R-Research – looking at how things were done before with a view of improvement
T-Training in all aspects of life
I-Initiatives, going forward to always do better
V-Valuing all women
E-Excellence – star quality
Aluta Continua'
(Elouise Edwards).

Although she would never use the term, Elouise Edwards was herself a phenomenal leader. Over a 50-year period, she founded or was actively involved in more than 35 organisations and campaigns tackling a gamut of social and health inequalities. She tended to minimise her role and it was left to others to point out that Mama Edwards had not simply been there but in many cases, had been instigator, leader, or strategist behind a particular initiative's success. She willingly squandered kindnesses for it was in her nature to be empathic and though she was not averse to confrontation, it was more her style to enter a room and quietly transform the distance between people into a space for negotiation. Elouise never commanded that anyone do anything, but it was clear she considered passivity in the face of oppression as complicity. Mama Edwards (as she was known) is one of eight radical anti-imperialist activists featured by the Manchester Guardian in its

Special Issue 'Cotton Capital' (2023) and is celebrated in this poem by Deanne Heron.

Salute! Chief Elouise Edwards MBE

African Queen to whom family, community and culture mean much,
From birth, so many across the world your benevolence has touched.
A stoic role model for Black women but sterling example for all,
When inequality raised its head in its many forms Chief, you stood tall.
Guyanese born wife of Beresford Edwards, aka Nana Bonsu, and mother of four sons,
Mama Edwards, tireless community and civil rights campaigner across decades, second to none.
The 'Pardner' savings club was instrumental in your early years in Britain combating financial strife,
It paid for your passage from the Caribbean to join your husband and start a new life.
In 1961 you established yourself in the terrace houses of the Moss Side community of old,
And began the fight for equality in the 'Mother Country's' debilitating weather of ice and cold.
The rag 'n bone man, black and white TV, coal fires with smoking chimneys and thick obscuring fog,
And offensive signs born of hate and ignorance in windows saying: 'No Blacks, No Irish, No Dogs.'
With family for cricket, you travelled on coaches linking England's West Indian Community Centres,
Rallies, demonstrations and marches against injustice, a vital role with other pioneering Black mentors.
For the racism of the narrow minded and unaware, in every aspect of our lives was rife,
In Enoch Powell's dark political era of 'Rivers of Blood', it was difficult being supportive mother and wife.
With music, Caribbean food, drink and jovial camaraderie, community support kept many sane,
The 'Sub Parties' provided stability, reassurance and allowed trampled self-esteem to be regained.
At the forefront of the formation of WIOCC, your precious time the only price,
Providing education and leisure activities as well as housing, employment, and legal advice.
Who can forget the terrifying race riots of 1981, the fires, broken glass and looting,
When 'SUSS' laws of Stop and Search gave police power, though no guns then, and no shootings.
The role you played in Abasindi Co-operative in treating the wounded regardless of colour,

political activism which was happening across so many different fields during Abasindi's lifetime. Everything from opposing the SUS laws and police harassment of Black people, through challenging mainstream feminism, e.g., at the time when women's right to choose abortion was high on the agenda for White women, Black women were fighting its imposition and the forced sterilizations and sexual assault on ethnic minority women by immigration officials. Belonging to Abasindi taught me that grassroots organising, and activism can have a real effect and I've continued to work with my local community. As Abasindi we were involved with a number of anti-deportation campaigns in support of African Caribbean and Asian women, all of which were successful. Our Saturday and summer schools are still remembered by those who attended, now adults with their own children, as instilling pride and confidence. Abasindi Drummers and Dancers not only contributed to the cultural awareness and fitness of the women and girls involved, but offered a vibrant spectacle to innumerable fundraising, women's movement, and community events. A younger friend of mine asked me to tell her about Abasindi, so I asked her what she knew already. She said that she knew that it involved a strong group of women, but also that it was seen as lesbian and anti-men. I laughed aloud! I marvelled at how homophobia and sexism had come together in that perception to negate the status of the group. We recognized that ours was a radical grouping, but we never took on the label 'feminist,' although there were members who defined themselves in this way. The group was certainly remarkably diverse involving older established community activists, students, local workers, girls, Rastafarian, religious, atheist, women who just wanted to do something useful with their time. This grouping taught me that labels do not define individuals, it is their relationships and interaction with others that give the fuller picture. Our defining terms were Black and women, yet our concerns and actions were about improving the quality of life for our whole community. It is great to see an upsurge of activism to challenge the self-serving greed and callousness of the ruling interests in the world. Everyone is made up of a complex mix of identities, today referred to as intersectionality, but I have learned to be cautious about becoming too hooked on the language we use. Working with all sorts of people, I have realized that it is behaviours, actions and outcomes that matter more than words. Being involved with Abasindi I learnt that doing is what makes the difference. It is more important than all the thinking and talking that frame one's actions. I was one of only a few (out) lesbians associated with Abasindi and one of the strengths of the group was that we drew on aspects of our individual identity and interests to be involved with a broad base of activism with a wide range of people. This has left me with an openness to talk to people and a willingness to make common cause with different groupings to work for the common good. This was a key transformation for me as experiences of racism had left me closed and self-protective in my earlier life. Members of Abasindi made a bridge to all sorts of different campaigns – Greenham Common, the Miners' dispute, seeking medical provision to tackle sickle cell anaemia, tackling racial and gender dis-crimination in education, arguing for appropriate provision for Black children in care. We did solidarity work with the Nicaraguan socialists, anti-apartheid activists, Women Worldwide. We hosted cultural events and built links with cultural groups in Africa and the Caribbean, initiated community work such as mentoring of school children, Roots Family History Project and the annual Roots Festival that ran for several years, gaining a recognition blue plaque for the 1945 Pan African Congress. We backed a hostel for Black women survivors of domestic abuse. We participated in the short-lived national organisations, the Organisation of Women of African and Asian Descent (OWAAD) and the National Black Lesbian Support Group, as well as Manchester based Black Sisters and local women's celebrations. All these involvements contributed to our political awareness and built up skills and confidence amongst the women involved with Abasindi, but the bedrock for me was the weekly Friday meeting, which provided succour against some of the tough times that were confronting us all. If laughter is the best medicine, we certainly had a lot of it at these meet-ings, along with no small amount of alcohol and cigarettes – not such healthy options. We talked about anything and everything, testing ideas and opinions. Several great learning points for me were instilled by the late Kath Locke; 'we have history and need to keep it in mind, learn from it and build on it. I can go on learning throughout my life from people and courses and through thinking. As a group we need to control funding, rather than let it control us.' I continue to act on these lessons. I was involved in development of the Ahmed Iqbal Ullah Race Relations Archive/Resource Centre and Education Trust. I research and present talks on Black History and I am active in building social capital in my community, which is based out of the efforts of local people, backed by appro-priate funding pools. In cautioning against taking ongoing funding Kath used to say, 'The State doesn't pay you to oppose it.' Indeed, the State now pays com-munity groups to keep its members in line and to denounce those 'radicals' who challenge state actions. Our lives are now under closer State scrutiny than ever before, for both legitimate and illegitimate reasons. The equality gains that we made in the 20th century – education, pay and conditions, housing quality, justice, anti-discrimination laws – are all under dire threat. Thanks to my grounding with my sisters in Abasindi I was under no illusions. We must fight for our rights and keep fighting to protect our gains.

Abasindi worked collaboratively with organisations such as the Manchester Black Women's Mutual Aid and the Moss Side and Hulme Women's Action Forum on a range of community development initiatives. The organisation's work with the Moss Side and Hulme Women's Action Forum included the 1997 'Women as Role Model Conference'. As part of the European Year of Anti-Racism and International Women's Week, this conference was organised

Fig. 2.7 Louise Da-Cocodia speaking at the 'Women as Role Model' conference

in celebration of the lives and achievements of Black women in Manchester. The event was chaired by the late Louise Da-Cocodia (Fig. 2.7), a founder member of the Moss Side and Hulme Women's Action Forum (MOSHWAF). In her opening address she concluded thus: 'The greatest challenge of the conference was to give voice to local women and women everywhere whose experience and aspirations go untested.'

The speakers at the conference included Sharon Beck, who spoke about the lack of recognition in management courses on issues of sexism and racism and its impact on the lives of women aspiring to management positions. On the issue of Black women's position in areas of management, the 1997 campaign of the Commission for Racial Equality found that traditionally Black women were more reluctant than men to complain about institutional racism. At the 'Women as Role Model' conference, Val Blake nevertheless highlighted the need for Black women to identify and celebrate their achievements. Carol Baxter emphasized the importance of recognizing and celebrating the contributions of Black women in the building of the country's National Health Service. Having mentored and supported two young women from an early age, Wilma Deane pointed out that even when as women we appear to have achieved success, our need for positive role models continues all through life. The conference was also an opportunity to pay tribute to women activists such as Elouise Edwards and Kath Locke (Fig. 2.8).

Bryan et al. argue that:

> If we are to gain anything from our history and from our lives in this country which can be of practical use to us today, we must take stock of our experiences assess our responses – and learn from them. This will be done by listening to the voices of the mothers, sisters, grandmothers, and aunts who established our presence here. And by listening to our own voices. (Bryan et al., 2018, p. 4)

Fig. 2.8   Kath Locke and Elouise Edwards

Judy Craven spoke about her experiences as an adult education tutor working with women who, because they had no educational qualifications, would often describe themselves as 'only a housewife'. In conversation it was not unusual for the women to start with a list of things they could not do, yet it was obvious to her that they were involved in a range of complex activities both at home and within the wider community. She concluded that:

> It is proven in communities all over the globe that one of the things we women excel in is fostering, encouraging, and drawing the potential out of sisters and the people around us. This is something we should be celebrating and if we get the GCSE in English or the degree, that is good and wonderful; but if we feel that we have supported and developed somebody else this is the real achievement. (Conference Report, 1997, p. 15)

In commenting on the findings of her own small-scale research on Black women's definition of achievement, one of the speakers found that the women

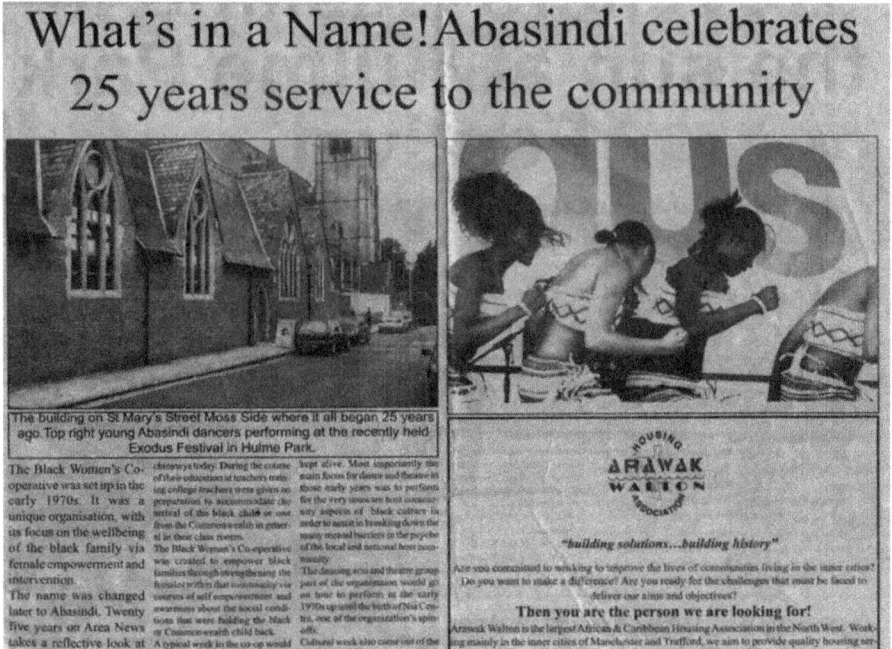

What's in a Name! Abasindi celebrates 25 years service to the community

Fig. 2.9   Abasindi celebrates 25th birthday

in her study had different views on the concept of achievement. These included staying sane, being a good mother, and creating a stable base for the family. The speaker argued that to encourage Black women to redefine achievement is not to diminish the concept generally or academic achievement, but rather to recognize that for many women, there are far greater achievements in their lives outside of academia. It was therefore important for them to recognize and value all aspects of their life experiences and to acknowledge that one of the characteristics of Black women in history was their ability to assess their situation and plan strategies aimed at overcoming adversity. This allowed them to move away from negative situations to a position of hope, faith, and strength. These are women whose experiences have been portrayed by Campbell in African-Caribbean poetry as 'history makers,' as 'women stonebreakers,' as 'hammers and rocks', and 'as builders' whose strength has provided not just the sustenance for survival but also the power to create a way of life.'

At the celebration of Abasindi's 25th birthday (Fig. 2.9), founder member Abina Likoya reflected: "There used to be something operating in the 70s called the Black Women's Co-operative, but it was run by men! We decided that perhaps it was time for community action run for women by women, taking a little ownership back – and everything developed from there."

3

Cultural Expressions of Resilience

Abstract This chapter explores Black women's activism in relation to the arts. The Abasindi Women's Cooperative was not only involved in the promotion of African and Caribbean art forms but its members were also creators of art. Abasindi women 'laid claim to spirit' and infused this notion into the music, songs, costume design, poetry, writing, photography and films they produced. We dismissed the notion that culture and the arts should be separated from politics as an artificial contrivance, and we not only used the arts to bring light to social justice campaigns, we simultaneously developed political strategies to highlight the marginalisation of African-Caribbean art forms. By placing Africa at the centre of these multiple means of cultural expression, we also identified ourselves as part of a broader anti-colonialist Pan-African struggle for recognition and representation. Through our community activism, we also ensured that local political struggles were infused by the celebration of African and Caribbean art.

Keywords African • Caribbean • Black women • Art • Culture • Representation • Community

> ***Black and Beautiful as We Are***
> *From where*
> *We do not know*
> *We find the strength to crawl off the back shelf*
> *Dragging the age-old mantles behind us:*
> *Low achiever*
> *Will not go far*
> *Chip on shoulder*

We have landed in the mire of history
And when we laugh if off
Our humour is considered intrusively loud
Fearfully aggressive
So we stop smiling
At those we do not know
Do not want to know
And the distance
Deepens over the years
But in the secret place of our dreams
Hope is never a stranger
We plot
Not like mutineers
We plan like generals
Determined to stop this war
We study
Write
Snip
At frugal budgets
Yet still we fashion ourselves
Sophisticate our styles
So that we may never be seen as
Third class
Because this ladder has missing rungs
We stumble
But still we ascend
The heavens may be out of reach
But achievement
Like retribution
Is the goal of possibility.
We are warriors
Amazonians
Mothers
Wives
Sisters
Friends
Standing at the edge of tides
We would never exchange for anything
Black and beautiful as we are

SuAndi ©2014

Resilience

Resilience has been described as the 'ability to climb more times than you slip or fall by discovering the faith, comfort, and inner power.' The celebrated African American civil rights activist, poet and writer Maya Angelou stated that 'To be successful is to be constant, to be patient and resilient – to accept things as they are. Resilience means…laying claim to your spirit.' (Riley, 2002, p. 243). This chapter explores the ways in which the women of Abasindi, by way of various cultural expressions have been resilient in withstanding and challenging racism and gendered forms of discrimination. Abasindi women laid claim to their spirit, but they did not accept things as they were. Beckles (1989) coined the term 'natural rebel' and 'rebel woman' to describe the experiences of enslaved and oppressed Black women whose power has been associated with their ability to transmit cultural norms and practices. This is a form of power which has no economic or political links. Furthermore, it is not based on the domination of women, it is a struggle of resistance and those spirits of resilience that have been central in ensuring survival and growth (Hill Collins, 1990). Nanny of the Maroons is noted for her legacy of resistance and resilience. She was an exceptional woman whose power was underpinned by material and cultural factors. Culturally she drew on the tradition of the Ashanti Queen Mother and materially on the control which African women had over agriculture (Campbell, 1992). In continuing along the path of resistance and resilience carved out by Nanny, the Abasindi Cooperative provided an opportunity for Black women to develop skills and strengths for themselves and the wider community (Fig. 3.1).

Alice Walker (1983) argued that experiences of suspension, assimilation and emergence were the three cyclical stages that are associated with Black women's movement from being victims of society and of men to that of having control over their lives. Based on her personal interpretation of Black women's history in America, the stage of suspension is in reference to Black women during the nineteenth and early twentieth century whom Zora Neale Hurston describes as the 'mules of the world'. Despite being the victims of racial and sexual oppression, Sojourner Truth's speech at the 1851 women's convention in Akron, Ohio nevertheless echoes the determination and resilience of these women.

That man over there say that a woman need to be helped into carriages and lifted over ditches, and to have the best place everywhere. Nobody ever helped me into carriages, or over mud puddles, or give me a best place…And ain't I a

Fig. 3.1 Abasindi Women—faces of resilience

woman? Look at me. Look at my arm! I have ploughed and planted and gathered into barns, and no man could head me… and ain't I a woman? I could work as much and eat as much as a man when I could get it, and bear the lash as well… and ain't I a woman? I have borned thirteen children and seen them most all sold into slavery. And when I cried out with a mother's grief, none but Jesus heard. And ain't I a woman (Sojourner Truth quoted in Davis, 1981, p. 61)

Amy Jacques Garvey of Jamaica also believed that Black women's experiences of what King (1973) termed 'multiple jeopardy' compelled them to cultivate inner strengths that rendered them natural leaders in the fight for equality. As a leading Pan-Africanist and Black nationalist for over 50 years, she held the post of Secretary General for the Universal Negro Improvement Association (UNIA). Based on the community social and economic development model, UNIA (and the African Communities League) was one of most powerful Black organisations of the early twentieth century. The African Communities League was the business arm of the organisation and established the Negro Factories Corporation which was responsible for managing UNIA's laundries, restaurants, tailoring and millinery establishments, printing press and doll factory. The doll factory was established to ensure that Black children had access to black dolls which was regarded as essential to the development of healthy self-esteem, positive self-concept, and pride in being Black (Carlton-LaNey, 2001, p. 81).

Although she was often described as Marcus Garvey's companion and 'nurturing spouse,' Amy Garvey is one of the most remarkable women in history. She was amongst the women of that period who developed a 'cultural resistance' that offered Black people an alternative to prevailing racist, classist, and sexist ideologies (Collins, 1990, p. 147). From 1924–27, Amy Jacques Garvey was the associate editor of the UNIA newspaper *The Negro World* and was responsible for introducing the page '*Our Women and What they Think.*' This page included contributions not only from women in America but also articles, poetry and, letters from women in the Caribbean and Africa. In her article on 'Women as Leaders,' she describes Black women as the ones who have 'borne the rigors of slavery, the deprivations consequent on a pauperized race, and the indignities heaped upon a weak and defenceless people. Yet she has suffered all with fortitude and stands ever ready to help in the onward march to freedom and power.' Matthews (1979) is critical of the tendency to minimise the work of Black women who played an integral role in the shaping of the Garvey movement. Whilst maintaining that the Jamaican feminist movement of the 1930's and 1940's was nurtured within the Garvey movement, Ford-Smith (1988) found little difference in the portrayal of Black women from the racialised image of the subservient woman upheld by dominant colonial ideology. During the period of Marcus Garvey's incarceration on charges of mail fraud in connection with the Black Star Line, Amy Garvey published volume two of *The Philosophy and Opinions of Marcus Garvey* and two volumes of his poetry *The Tragedy of White Injustice* and *Selections from the Poetic Mediations of Marcus Garvey*. The proceeds from the sale of these publications were used towards Garvey's defence. After his death in 1940, Amy Jacques continued the struggle for Black nationalism and played an instrumental role in the organisation of the 1945, fifth Pan African Congress which was held at the Chorlton Town Hall in Manchester. She was also one of the sponsors of the 1974, 6th Pan African Congress in Tanzania. In 1963, she published her own book, *Garvey and Garveyism*, and later published two collections of essays, *Black Power in America* and *The Impact of Garvey in Africa and Jamaica*. In her article on the role of women in liberation struggles, Amy Jacques wrote

> As a Black woman I was trained by my father who lived in Cuba for years and spoke Spanish fluently; he also lived in Baltimore. He married my mother, and settled down in Jamaica, West Indies. For five years they had no children, so my mother prayed for a 'son and heir.' I came a girl, but my dad trained me as if I were a boy. He took me around the property, explained to me how tobacco was

grown and cured, taught me to use a gun to shoot stray goats. On Sundays, after dinner, he would collect his foreign newspapers, and I had to get a dictionary and read editorials and news items; he would explain everything to me and answer all my questions. Sometimes he would give me an essay to write on a news item or article. This made me learn to think independently on world affairs and to analyse situations. So, when I met Marcus Garvey the International Black Leader, he found in me an understanding and dedicated partner. (Jacques Garvey, 109–112)

Prior to her death in 1973, Amy Garvey was awarded the Institute of Jamaica Musgrave Gold Medal (http://blackhistorypages.net/pages/agarvey.php).

The 1940's and 50's are described as the period of assimilation and are associated with Black women's experiences of psychic violence. This was a consequence of their desire for white acceptance at the expense of their own racial identity. Within the British context, it was at a time when the Jamaican poet and journalist Una Marson (Fig. 3.2) was being described as:

…a major figure in 20th century feminist black and literary histories. Her story arcs towards untouched visions for black people and for women and confronts the complexities of 'identity' in the modern world. And yet it has been erased because it is alternative, and discredited because it is critical. So often, even now, black women of Una's stature appear only as token women in black texts or as token blacks in feminist ones. When their contributions are noted, they might be represented superwomen – separate from their peers. (Jarrett-MacCauley, 1998, p. viii)

Born in 1905, Una Marson encouraged women to develop their intellects and extend their activities beyond that of home and work. She was one of the founder members of the Jamaica Business Women's Association (JBWA) and was amongst those who gave evidence to the West Indian Royal Commission on the condition of women in the British Caribbean. This Commission was appointed in 1938 as a direct result of the labour rebellions in Jamaica and the other Caribbean islands (Shepherd, 2006). In 1932, Marson arrived in England aboard the SS Jamaica Settler. Within three years she had become a leading Black feminist activist in London. At the request of the Women's Social Service Club in 1935, she attended the 12th Annual Congress of the International Alliance of Women for Suffrage and Equal Citizenship. This event took place in Turkey and was attended by over 250 delegates. In commenting on her speech to the Congress, the Manchester Guardian reported that: 'This negro woman of African origin from the former slave world of

Fig. 3.2 Una Marson

Jamaica brought a new note into the assembly and astonished them by the vigour of her intellect and her feminist optimism.' (Jarrett-MacCauley, 1998, pp. 87–91). As a Black nationalist and feminist writer, she made several attempts to organise women into an active force in the nationalist movement through cultural expression. Sistren Theatre Collective attributes their existence to Marson's pioneering work in the use of her own experiences as the raw material for her poetry and drama. Marson also emphasised the 'link between art and nationalist struggle…' (Sistren Theatre Collective and Ford-Smith, 1986, p. xxiv).

Walker's third cycle consists of 'emergent' women who were influenced by the political activism of the 1960's and 70's. It was a period when African Americans such as herself, were encouraged by Black activists and musicians to 'Think Black, Talk Black, Create Black, Buy Black, Vote Black and Live Black' (Gilroy, 1987, pp. 176–177). In Manchester, the period of Walker's emergent women also gave rise to the activism of women such as Elouise

Edwards, Ada Philips, Shirley Innis, Paula May, Louise Da-Cocodia and Kath Locke.

Of all the women to have played a role in the success of the Abasindi Cooperative, it was the political philosophy of Kath Locke that was its driving force. Long-standing friend of Abasindi is the lawyer and university lecturer Paul Okojie, who stood beside us in many of our human rights struggles. He knew Kath well and below reflects on her contribution to improving the lives of Black people in Manchester.

Kath Locke was born in Manchester in 1928 but lived her early years in Blackpool. She remembered her school years in Blackpool and how her school deprived her because of racist reasons of a place in a grammar school despite passing the 11 plus (11+) examination. This had an unforgettable effect on her life and the experience strongly influenced her politics and activism. In a video conversation with the author just before her death, she recalled her parent's effort to right this cruel racism only for them to be thrown into a Kafkaesque world that led nowhere. Her parents were dealing with a school system lacking in accountability and transparency.

Kath Locke returned with her parents to the red bricked two-up, two-down terraced houses of Moss Side, Manchester, still in her early teens. Moss Side at the time had a large Irish immigrant population and some East European Jewish communities. African and Caribbean people started to settle in Moss Side from the 1930s, and in large numbers in the immediate post-war period. She returned to a Moss Side – a concentric zone of Black Commonwealth citizens within the periphery of Manchester city centre; it mirrored experience elsewhere in Britain where the more affluent white population moved to more prosperous suburbs. Despite 'white flight,' the Moss Side of her youth was a thriving community – culturally and commercially, for example, the Guyanese, Ras Makonnen, owned many business enterprises earning enough income to enable him to finance the 5th Pan African Congress held in Manchester in 1945. The area was buzzing with African-Caribbean clubs with names such as the Palm Beach, the Reno and the Nile, the Cotton Club, and the Kroo Club.

Although she travelled to many countries including China where she met some of China's top political leaders, Manchester was her home. She lived on the Alexander Park Estate, Moss Side where she brought up her three children (Fig. 3.3).

As a community activist, Kath was concerned about the housing conditions on the estate. She campaigned vigorously against the neglect of housing: organising petitions, leading demonstrations, and marches. Manchester Council eventually responded by improving the housing stock in the estate by the late 1960s and early 1970s. This was proof to her of how the balance of power can be tilted in favour of political activism and solidarity. She was the perpetual

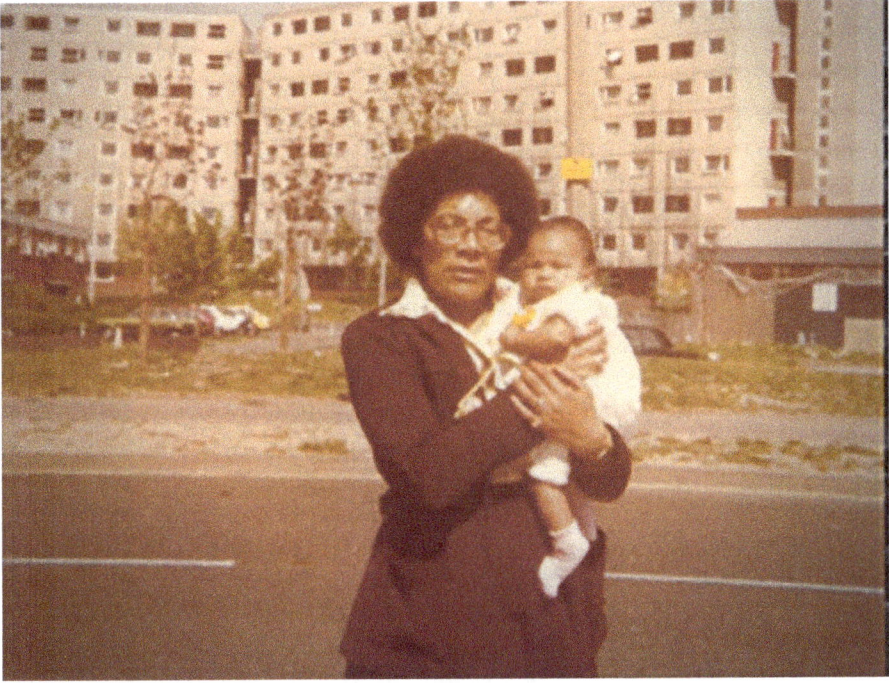

Fig. 3.3   Kath with one of her children in the Hulme/Moss Side district

idealist and inspiration to many young people. Kath believed strongly in the power of the community to change their situation. At the heart of this belief is the idea of self-empowerment of which the Abasindi Black Women's Cooperative was an example. She would enumerate several conditions for achieving self-improvement: clarity of purpose, not keeping silent in the face of evil or injustice, social solidarity, sound organisational strategies and financial self-reliance. She was fastidious about the principle of not seeking financial help from the group against whom one is opposed. Thus, Abasindi remained a self-financing entity. It was her cardinal belief that power relationships between the community and the economically powerful cannot be redressed if activists do not resist the temptation of the 'begging bowl.' She often recited how many radical community groups had become neutered in their politics because of financial dependency on the group there were supposed to be opposing. Pressure groups, she would argue, should remain true to their cause, and avoid undermining their message by compromises. The success of the campaign for the slum clearance on the Alexandra Park Estate was a great lesson in shaping her activist politics. For example, following Kath's self-belief as an activist, the campaigners funded their own campaign. In spite of the undoubted success of the slum clearance campaign, Kath remained disappointed at the depth of social deprivation in Moss Side. She blamed this on several causal factors, key among these being the school system. She would cite Bernard Coard's book, 'How the West Indian Child was made Educationally Subnormal in the British School System'. The book had a dramatic impact on the ongoing debate about the causes of under-achievement of Caribbean children in British schools and became part of the manifesto for those resisting racism in the education of Black children. Coard's view of Black children's experience in school chimed with Kath's experience as a school child in Blackpool. Although Coard's work was based on a study of inner London Schools, Kath believed the same was true of the experience of Black children in Manchester. She used to say that no child is uneducable and that teachers who think otherwise should not be in school. As with housing, she was very strong in supporting parents whose children were facing expulsions or disciplinary hearings in school. Apart from racism in schools, Kath also believed lack of opportunity in the labour market due to racial discrimination was a major factor in the poverty in the area. It was through Kath that I first became aware of the work of Arthur Lewis in the Black community in Hulme and Moss Side. He was the Black Professor of Economics at Manchester University who won the Nobel Prize for Economics in 1979. She drew attention to his work to show how long the people of Moss Side had been forced to live with poverty and deprivation due to neglect on the part of the civic authorities. She would remark repeatedly that this was due not to lack of knowledge, but wilful blindness. Prof Lewis who died in the same year as Kath Locke (1991), came from St Lucia and like Kath he was concerned about the economic position of Black people in Manchester. They also both had wider concerns about the police, the criminal justice system and general racial discrimination. Following the 1981 Moss Side Uprising (during which Abasindi was the centre where those wounded by the Tactical Aid Group (a para-military force) within the Greater Manchester Police were taken for first aid treatment prior to going to hospital) Kath became an ardent campaigner against the abuse of police powers against Black people. Kath Locke pondered all her life about what the community should do about racism. In a way, she provided the answer in the establishment of Abasindi. Visitors found that Abasindi was not only a community centre, but also a kind of school without borders and Kath was the Mwalimu; an inspiring community educator – she could be said to have embodied Paulo Freire's idea of communities as their own educators. Kath was a strong advocate of the Black community harnessing their social capital in responding to its myriad problems: schooling, housing, unemployment, racial discrimination and the menace of the National Front and she regarded identity as the 'pull' that would bring the community together to act in their interests. As well as her local activism, Kath was also a political activist at the international level. This was most evident when she discussed the impact of the 5th Pan African Congress held in Manchester in 1945. Although she was too young to participate in the conference, she recalled with pride meeting some of the key conference delegates such as Jomo Kenyatta and Ras Makonnen through her father's connections. Throughout her life she believed that the problems facing Black people, whether local or international could be solved through unity and collective solidarity. She will always be remembered as one of Manchester's most powerful and feisty fighters for the people's rights. (Paul Okojie).

Disconnections and Re-unification

Although most of the Abasindi members were either born or had strong family links with the Caribbean, the sense of Africanness is what informed the individual and collective identity of the group, despite the disconnection and divisions that had been sown through colonialism. 'Colonisation is not satisfied merely with holding a people in its grip … by a kind of perverted logic, it turns to the past of the oppressed people, and distorts, disfigures and destroys it' (Fanon, 1968, p. 70). In 1840–41, the decision by the Mayor of Kingston in Jamaica to ban John Canoe (also called Jonkonnu/Junkanoo) festivals during Christmas celebrations was based on what was seen as the festival's 'barbarous' African links. The mayor was of the view that, the 'wild' dancing and the 'noisy' drumming had to be curtailed if the formerly enslaved were to acquire new habits of 'civilisation' and decorum (Shepherd et al., 1995, pp. 286–287). The disconnection from Africa was indeed central to the experiences of Caribbean people. By placing Africa at the centre of its cultural expressions, Abasindi provided women with the space to both 'recover' and 'discover' themselves. This journey of re-unification with the ancestors is in keeping with the fundamental tenets of traditional West African religious practices and ancient theological beliefs in the existence of two or more souls. The Yoruba people of Nigeria and the Fon of Dahomey identifies four souls. The first is the life soul which comes from the Supreme Being and enters us at the time of birth. The second is the personality soul which differentiates us from each other. The third soul is that of the guardian soul commonly referred to as the guardian angel. Fourth, there is the shadow soul, which is indistinguishable from the guardian soul. In the Caribbean, this belief in the hereafter is a mixture of both Christian and African practices. At death and after three days, the soul that comes from God goes back to God. The personality soul returns to the land of the ancestors and may be reborn repeatedly in children of the lineage. The guardian and/or shadow soul usually remains with the family for nine days to ensure that all the funeral rites are completed. The soul may also stay indefinitely, depending under what circumstances death occurred. Whilst taking their leave from the family they remain in the land of the living and communicate with them either through dreams or visions (Barrett, 1976, p. 108).

The extent of the colonialist fear and suspicion of traditional religious practices such as voodoo—derived from Vodun, the principal deity of the Yoruba people, can be found in the following extract from a speech given by Jules Renkin, Governor of Kinshasa. This speech to the first group of missionaries to the Congo in 1883 was published in a Belgian newspaper in 1951.

> Reverend Father and dear Compatriots, the task, I ask you to accomplish is very delicate and demands much tact and diplomacy. Fathers you are going to preach the Gospel, but your preaching must be inspired by first, the interest of the Belgian State…To do so, you will see that our savages be not interested in the riches that their soil possesses, in order that they will not want them…You will cause them to follow the Saints who turned the other cheek. You will take them away from any thing and act that procures them with the courage to confront us. I am alluding myself here to their magic, i.e., Juju, Voodoo. They should feel like abandoning their Juju and you will do your best to take them.

Obeah and Myal are two of the terms that were used in Jamaica to describe religious and quasi-religious activities among the enslaved. Section 3 of the 1760 Jamaica Obeah Act clearly pointed to the belief on the part of the colonialist of a relationship between religion and rebellion (Alleyne, 1988, p. 83). Among the explanations given for this association is the fact that irrespective of their ethnicity, the enslaved in preparing for war would invariably appeal to Loa Ogun, the Yoruba god of war (Campbell, 1992, p. 4). Abasindi was a secular organisation, but it was important to our understanding of resilience that we educated ourselves about the role of religion in African and Caribbean survival stories.

'Naming' and 'Renaming'

For the women of Abasindi, names were an important part of their identity. According to Woodward (1997, p. 1) 'identity gives us an idea of who we are and how we relate to others and to the world in which we live.' During the period of enslavement 'un-naming' and 'renaming' of newly arrived enslaved people from Africa was one way that slave owners employed to establish possession of people and their descendants, whom they regarded as their property. In his book on *Slave Ships and Slaving*, Thomas Watson who was a sailor on the *Slaver* is quoted as having once said:

> I suppose they…all had names in their own dialect, but the effort required to pronounce them was too much for us, so we picked out our favourites (slaves) and dubbed them *Main-stay, Cats head, Bulls eye, Rope-Yarn*, and various other sea phrases. (Dow in Fitzpatrick, 2012, p. 41)

Giving their children Yoruba, Zulu, and Xhosa names such as Olayinka, Dkizo, Nkosi, Thembikile, Zindiwe or Sibongile represented not only a 'recovery' of ancestral names but also an expression of Abasindi's support for struggles against apartheid in South Africa and colonialist oppression in other parts of Africa. Abasindi member Malaika epitomised the practice (Fig. 3.4) when naming her son.

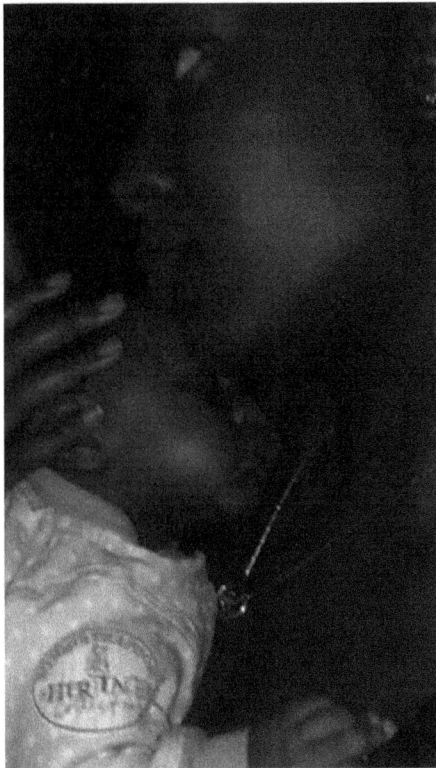

Fig. 3.4 Malaika and her son who carries the African name Nosakhare meaning 'God's will'

Fig. 3.5 Olajumoke Sankofa

Some of the women at Abasindi also adopted African names. Olajumoke Sankofa (Fig. 3.5) explains why this was important to her:

> In the spirit of Sankofa the traditional name Olajumoke Sankofa was bestowed upon me by Elder Lartey Addico. Olajumoke is a Yoruba name which means "All wealth combined to pamper" the child. Ola refers to wealth, affluence, or richness. Ju mo (combine effort, thoughts, and plans), ke (pamper, treat well, spoilt child, shower the child with lots of love and affection.) Jumoke means combined efforts; shower her with love and affection. Sankofa is an Akan word that means 'we must go back and reclaim our past so we can move forward so that we might understand we are today'. We can reach back and take the best of what our past can teach us, so that we can fulfil our potential as we strive to go forward. Regardless of what we may have lost, forgotten or has been stolen we can reclaim, revive, preserve, and perpetuate repeatedly. As a Diasporan African born and raised in Moss Side and growing up within the Abasindi family, the name Olajumoke Sankofa resonates with the heartbeat of Africa, reconnecting me back to the authentic essence of who I am. A constant reminder of why I am here, and what I am here to do in service to my community, race, and nation. (Sankofa, also known as Jumoke).

This process of re-naming was prevalent amongst African/Caribbean and African American people during the Black Power era and the Civil Rights

Movement in the 1960s and 70s. Amongst African Americans the most notable and highly publicised name changes were of Malcolm X and Mohammed Ali. On joining the Chicago Chapter of the Nation of Islam, Malcolm Little replaced his surname with an X to represent how enslavement robbed African people of their identity and cultural heritage. Fanon maintained that this loss produces 'individuals without an anchor, without horizon, colourless, stateless, rootless – a race of angels' (Fanon, 1968, p. 176). On his return from Mecca, Malcolm X again changed his name to El-Hajj Malik El-Shabazz.

Mohammed Ali, the world heavy weight boxing champion, said that his birth name 'Cassius Clay,' lacked "divine meaning" … "I am Muhammad Ali, a free name which means 'beloved of God' – and I insist people use it when speaking to me." "Get used to me… Black, confident, cocky – my name, not yours. My religion not yours. My goals, my own. Get used to me." Prior to his involvement with the Black Power movement and the struggle for the liberation of African people, Trinidadian born Stokeley Carmichael described himself as someone who dated White girls and was 'the good little nigger' (Belton, 2007, p. 74). After his marriage to South African singer Miriam Makeba in 1969, Carmichael left America and went to live in Guinea, West Africa, changing his name to Kwame Touré in honour of the African leaders Kwame Nkrumah of Ghana and Sekou Touré of Guinea. Both leaders were known for being totally opposed to Europe's colonisation of Africa.

Following the release of Alex Haley's book and the film Roots, in 1977, Kizzy was the 17th most popular name given to African American girls. Similarly, the name Marcus, due to Jamaican Pan-Africanist Marcus Garvey, was the 13th most popular name in the 1970s and by 1983 was the fifth most popular name for African American boys in Illinois. Playwright and poet Ntozake Shange changed her name from Paulette William in 1971. In Xhosa, Ntozake means "she who has her own things," and Shange means "she/he who walks/lives with lions" in Zulu. In her biography, Assata Olugba Shakur, a former political prisoner, wrote that 'the name JoAnne Deborah Byron Chesimard began to irk my nerves. I had changed a lot and moved to a different beat, felt like a different person. It sounded strange when people called me JoAnne.' In Yoruba, Assata means 'she who struggles,' Olugba means for the love of the people' and Shakur which means 'the thankful one,' was the surname adopted in honour of Assata's friend Zayd Shakur (Belton, 2007, p. 125; Fitzpatrick, 2012, p. 67).

For the first twelve years of his life, Lemn Sissay believed he was Norman Greenwood, the name 'Norman' given him by his foster parents in honour of the Social Worker that had overridden an Ethiopian mother's wishes and put him up for adoption. 'Greenwood' was his foster family's surname although

Lemn would later say that the Greenwood turned out to be a false promise—he never fully belonged with them. It is one thing to take a child but to take their name too is to forever set them adrift from their roots and is to declare the child's history unworthy. Finding out his birthname set Lemn on a search—'Lemn' means "Why" in Amharic, the official language of Ethiopia and unsurprisingly, Lemn had a million questions. He searched for his birth family, for who he was, why he had been in care and at eighteen, was given his case files which included letters written by his mother showing her desperation to get her child back. The discoveries Lemn unearthed about his past have been crucial to his becoming (Sissay, 2019).

> In Africa, a name is considered to be very much part of the personality of the person. It is chosen with a great deal of care and consideration, often through divination…It is believed that people assume the character life and personality traits after whom they are named…Among the Akan of Ghana a person has two names. The first name is the one he/she automatically assumes on the day they are born. This is the name of the day that they are born. The second name is a family name given to the child by the father. (Kirwen, 2008, p. 26)

The re-claiming of African names is not limited to African people in the Diaspora. Kamau wa Ngengi was the birth name of Jomo Kenyatta who, on the eve of Kenya's independence in 1963, became the country's first prime minister and in 1964 he was elected the country's president. Kenyatta was amongst the Kenyans imprisoned by the British for alleged involvement in the Mau Mau struggle for land, freedom, and self-governance (Maathai, 2007, p. 67). After his conversion to Christianity, Kenyatta had changed his birth name to that of John Peter which he later changed to Johnstone Kamau and then to Jomo Kenyatta. Ironically, this was not so in the case of South Africa's first black president, whose Xhosa name Rolihlahla was changed by his teacher Miss Mdigane, to Nelson (Fitzpatrick, 2012). The *Telegraph* article 'Nelson, Madiba, Tata – What's in a name?' (2013)

suggested that the use of the clan name Madiba carried far more importance than Nelson's surname, Mandela. Peter Alegi, a specialist in South African history at Michigan State University highlights the link between re-naming and colonialism: 'Using the Madiba name is to reclaim his Africanness and to downplay the Nelson part, which is a colonial legacy that unfortunately shackled much of the African continent for a long, long time' (www.usa.today.com/story/news/nation.now.mandela..388469).

In his research on African-Caribbean family history, Guy Grannum outlined the difficulties faced by African-Caribbean people and the African Diaspora in tracing their ancestry and family history. According to Grannum, standard genealogical research in the UK relies on people having surnames that are passed on from father to child. After emancipation freed men and women could also choose their own surnames or accepted names given to them by the church or the State. Although it was the practice in traditional African culture to have one or more personal names, it was uncommon for families to have a name that was handed down from generation to generation (Fitzpatrick, 2012). There is also the assumption that parents were married before or soon after the birth of their first child. Such assumptions do not reflect the reality of enslaved people whose surnames were likely to be that of their last owner or former master or that of their mother or grandmother. Adéle Jones, co-author of this book acknowledges the significant of this point and explains what her name means to her and why she considers the name 'Jones' is an important reminder of the resilience of her enslaved ancestors (Fig. 3.6).

Although I was given the name Adéle, it turns out that I was really named for my Sierra Leonean Aunt Ayodele who died in childbirth; the baby she birthed (also a girl) being named after my mother Beatrice. As if they knew, all my

Fig. 3.6 Adele Jones—sitting by the ocean that connects her adopted home in the Caribbean with her ancestral home in Africa

Abasindi sisters pronounced my name the African way – 'Ade-lay'. I never met my aunt, but this connection is something that binds us – her, me, my mother, and her daughter and for some reason I cannot explain I find this ancestral bind deeply comforting. The name 'Jones' is undoubtedly the name of the slaver that 'owned' my ancestors who eventually found their way back to Africa. They settled in Freetown, the capital of Sierra Leone and so named for formerly enslaved Africans. Once, on a visit to Freetown I told an elderly relative that I wanted to find and reclaim my original African name. He was outraged. He told me that freed slaves built the city, and it would be a dishonour to disown the name that signified what they had endured. He also explained that it would mean I would be forever lost – changing my name would mean that I could not be claimed by the Jones's of Freetown, and I could not claim them – "which people would I belong to?" he wanted to know. Freetown is full of surnames that originated from slave owners – Jones, Smith, McAuley, Thompson, Smythe, Johnson and on and on – it is an important history, and I am thankful that the resilience of the Jones's before me has engendered the resilient person I am today. Now I have reclaimed 'Jones' and I have reframed the narrative of my name – it is not proof of identity theft but proof of resilience.

During the period of enslavement, a man could be sold or transferred to another estate, leaving behind his children and their mother who, later, might be sold without her children. In such a case it was customary for the slave owners to place the children in the care of the woman's mother (Henriques, 1960, p. 146). These women not only reclaimed the children but as Walker says, 'more often than not [they] anonymously handed on the creative spark, the seed of the flowers they themselves never hoped to see' (Walker, 1983, p. 240) and in this way cultural knowledge was often transmitted. Issues of re-naming, re-claiming, culture, and the creative spark of women under-pinned the role played by Abasindi women in the development of the Nia Centre for African and Caribbean Culture and Art (Fig. 3.7).

The NIA Centre was the first 'cultural' space in the North West of England to focus explicitly on African and Caribbean art forms. NIA was the site of many exhibitions and concerts and particularly memorable was the 1991 concert featuring Nina Simone, not only for her incredible voice and presence, but because as a civil rights activist herself, the songs she sang about racial inequality chimed with the Black women present—this performance embedded itself in our collective cultural memory. These forms of cultural activities were in fact building on the work of the West Indian Overseas Co-ordinating Committee, (WIOCC) and the Roots Festival and as they were taking place in a locality characterised by the City Council as having 'high levels of unemployment, social deprivation and environmental decay', they provided crucial

NIA CENTRE
for African & Caribbean culture

NIA CENTRE, CHICHESTER ROAD, HULME, MANCHESTER M15 5EU

Fig. 3.7 Nia: Centre for African and Caribbean Culture and Art

spaces and opportunities to both 'recover' and 'discover.' It was Abasindi, for example, that gave the famed author and broadcaster Lemn Sissay his first opportunity to perform—we made space for him, a Black man, in our International Women's Day celebrations. Part of the process of recovery and discovery involves the exploration of the politics of 'naming' and the recognition for example, that most of the European names we carry have their roots in enslavement. For one woman, this recognition led to her renaming herself—she explained why this was so significant for her: "the name Olajumoke Sankofa resonates with the heartbeat of Africa, reconnecting me back to the authentic essence of who I am...". A crucial aspect of Abasindi's work was to partner with other organisations to create the spaces and places in which Black people could be their authentic selves.

During the 1980s the women of Abasindi were amongst the community groups and local people who became involved in the development of the Nia Cultural Centre which was located in the former BBC Playhouse in Hulme. The steering committee members and officers for the launch of the Centre in 1986/7 were Conway Mothobi, Pat Osborne, Keith Stephens, Elouise Edwards, Yasmin Hack, Tony Gordon, Trevor Plummer and John Lyons. The Abasindi members on the committee were Abina Likoya, Yvonne Ahimie, Pauline Anguin, Yvonne Hypolite and Diana Watt. There was also Linford Sweeney who was the leading founder member of Moss Side Arts Group which was established in 1962. The extract from Moss Side Arts Group annual report 1983/84 stated that the Moss Side Arts Group (MAG) was formed in December 1982 by 'local members of the 'Afro-Caribbean' community who strongly support the need for the development of Afro-Caribbean arts within the Moss Side area'. Alongside improving access in Moss Side to the best of African-Caribbean art forms, the group's long-term aim was the centralisation of these activities in a suitably equipped single venue in or near Moss Side.

The implementation of these aims involved the regular promotion of events as well as the participation of both local and visiting artists. As a result, MAG achieved a varied and balanced programme covering a wide range of art forms, namely dance, music, poetry, and theatre. The promotion of events at different venues in and around Moss Side was an integral part of MAG's activities. Events took place at several Manchester organisations: Birley High School, 8411 Community Education Centre, Abasindi Co-op, West Indian Sports and Social Club and the West Indian Centre (Bennett, 1987, p. 26).

The first event was held at Birley High School in Hulme on Sunday 20 March 1983 and featured two Liverpool based artists, Levi Tafari (poet) and Delado Dance and Drumming Group which specialised in West African dance. During 1983 and 84, local artists included Yootman Sound, poets Tshaka, Monique, Pat Berkeley, Keith Stephens, and the Kantamanto Drumming Group led by Kwesi Asare. Kantamanto sought to give authentic expression to Ghana's traditional way of life both in terms of spiritual development and ritual performances. Female vocalist Abina, whose repertoire embraces blues as well as contemporary and traditional songs from various countries in Africa, was also a regular performer as were Waduku, a band which specialised in fusing traditional Ghanaian music, highlife, and Afro Jazz. The evening of poetry in April 1985 was organised by Grass Roots Bookshop and Abasindi Co-operative. The event brought together women from different racial and cultural backgrounds. Abasindi dance and drumming workshops were held at the West Indian Centre Youth Club and the 8411 Community Education Centre and aimed to involve young people in the development and performances of various African-Caribbean art forms. In addition to local performers, international artists were featured such as the Jamaica National Dance Theatre and Sistren Theatre Collective. The performance by Sistren Theatre Collective was organised jointly by the women of Abasindi Co-operative and the organisation 'War on Want,' together with members of the Moss Side Arts Group. Over a period of around forty years, the Sistren 'grass roots' Theatre Collective initiated programmes aimed at:

... educating working-class women about alternate ways to circumvent as well as dismantle the system that oppresses them economically, sexually, and politically... Of equal importance are the strong cultural links and pride in the indigenous culture that the group advocated. Sistren speaks the language of the masses and incorporated the folklore and songs of the islands into its theatre productions. (Boyce-Davies & Ogundipe-Leslie, 1995, p. 34)

Sistren was established in 1977 by thirteen women who lived in the poorest areas of Kingston, Jamaica and in addition to their social justice programmes and plays, they also produced craft to generate funds to finance their activities (Fig. 3.8). It was the time when, as part of the Democratic Socialist Government Emergency Employment Programme for Unemployed Women, the group's members were working as street sweepers—several later became teaching assistants. In the book *Lionheart Gal (1986)* Honor Ford-Smith, who was the group's artistic director for some years argued that her work with Sistren represented 'an extension of her involvement in popular theatre and her belief in its importance for Caribbean identity'.

By way of drama, poetry, songs, music, dance, personal testimonies, oral history, rituals, role play and traditional ring games, Sistren addresses issues that adversely impact on the lives of Black working-class women. Sistren's first production 'Downpressure get a Blow' focused on the struggles of garment workers to form a union. Lana Finiken who had been a member of Sistren since it was established in 1977 and is its director commented on the fact that

Fig. 3.8 Annette admiring craft work by Sistren Theatre Collective

the group's first production was the result of hours of group discussion and storytelling. The act of storytelling is concerned with issues of survival at two levels. It is about the survival of the storyteller who lives to tell the tale and the listener who has survived having learnt from the story (Nnaemeka, 1997, p. 7). Merle Collins, novelist, and performance poet observed that anyone seeing Sistren performance would have the:

> Sensation of sharing in the lives of women who have been held within the grip of poverty, alienated by a brutal neo-colonial political system, brutalised by the police who also brutalise their men, who in turn brutalise them. Their stories are those of women who have learnt to confront life with the same toughness with which it has confronted them, who want love and tenderness and caring but have learnt to carve a niche which ensures their survival in an unyielding atmosphere. Their experiences have given the strength and resilience which makes life possible even when it continues to be a constant struggle. (Collins, 1988, p. 20)

The play QPH (1981) which Sistren performed at the 8411 Centre in Moss Side was based on the lives of three women, Queenie, Pearlie, and Hopie who had lived together at the Eventide Home for Destitute Women in Kingston, Jamaica. Pearlie died in 1979 and in 1980, more than 150 women including Hopie, lost their lives in a fire that destroyed their 'home'. Although badly scarred, Queenie was amongst the survivors of the fire. In their exploration of the lives and aspirations of these women, both for themselves and their children, Sistren used the Etu ritual, a 'celebration for the dead through singing, dancing, and feasting to tell the story. In this way, the production provided a space for participants to truly mourn the death of the women who were not projected as hapless and destitute but as our companions on the journey of life,' (https://www.nytimes.com/1980/05/21/archives/157-elderly-women-die-in-jamaica-fire-14-missing-at.html., Gilbert, 2001).

These cultural activities were taking place at a time when Moss Side was one of the wards described in a City Council report as 'characterised by high levels of unemployment, social deprivation and environmental decay.' Following the disturbances in 1981 (commonly known as the Moss Side riots, see Chap. 7), the Head of Personnel and Administration at BBC Manchester decided to vacate the premises they held in Hulme, which borders Moss Side. This was partially influenced by the fear that audiences might be reluctant to attend performances at the Hulme Playhouse. For members of the Nia Committee this was an opportunity to reverse negative perceptions of the area. The Nia Centre planned a programme of music, visual and creative arts that would enhance the community's sense of pride and identity. This period coincided with the launch of the Arts Council of Great Britain Ethnic Minority Arts Action Plan in January 1986. The rationale for increasing funding for Black arts and the spending of a minimum of four per cent of its budget on the development of African-Caribbean and Asian arts was influenced by several factors as outlined in the Council's 1985/6 annual report.

> The last two decades have seen a growth of arts activity amongst British people of Afro-Caribbean and Asian origin. African dancers and musicians have enjoyed an increased awareness and appreciation amongst audiences of all ages, artistic inclinations, and ethnic origins...Influenced by a consciousness of ancestral heritage and the immediate experience of life in contemporary Britain, these artists have developed a powerful voice which, heard and acknowledged, will have a profound and enriching influence upon the artistic life our multi-cultural society. (Bennett, 1987, p. 14)

In the spirit of Ujima (which means collective work and responsibility), the aims of Moss Side Arts Group were consistent with that of the Nia Centre. The name NIA refers to one of the seven principles of Kwanzaa, an African festival which originated among the African American community (Kwanzaa is also mentioned in Chap. 4). Dr Maulena Karenga is the founder of Kwanzaa which was first celebrated on 26 January 1966 in Los Angeles. The seven core principles of Kwanzaa are referred to collectively as the Nguzo Saba, a Swahili term. Beginning on December 26, the celebration lasts for a period of seven days. The history of Black art forms in England was perceived by the Nia Committee as one of exploitation and neglect. It was therefore important for Black people to provide a focus for their own culture and to not rely on the efforts of others. This was in line with Umoja, the first principle of Kwanzaa which represents unity, self-reliance, and independence. This required self-determination and persistence, qualities which constitute the second principle: Kujichagulia. The relevance of the third principle, Ujimaa, was reflected in the letters of support from a number of organizations including the African Methodist Evangelical Church, Birley High School, Claremount Junior School, Churches Work Scheme, Central Area Community Education, Information Technology Centre, Family Advice and Community Resource Centre, West Indian Centre (WIOCC), Manchester Teacher's Centre, the Chief Constable and Members of Parliament. The fourth principle Ujamaa (co-operative economics), and the fifth principal Nia (purpose) are celebrated within Kwanzaa on December 30. This sense of 'purpose' and 'co-operative economics' was captured in the letter of support from the Family Advice Centre:

As a Moss Side-based organisation, the Advice Centre has for many years been an advocate of the aims and objectives of the Nia Centre...We are conscious that the absence of job prospects within the area of Moss Side has made it necessary for the inhabitants to create their own job market areas of music, art, dance and all aspects of cultural forms. Unhappily however, the area is devoid of the space and venues to enable the proper advancement of cultural activities, and this has caused the cessation of some very promising groups and individuals who could have made a positive contribution to music and drama etc.

Drawing upon the sixth principle, Kuumba (creativity), the Nia Committee was committed to the development of an arts centre specialising in African-Caribbean culture. The Committee wanted a venue that was equipped to the highest professional standards and would nurture, enhance and dignify the work of Black artists and would provide a creative space for young people and children in the community.

What kind of people we become depends crucially on the stories we are nurtured on; which is why every sensible society takes pains to prepare its members for participation in its affairs by among other things, teaching them the best and the most instructive forms of its inheritance stories...drawn from both the factual and the imaginative literature bequeathed by its ancestors: songs, poems, plays, epics, fables. (Riley, 2002, p. 247)

The seventh principle, Imani (faith), was a key component in the Nia Committee's determination to establish the centre. The group's unsuccessful attempt to acquire the Star Cinema on Withington Road, which was subsequently sold and later demolished, did not deter them from pursuing their goal. In commenting on the failure to acquire this building, Barrett (1976, p. 11) wrote, "Although the objectives of the Nia Group have not yet been achieved, they have been tenaciously pursued over a two-year period by a responsible group of people, clearly committed to seeing the Centre established and properly managed."

Following the 1981 disturbances, the establishment of the Nia Cultural Centre was significantly influenced by the work of men and women who were involved in the West Indian Overseas Co-ordinating Committee (WIOCC). Throughout its history in Manchester, the WIOCC had been at the forefront of promoting events that aimed at raise awareness about the educational, political struggles, the cultural experiences and achievements of Black people as expressed in its supplementary educational programmes, conferences, workshops, and culture week celebrations. The annual Caribbean Carnival in Alexandra Park started in 1972 and the Roots Festival, involving collaborative work with local schools and community groups was initiated. The Roots Festival not only placed emphasis on providing a platform for local children and young people to display their talents and ability but was also committed to raising awareness about their cultural heritage. In its 1990–91 Annual Report, the Chairperson of the Nia Centre's Committee Elouise Edwards stated:

> The Nia Cultural Centre has begun a process of re-awakening our cultural traditions. For the first time in its history, this England has an African Cultural Centre of local, national, and international fame. A Centre devoted to bringing together the talents and aspirations in art, theatre, music, dance, education etc., from people of diverse backgrounds and cultures. People who had been denied that opportunity – until now.

Artists that performed at the Nia Cultural centre included Nina Simone, Gill Scott Heron, The Mighty Sparrow, Uncle Tommy Odueso, Fela Kuti, Ziggy Marley, Gregory Isaac, Jean Binta Breeze, Baba Maal, Dennis Brown, Talawa Theatre Company, The Ghana National Dance Company, Culture, Roaring Lion, Beres Hammond, Luke Dube and John Amos. Despite its determination to succeed, the organisation's dependence on public funds together with difficulties in translating the principle of co-operative economics (Ujamaa) into practical financing, meant that the centre was unable to sustain itself within the first five years, as was initially envisaged by the Nia Centre Committee.

The Rise of Manchester's Nia African Cultural Centre

I became involved in the arts of my community as a teenager in 1973 when I was a member of what could have been the first Black youth theatre in Manchester, led by Prince Miller, and operating out of Moss Side Youth Club. In 1976, I graduated to sitting on the Committee of MAAS NW (Minorities Arts North West) which had been established to develop and promote the arts and culture of minority ethnic communities living in the region. In 1979, whilst serving on the committee, the Coordinator of MAAS NW, Pnina Werbner pointed out that African and Caribbean arts were not being sufficiently exposed to the North West of England. We considered this to be a distinct and crucial gap in our cultural expression. It was clear that there were no specific venues to highlight the richness of African and Caribbean arts. In addition, existing venues were inadequate and performances in traditional theatres and other venues did not reach such communities. For example, on the odd few occasions when

African and Caribbean touring performers were funded and staged by traditional venues, the African and Caribbean communities would not become aware of ticket availability until the event had taken place. This situation then led to a call by individuals within the communities for more accessibility, which the traditional venues found hard to answer owing to their lack of understanding about how to reach African and Caribbean communities. At that time there were several Black-led arts groups in Manchester, including Kutamba (an African and Caribbean performance troupe led by Abina Likoya and consisting of dancers and drummers that toured the country from time to time), Black Kulture (my own youth theatre) and later Kantamanto, led by Kwesi Asare, an African percussion group. My own interest was stirred by the 1981 tour of the UK by the Black Theatre Cooperative performing at the West Indian Sports and Social Club. Although a venue within the community had been used, it was inadequate for staging professional theatre. Other venues had been suggested such as the West Indian Centre in Carmoor Road and Abasindi. However, these venues were not properly equipped or even accessible enough to stage professional work. It was clearly a frustrating time for the whole community who wanted to attend more performances that spoke about and displayed their cultural backgrounds. And yet, in cities such as London, Liverpool and Birmingham such performances were taking place. After speaking with several people, Pnina suggested that I contact Abina Likoya at Abasindi to see whether anything could be done to rectify the situation. At that time, Abasindi (formerly the Black Women's Cooperative) was the hub for many African and Caribbean arts and cultural activities in Manchester and had become a focal point for visitors, including artists, singers, dancers, musicians and more. I approached Abina in 1982 and with several other people, including Diana Watt, Terry Brandy, Pauline Anguin, Shirley Gordon, and Keith Stephens, we formed Moss Side Arts Group. Its initial brief was to provide access to touring African and Caribbean arts groups and companies and to identify an appropriate venue which could be developed to provide the professionalism and quality required to both house the arts and stage regular educational and cultural programmes of activities and events. We approached North West Arts for funding and they gave us £350. Before Moss Side Arts Group was formed, several individuals and groups within the community had tried to initiate the development of a professional venue for the arts of African and Caribbean people. By 1983 the drive to obtain such a venue had become much stronger, with the Moss Side Arts Group regularly staging performances. Some events attracted up to 150 people. This meant that many different venues were used, many of which were unsuitable. The emergence of the new group, led by Mrs Elouise Edwards, and including Richard Davis, Conway Mothobi, Kwesi Asare, a host of young people and many others, created unity of expression and a determination to find a solution to a growing problem. These meetings sometimes attracted up to seventy people and resulted in the establishment of the Nia African Cultural Centre which I chaired for the first three years. Eventually Moss Side Arts Group became a part of this organisation. As Nia grew, it attracted more funds and its own full-time staff. Ervine Okuboh became its first Coordinator. Later, Alti Daniel became Nia's second Coordinator. The project was originally based at Abasindi. Eventually Nia became a limited company by guarantee and obtained charitable status. Buildings were identified and feasibility studies were undertaken from around 1987, with the assistance of Judy Lancaster from MCCR, until a suitable building was located: the 'BBC building', as it was known, on Chichester Road in Hulme – a listed building. It had been in use as a hippodrome for many years until the BBC used a part of it as a rehearsal space for orchestras. The other half of the building had been used as a bingo hall. It was ideal. It boasted a 550-capacity theatre space, a large stage, room for expansion, and its location in the heart of the community suited everyone. Around 1988, negotiations began to secure the 'BBC building' as the African and Caribbean communities' showcase venue of excellence. This was a long drawn-out process that included Manchester City Council and its Urban Fund, North West Arts Board (where I was first a panel member and then non-executive Director), and local residents. At that time too, we had the full support of the North West Arts Board and their Community Officer was instrumental in assisting us to manage the process of funding acquisition. Eventually, the project received £2.1 million from a combination of funding bodies and a acquired a seven-year lease. In 1989 refurbishments began to repair a damaged roof and many internal changes were identified including a new reception area, offices, a kitchen, a spectacular skylight, and a sturdier stage. The Nia Cultural Centre opened in 1990, with a staff complement of around twenty, including a Director (Morenga Bambata), Events Manager (Alti Daniel), and several other managers, box office, kitchen, and cleaning staff. At the time, it was the largest and only project of its kind in Europe. The launch highlight was the appearance of Nina Simone! The African and Caribbean community were proud of the new facility and supported all its activities. (Linford Sweeney, African heritage historian and author).

The cultural work undertaken by Abasindi Black Women's Co-operative is akin to the role of their foremothers in ensuring the protection of African heritage. Significantly, Algerian feminist Awa Thiam argues that the survival of African customs was not an accident but instead resulted from the fruits of 'continual resistance,' whereby the women in particular 'took it upon themselves to preserve certain customs' (Thiam, 1978, p. 123). In this chapter, we have demonstrated the importance of our adoption of an Afrocentric feminism—this enabled us to work with a variety of organisations and with men who shared our aspirations to uplift our communities and reclaim and reassert positive representations of Black art and culture. It has been argued that a community can provide both space and opportunity for women to begin to

Fig. 3.9 Shirley Gordon with a collection of Abasindi's cultural artifacts

determine and redefine some of its conditions (Williams, 1997). In their role as community and cultural activists, Abasindi Co-operative was an important space for Black women to have their voices heard. Alice Walker's various writings are concerned with rescuing Black women from silence, through the establishment of sisterhood and 'womanist prose.' From a standpoint of resistance and resilience, the cultural work of Abasindi (Fig. 3.9) challenged the silencing of Black women and instead created a space for their involvement in wider struggles linked to the development of self and the community. Both the work of Abasindi and that of the Nia Centre provided empowering spaces for Black arts to be used as a vehicle through which the community were able to play, celebrate achievements and resist both individual and collective experiences of oppressive practices.

4

Ancestral Journeys and Diasporic Connections

Abstract This chapter explores African-Caribbean music and dance as political activism. If the Abasindi Black Women's Cooperative was focused primarily on transforming systems of inequality at home within its local communities, the reach of the organisation's drumming and dance group was unbounded. Here, we discuss the political significance of African dance; we show how we used dance and drumming to engage with our mis-remembered enslaved African ancestors. This takes us into a discussion of the function of the drum as a communication tool within slavery and the role of dance in African societies more widely. We relate this to the current struggle for reparations and move on to talk about the development of Black dance groups in the UK as a means of reclaiming representations of self and celebrating black culture. The chapter concludes with a description of two most memorable events—our participation in the Pan-African festival in Ghana (PANAFEST) and in the Crop Over Festival in Barbados.

Keywords Black women • African dance • Ancestors • Slavery • Reparations • Culture

A Meeting of Memory

One of the most visually dynamic elements of the Abasindi Cooperative was its dance and drumming group: the Abasindi Pan-African Drummers and Dancers (commonly known as the Abasindi Drummers and Dancers). The group was established shortly after the organisation's inception but its legacy was to outlast

Fig. 4.4 Master Drummer Thomas Odueso (Uncle Tommy)

Like the organisation itself, the drumming and dance group was a loose and fluid collection of women who passed through, stayed or moved on from the group as the shape of their lives dictated. From initial tutelage by Nigerian Master Drummer, Thomas Odueso ('Uncle Tommy') (Fig. 4.4), a legend in Manchester at the time, the women learned to play bongo drums, conga drums, the Djembé, talking drums and percussive instruments.

Another local legend Peddy, an expert in the creation of Carnival 'Mas (Minshall, 2000) helped build costume design skills, and from within the group came the talents for singing and dancing that we never knew we had. In the process, women found or reaffirmed an African heritage that enriched their lives.

We learned many different dance styles from different parts of Africa… from Ghana, Zimbabwe, South Africa… I learned a lot about African culture through dance and song…It was a place where I built my confidence up as well. It was kind of a journey, through developing myself. (Dahlia).

I think Abasindi has made a tremendous impact on my life, it gave me the opportunity to meet so many people from all over the world really, and to travel. For my own personal development, I've always been interested in Arts… meeting people from Africa gave me the opportunity to develop my skills in that area…It's really enriched my life… (Abina) (Interview extracts reproduced with permission from Tara Schaffe, 'Abasindi', MA Television Documentary, University of Salford, 2009).

Sometimes the group could count on 12–15 women for its performances while at others, it comprised only five or six. Over the years though, many women played the impressive array of traditional African instruments the Cooperative had acquired and still more learned the dances passed on by visiting artists from Africa and the Caribbean; a favourite being the war dance (Fig. 4.5). Abina, Diana, Pauline, Shirley, Abiola, Moiwale, Dahlia, Kaya, Liz, Francia, Magdalene, Adele, Evadney, Lorraine, Tara, Sam, Caroline, Maria, Louise, Chalana, Miselo, Patricia, Esther, Mumba, Joy, Pauline, Madge, Joy, Dorette, Estree were all performers with the group at one time or another, but there were others also.

There were children too (Fig. 4.6). Although public drumming and dance performances were always performed by women, Abasindi ran workshops for the children of the community, and those whose mothers were members of the group came to rehearsals and emulated our dance movements or joined the chorus to our songs.

A swollen-bellied woman in her seventh or eighth month of pregnancy wedged behind a bongo drum was a common sight and nothing soothed an Abasindi baby more than the steady drumming that is the heartbeat of any

Fig. 4.5 Abasindi—'War Dance'

Fig. 4.6 Abasindi girls dancing

reggae rhythm or the South African Lullaby 'Thula Baba' which became one of the group's most popular songs:

> *African…*
> Thula thul', thula baba, thula sana,
> Thul' ubab' uzofika, ekuseni. (repeat)
> Kukhon' athologi, eholel' ubaba,
> Ekhanyisela indlel' eziy' ekhaya,
> Sobe sikhona xa bonke beshoyo,
> Bethi buyela ubuye le 'khaya,
> Thula thula thula baba,
> Thula thula thula sana,
> Thula thula thula baba,
> Thula thula thula sana.
> *English…*
> Keep quiet my child
> Keep quiet my baby
> Be quiet, daddy will be home by dawn
> There's a star that will lead him home
> The star will brighten his way home

The hills and stones are still the same my love
My life has changed, yes my life has changed
The children grow but you don't know my love
The children grew but you don't see them grow
(Soweto Gospel Choir, http://www.metrolyrics.com/thula-baba-lyrics-soweto-gospel-choir.html)

Growing up, I remember there would be huge debates and many a raised voice in support of many causes.... This would be followed by songs and music, reflected by a multitude of different African/Caribbean songs, sometimes accompanied by drumming. My earliest memory to reflect this was marching and singing in a procession to demonstrate our pride. "We are the children of Mother Africa; you better clear the way let me pass." With powerful mantras like these as opposed to meaningless nursery rhymes, I felt connected with those who had come before me. (Melanie).

As a cooperative, run on democratic and participative lines, the organisation did not single out or acknowledge the role of leader as part of its structure. Nevertheless, one woman *does* stand apart for her singular contribution to the group and for promoting African music and dance in Britain more widely—Abina Likoya (Fig. 4.7).

Fig. 4.7 Abina with some members of the group: from left to right: Kaya, Abina, Abiola, Lorraine, Francia

Abina, one of the founder members of Abasindi and an accomplished jazz and blues singer and musician in her own right was the backbone of the group. During the 30 years when the Drummers and Dancers were most active, she was lead vocalist, lead drummer and manager, organising and directing the choreography, costume design and compositions for shows across the UK and internationally. There was always a political context to our performances and this was not only in relation to content, but often to location too. For example, when invited by a women's organisation, to perform in Belfast, the fact that many in Northern Ireland were still engaged in anti-colonialist struggle was brought home to us when our mini-bus was stopped and searched by British soldiers wielding rifles. This only heightened the energy with which we later performed and it also underlined the importance of debriefing together afterwards (Fig. 4.8).

Abina was also to take the group to Africa and the Caribbean; trips that evoked intense personal feelings and which cemented the Diasporic connections we discuss in this chapter. Reflecting on Abina's influence, Diana Watt (a co-founder of Abasindi) states:

> Within the group, this was indeed Abina's area of specialism and she can be counted amongst those people whom the Arts Council concluded were 'influenced by a consciousness of ancestral heritage and the immediate experience of

Fig. 4.8   Relaxing between gigs—on tour in Northern Ireland

life in contemporary Britain, these artists have developed a powerful voice which if heard and acknowledged, will have a profound and enriching influence upon the artistic life of our multi-cultural society'. Although Abina worked tirelessly to encourage other women such as myself to move from a position of spectator to that of performer, initially I resisted in that I could not see the relationship between community activism and grass skirts… However, an early visit to Barbados to the Caribbean Festival of Arts (CARIFESTA) was a significant turning point in that the relationship between performer, spectators and audience were all interlinked. On our return to the UK… the group agreed to establish the Abasindi drummers.

Abasindi was committed to promoting African and Caribbean culture and in facilitating workshops in schools, colleges, community centres and other venues throughout Britain; the drumming and dance group was one of the means of achieving this. However this was not the group's only role, or even, its most important. In this chapter we explore the political relevance of African dance in Britain during the 70s and 80s and in examining some of the journeys undertaken by the group, we unearth buried discourses of the function of dance and song within Black communities. For those whose recollections we have drawn on, this retrospective reflection represents a 'meeting of memory':

Memory
We meet in the middle of memory
Colliding against each other
Like bats without radar
Trying to find our way home
Our voices are confused by languages
That we are not always able to translate
Yet we know the timbre of the sound our lips
Vibrate upon
Like drummers, we are masters of rhythm
Beating a time of yesterday
So that our spirits might soar on tomorrow

We discover ourselves on continents south
And even more southern
On islands adrift from the mainland by centuries
And remember the taste of our grandmothers cooking
In pots we have never seen before
Our rituals are not similar but the same
Only the timing of dawn to dust makes the difference
Because our ancestors
Once held hands in laughter

Before the sorrow
We are not trapped in memory
We carry these memories inside of we
What for you is history captured in a book sealed paint on canvas
Is the nightly wail of terror
That wets our eyes each morning
And for a moment
The midst of dawn is tinged with sorrow

Anger is an ailment long ago pacified by endurance
And the possibility that tomorrow
Our ancestors will not simply be honoured
But revenged
So that the true history will be recorded
For all our children to know
And never let each or anyone of them enslave another
"REMEMBER we were AFRICANS before we were slaves"
'Memory', SuAndi © 2007

SuAndi reminds us to be cognisant of Africa's rich pre-slavery history. However, there is no doubt that slavery disrupted the dance form in irrevocable ways. If African dance was not political before slavery, then it certainly became so during it. The symbols and rituals of African dance and drumming became a source of resistance, communication and affirmation of identity among enslaved Black people that slave masters could not control and which have informed the development of dance in contemporary Caribbean societies to this day (Nettleford & LaYacona, 1985). Beckford (2000, p. 13) points to the importance of the reworking and restoration of 'memory of the African and Caribbean past' to inform how we move forward, precisely the ethos that underpinned the work of the Jamaican National Dance Company that Nettleford and LaYacona wrote about.

Politics and culture are often discussed as though these are separate domains. They are not. The disparagement, distortion or misappropriation of cultural representations are politicised processes in so much as they contribute to hierarchies of oppression. Through dance we were reworking memory and affirming an aspect of African cultural heritage, which as Black women living and working in a society ridden with racism was itself a political act. As if to keep us on our political toes, Kath Locke, one of Abasindi's founders, would comment: *"always keep your culture political"*. Our performances were infused with subliminal and overt messages about women's empowerment—what could be more political than that. For example, in our performances of the 80s, we would often include 'Winnie', a song dedicated to Winnie Mandela's tireless struggle against apartheid. Later revelations about her involvement in the assault and kidnapping of a 14-year-old boy who was subsequently murdered were deeply disturbing but at the time Winnie Mandela was emblematic of Black women's combined struggle against racism and gender oppression. The imprisonment she suffered and the enforced separation from her husband during his long incarceration testified to the lives of many families who had been torn apart by apartheid and social injustice and we felt it important to remind people of the role of women in this political struggle (Ato Qyason 15 February 2014, http://africasacountry.com/what-is-it-to-be-winnie-mandela/).

Given Abasindi's wider political goals it was unsurprising that the central narrative for Ancestral Journey, a production designed by the drummers and dancers and from which this chapter draws its title, was spun around Hetty, a Black slave from the former British colonies. We danced for Hetty as perhaps she once danced for her survival:

> African slaves, surreptitiously and openly, re-created an environment for their survival in the Caribbean, one in which their traditional belief systems were deeply planted. Dance, as non-verbal communication required no particular circumstances to reintroduce itself in the Caribbean and found regular expression as slaves celebrated birth, marriages, harvest, worship and death. In spite of the attempts by the governing nations to silence their cultural traditions, traditional religious rituals, music and dance seeped into everyday practices. (Ramdhanie, 2005, p. 84)

What follows is a description of the 'Ancestral Journey' production and its meanings. We then discuss African dance within the context of British society in the 80s and 90s and in the final section we describe the Abasindi Drummers and Dancers' performance at two iconic festivals, one in Africa and one in the Caribbean. These events are used to explore the social significance of African music and dance in their Diasporic connections.

Hetty

The most significant production of the Abasindi Drumming and Dance Group was 'Ancestral Journey' a dance drama developed in 1994 which, reflecting Beckford's point, aimed towards restoration of connections by linking the Diasporic experience to the historical legacy of slavery but also aimed to introduce the spectator to the tapestry of African dance, for which slavery was not necessarily a key reference point at all. Our programme read:

Embracing the diversity of African women we travel the Ancestral journey. We remember and celebrate in ways handed down over generations… Featuring songs and dances that originate from East, South and West Africa, the drummers and dancers add their own inimitable style and celebrate the survival and vitality of African peoples.

Hetty was a plantation slave in the British Caribbean colonies. She has no autonomous voice in the literature and we only know of her from a fellow slave, Mary Prince. Prince was 'freed/ abandoned by her owners after she had travelled with them from Antigua to England' (Banner, 2013, p. 298) and was encouraged by abolitionists from whom she sought support to recount her story for publication. Prince claimed to represent not only her own voice but also the voices of other slaves- she asks that we take her account as authoritative: "I have been a slave myself – I know what slaves feel – I can tell by myself what other slaves feel, and by what they have told me" (Prince, 1831, p. 23). In her narrative Mary speaks for Hetty but it seemed that Hetty had also 'spoken' for Mary since her brutal treatment was to portend what was to come for Prince: one beaten-to-death slave simply replaced by another.

The person I took the most notice of that night was a French Black called Hetty, whom my master took in privateering from another vessel, and made his slave. She was the most active woman I ever saw, and she was tasked to her utmost. A few minutes after my arrival she came in from milking the cows and put the sweet potatoes on for supper. She then fetched home the sheep and penned them in the fold; drove home the cattle and staked them about the pond side; fed and rubbed down my master's horse and gave the hog and the cow their suppers; prepared the beds, and undressed the children, and laid them to sleep. I liked to look at her and watch all her doings, for hers was the only friendly face I had as yet seen, and I felt glad that she was there. She gave me my supper of potatoes and milk, and a blanket to sleep upon, which she spread for me in the passage before the door of Mrs. I——'s chamber. (Prince, 1831, p. 6)

The History of Mary Prince, A West Indian Slave, Related by Herself was published in 1831. This, the first account from a female Black slave woman from the British colonies, was one of several autobiographies of the time around which was spun an 'enlightenment' discourse that linked the freeing of the slave with the acquisition of literacy (Larrabee, 2006, p. 454).

The production of literature was taken to be the central arena in which persons of African descent could establish and redefine their status within the human community. (Henry Gates Jr. cited in Larrabee, 2006, p. 454)

Within a year of being published, the *History of Mary Prince* was into a third edition—its emotional weightiness considered a timely addition to the debate on the abolition of slavery (Deck, 1996). In 1833, two years after Prince's pamphlet came out; The Emancipation Bill was passed in the House of Lords, followed in 1834 by a law to establish apprenticeships for freed slaves in the 'British' Caribbean and in 1838, England abolished slavery in the Caribbean completely (Deck, 1996, p. 3). Though Prince declares herself a 'more reliable authority on the subject than white men' (Deck, 1996, p. 3), the slave narratives of the eighteenth and nineteenth centuries were often considered incomplete unless accompanied by introductory or concluding text by a White person (often an abolitionist) which attested to the 'author's intellectual abilities and good moral character' (Banner, 2013, p. 298). The reliable authority of the voice of the slave, even the free slave was considered in itself, to be neither reliable nor authoritative. For believability to be established it had to be corroborated; 'slavery's truth ostensibly made doubly true by the authenticating aid of a white voice' (Banner, 2013, p. 298). In Mary Prince's account, Thomas Pringle, the Scottish abolitionist who helped her to publish her narrative, imposes his authority for establishing believability so completely that despite Prince's assertion, the control she exercises over her own voice is mediated through his greater power (Baumgartner cited in Banner, 2013, p. 298). Banner argues that in addition to the 'editorial infiltration' (298) of the abolitionist's voice, scholars have often overlaid their own meanings onto the stories told by slaves. Guided by the supposition that "what the text means is what it does not say, which can then be used to rewrite the text in terms of a master code ... the [symptomatic] critic restores to the surface the deep history that the text represses" (Best & Marcus, 2009 in Banner, 2013, p. 298). Banner's work shows how these imposed voices stand in hierarchical relationship to the voice of the slave herself and reveal a 'racial power at work within the genre' (p. 298). But if Mary Prince cannot even speak for Mary Prince, then who is to speak for Hetty?

Ancestral Journey invoked the notion of performative agency (Banner, 2013) through which the drummers and dancers provided a platform for the slave voice un-interrupted by overlaid meanings or white affirmation. The performance begins with a narrator delivering a slow-paced reading as Prince bears witness to Hetty's inhumane treatment and ultimate death. The narration is accompanied by continuous harmonic drumming—the drummers spontaneously break into explosive rhythm, they might beat a soulful or mournful melody, or then: krrrakk..krak…krak—staccatto slaps that reproduce the lash of the whip. All the while, the principal dancer moves freeform in response to the call of the drum or the sound of the narrator's voice, expressing what she feels in the moment.

Poor Hetty, my fellow slave, was very kind to me, and I used to call her my aunt; but she led a most miserable life, and her death was hastened (at least the slaves all believed and said so,) by the dreadful chastisement she received from my master during her pregnancy. It happened as follows. One of the cows had dragged the rope away from the stake to which Hetty had fastened it and got loose. My master flew into a terrible passion and ordered the poor creature to be stripped quite naked, notwithstanding her pregnancy, and to be tied up to a tree in the yard. He then flogged her as hard as he could lick, both with the whip and cowskin, till she was all over streaming with blood. He rested, and then beat her again and again. Her shrieks were terrible. The consequence was that poor Hetty was brought to bed before her time and was delivered after severe labour of a dead child. She appeared to recover after her confinement, so far that she was repeatedly flogged by both master and mistress afterwards; but her former strength never returned to her. Ere long her body and limbs swelled to a great size; and she lay on a mat in the kitchen, till the water burst out of her body and she died. All the slaves said that death was a good thing for poor Hetty; but I cried very much for her death. The manner of it filled me with horror. I could not bear to think about it; yet it was always present to my mind for many a day. (Prince, 1831, p. 7)

In their interpretation, the Abasindi women who performed this scene were perhaps as guilty of over-layering meaning as are the scholars who study the genre of slave narrative. But there are some important differences. The first is that the interpretative power of performative agency was filtered through the experiential lens of Black women who felt a visceral connection to this ancestral heritage.

Like drummers, we are masters of rhythm
Beating a time of yesterday
So that our spirits might soar on tomorrow
(From 'Memory', SuAndi, 2007)

Secondly, in contrast to the domination of cognitive forms of knowing (Larrabee, 2006), we believed the idiom of dance affirmed the agency of the spectator as much as the performer—what was knowable about Hetty's experiences was as much up to those who witnessed the performance as those who played it. A third difference is that we were part of the Abasindi Cooperative, informed by the everyday struggles of Black women of which we too were a part, a reality that sometimes left us depleted of energy but at other times infused us with determination.

Any dance drama that focuses on slavery is political. The trans-Atlantic Slave Trade is a highly politicised subject and this is nowhere more keenly evident than in the intention of Caribbean governments to seek reparations from the former European slave-trading nations (the UK, France, Spain, Portugal, the Netherlands, Norway, Sweden and Denmark). In March 2014, Heads of State from 15 Caribbean countries unveiled a plan demanding reparations from Europe which aims to achieve "…justice for the people who continue to suffer harm at so many levels of social life" (Sir Hilary Beckles, (Chair of the Reparations Commission, quoted in *The Guardian* (UK), 9 March 2014). One of the most important demands of the plan is for 'European countries to issue an unqualified apology for what they did in shipping millions of men, women and children from Africa to the Caribbean and America in the 17th and 18th centuries' (ibid). Other reparations called for include:

- diplomatic help to persuade countries such as Ghana and Ethiopia to offer citizenship to the children of people from the Caribbean who 'return' to Africa
- a development strategy to help improve the lives of poor communities in the Caribbean still devastated by the after-effects of slavery
- cultural exchanges between the Caribbean and West Africa to help Caribbean people of African descent rebuild their sense of history and identity
- literacy drives to improve education levels in Caribbean communities where this is needed
- medical assistance to a region struggling with high levels of chronic diseases such as hypertension and type 2 diabetes that have been linked to the fall-out from slavery

Although outside the scope of this chapter, one of the challenges for the reparation movement is how to address the role of African nations in this trade. Slavery in West Africa preceded and outlasted the Atlantic Slave Trade, existed alongside it and oiled its machinery (Schramm, 2009; Kankpeyeng, 2009) and as Schramm states: 'In royal armies and courts as well as in agriculture, slaves constituted a major workforce' (2009, p. 71). Domestic slavery and trans-Saharan slavery continued in West Africa for more than a hundred years after the abolition of slavery in Britain and was only outlawed in 1928 on institution of the Abolition of Slavery Ordinance (Kankpeyeng, 2009, p. 209). The prevalence of slavery in Africa before the Atlantic trade made ready accomplices for the Europeans among those who had already established systems of domination. Slavery clearly has a complex history but few would argue that the trans-Atlantic Slave Trade, which went on for more than 300 years, was particularly brutal, resulted in mass dislocation and genocide and has had more profound global ramifications at social, economic and political levels than any other historical event (Schramm, 2009, p. 71). Relevant to Abasindi's production of Ancestral Journey is Beckles' observation that the symbolism of acknowledgement and apology for the costs of the trans-Atlantic Slave Trade play an important part in the restoration of human dignity and human rights. Beckles observes that: "America has made efforts to reflect on their own history, but Britain has made no such effort to do so. If the British public were shown slavery in their own society seen through the eyes of the enslaved, they would get a much better understanding". Abasindi's Ancestral Journey was an attempt to do just that—to portray slavery in British society through the eyes of the enslaved.

There were more opaque meanings too. Drumming and dance were used by slaves to communicate through a language not accessible to their masters, though prohibitions and punishments for doing so were severe. There was an irony in Abasindi using African dance and drumming to foreground slavery when slaves had been brutalised when they danced for themselves and brutalised to make them dance for the master:

> The African was forced to dance in bondage and under the lash. He danced because the White ruler wanted his stock in good condition. He danced not for love, nor joy, nor religious celebration or event, or to pass the time; he danced in answer to the whip. He danced for survival. (Ramdhanie, 2005)

The trans-Atlantic Slave Trade represents a traumatic interruption in the evolution of African societies and has had enduring effects. In marking its abolition, Ancestral Journey included emancipation songs from the Caribbean. Emancipation Day was first celebrated in the former British Colonies of the Caribbean on 1 August 1834, a year after the 1833 Abolition of Slavery Act, and continues to be widely observed in the region and parts of Africa (www.understandingslavery.com/index.php?...id...emancipation). Slavery is not, however, the whole or even a small part of Africa's story and in traditional African dance it is not a defining factor at all since the meanings and function of dance have long existed outside of this context. For this reason Ancestral Journey also showcased dances and songs from different regions of Africa. The varied dances included those reflecting war and resistance, courtship, play and celebration and though largely based on traditional dance, the movements were interpreted through the perspectives of Black women from the UK whose lineage to Africa was far from straightforward.

The Politics of African Dance

Larrabee (2006) deconstructs the narrative of Mary Prince in order to critique what she calls the 'standard' epistemological viewpoint. She draws on an extensive body of feminist literature to challenge the logocentric dominance of cognitive forms of knowledge which place the mind in 'dichotomous relation' to the body and which, she suggests, presents the subject 'as too narrow, as disembodied, as "autonomous" and therefore non-social' (456). From Abasindi's viewpoint, the meshing of dance, drumming *and* political activism was a means of achieving the 'embodied and culturally adumbrated' knowledge Larrabee argued for. Drumming and dancing gave us the opportunity to express our representations of socially significant but invisible events, and though there was often opacity to our performances we also validated literal, surface meanings; our target was not the 'rational' subject but the social being.

In Hetty, through the story telling of Mary Prince, we connected ourselves as Black women to a long line of female ancestors who had faced and fought racialised and gendered subjugation. Though the trans-Atlantic slave trade is historic, as other chapters in this book show, contemporary life in the UK is fraught for many Black women. The drumming, drama and dance in Ancestral Journey was a means of weaving history to these contemporary realities. The 'knowledge' produced through our performance was not easily categorized. For the performers, learning was internalised—this was about discovery, self, identity, place, belonging and connectedness; performing to Mary Prince's narrative about Hetty was intensely moving and we were deeply affected. What the spectator gained, only the spectator can say, but our aim was to showcase drumming and dancing as a vital aspect of African and Caribbean culture, not as reified or fossilised artefact but as a dynamic, organic art form that has history, social context *and* contemporary relevance.

We had learned traditional African dances from visiting artists and from professional dancers/choreographers; people like Peter Badejo and George Dzikunu (of Adzido Dance Company, Ghana). These men were among the most influential promoters of African dance in the UK, but our interpretation of the dances were inevitably filtered by our varied Diasporic experiences and were anything but traditional. For example, the Zulu war dance (Fig. 4.9) taken out of its South African context could only claim a loose connection to the history of KwaZulu-Natal but as a symbol of resistance and agency, it could not have spoken more loudly of that connection.

If this was indeed traditional dance, then we were rewriting history because all these 'warriors' were women. But this was not history rewritten and neither was it parody—we used African dance to symbolise the role of Black women

Fig. 4.9 Abasindi Drummers and Dancers- Zulu War Dance: from left to right: Emense, Evadney, Mumba, Abiola (drums), Magdalene, Adele, Estree (other drummers are hidden from view)

at the forefront of struggle within a specific socio-historical context, while at the same time passing on 'culturally adumbrated' knowledge, or so we hoped. Beyond mere entertainment, the strength and determination we sought to convey through dance were unequivocal and when the drumming in our war song called the warrior to raise up and stamp the ground, the message "come no closer, you don't know who you are dealing with" seemed more resonant of everyday life than the preservation of tradition. As Magdalene (third from the right) danced her solo—body taut, crouched low and spear held high, her eyes daring her potential violator to cross the line, it was electrifying—we were glorious ferocious Black women. We danced for others but clearly we also danced for ourselves—the affirmation of Black history, culture, identity and womanhood interlocking in one to locate the self.

I was brought up with a Black father and a White mother; I had no influence from Black women, at all. As I got older, I felt kind of like quite isolated and then when I started to get involved in Abasindi, it was like I'd found my Black women. (Liz); interview extract reproduced with permission from Tara Schaffe, 'Abasindi', MA Television Documentary, University of Salford, 2009).

This is the second edition of the only book to comprehensively document the role of the Abasindi Cooperative in Black women's activism and though several references to the Abasindi Drummers and Dancers can be found (see for example Ramdhanie, 2005), the group did not conform to any attempts to classify it. In Rhamdanie's impressive thesis, he mistakenly classifies the Abasindi Dancers and Drummers as a traditional African dance group:

> [Traditional African Dance] TAD refers to practice that maintains its repertoire when it is transferred from traditional African communities to performance spaces 'outside' of this setting. For instance, a dancer in England researches and re-presents a dance that he/she has practiced or observed on the continent. The dancer expresses creativity in reproducing the traditional form through the execution of floor patterns. In this sense he/she is not a choreographer but a "dance arranger" of traditional dance practice. The presentation maintains its 'narrative' and provides a context of a particular community. This maintains the traditional form in the Diaspora and ensures that besides the exactitude of the vocabulary in terms of gestures and symbols, costuming, musical accompaniment, religious and spiritual invocations, the forms provide continuity, meaning and a 'reaffirmation of self' for various Black communities in the Diaspora. Adzido Pan-African Dance Ensemble, AfiDance, ADANTA and Abasindi Dancers and Drummers etc., most notably mirror the TAD movement in England (24).

There are hundreds, possibly thousands of traditional African dances. It is important that the movements and gestures of some dances are preserved since as with oral language, changing a word can change meaning. However other dances might permit a degree of improvisation and modification depending upon the age, kinship and status of the performer (Welsh, 2004). Traditional dance in African societies is an integral part of everyday life. Used to mimic, mark or celebrate the ordinary as well as the exceptional, it accompanies birth, death, work and play, is a medium for the transmission of social values and enables people to encounter the Gods they wish to appease or worship (Welsh, 2004). Traditional dance is also about relationships and is often segregated by gender, reinforcing gender boundaries and roles. Both men and women dance (often separately) but in most traditional dances it is the men who provide the drumming. The Abasindi drummers were all women—literally and figuratively the women of the group were foundation, keystone and castle.

> I always admire drummers….the fact that they are the mainstay, they still keep going no matter what. (Francia).

The rebuttal of the imposition of the woman's place implicit in the term 'traditional' signified by women taking up the drum suggests this was a political position. It was. It was also joyously empowering. On several occasions Abasindi drummers were invited on stage to perform with other bands; the skill of the women in keeping pace with accomplished male drummers engendered mutual respect that was seldom evident otherwise. Spectators familiar with West African dance and music were sometimes astonished to see the proficiency of our drummers on the Djembé, as this instrument is rarely played by women (Flaig, 2010).

Our distancing from the term 'traditional' was also based on deep respect for the religious connections of some dances in African societies (see for example, Turner's 1968 text *Drums of Affliction*; Euba (1977) on drumming for Yoruba religious rites; Dargie (1992) *Musical Practices of the Xhosa People,* and Impey (1998). As a secular organisation encompassing faith-holding and non-faith-holding women alike, we did not seek to promote the religious meanings of any of the songs we sang. Being non-traditional was an important creative standpoint too, as the Abasindi Drummers and Dancers operated a pluralistic, rather than dualistic positionality which embraced the cross-pollination of African and Caribbean cultural modes of expression. If we did not represent traditional African dance, we could not be classified as a contemporary Black dance troupe either. We learned traditional African dances but danced them in our contemporary realities which, for us, as women of the African and Caribbean Diaspora, were loaded with multiple, often contradictory meanings. For example, we were as comfortable dancing a modest courtship dance of the Luo people of Kenya as we were spicing up the dance by throwing in a 'wine' (a contemporary Caribbean dance movement which involves an emphatically sexualized gyration of the hips, usually danced to calypso and soca music (http://www.urbandictionary.com/define. php?term=wine). Though we appreciated the importance of cultural, spiritual and social meaning of the dances we learned, we were outsiders to their nuanced contexts. We did not perform dances we had learned on the continent of Africa; on the contrary, visitors from Ghana, Nigeria, Sierra Leone, Zimbabwe, Kenya, Uganda and South Africa brought the continent to us. Though we kept dances true to their original form where we could, being performed by Black women in Britain, outside their historic and social locations meant they melded with other influences and became something else. The ambiguity and hybridization we created we thought worthy of celebration although traditional dance purists must have shaken their heads in dismay. That this hybridization was as much evident in our costumes as in our dances can be seen in the photograph below (Fig. 4.10): the hats take their

Fig. 4.10 Dance costumes—African and Caribbean fusion

shape from those worn by the Zulu women of South Africa while the dancers' manipulation of the long flowing skirts is reminiscent of the quadrille dress, the folk costume of the Caribbean.

The social and political context in which the Abasindi Drummers and Dancers performed was informed by the wider Black power and anti-racist activism that emerged during 70s and 80s Britain. The resurgence in the celebration and reclaiming of African and Caribbean culture, of which dance was a part, is described by Ramdhanie (2005, p. 36, citing Fielding Stewart) as 'Black resistance in the social, political and personal realms'. Black dance or 'African Peoples' Dance' defined as that 'which draws its main influence, sensitivities, means of experience and technical base from the cultural heritage of Africa and the peoples of Africa living in the Diaspora' (http://www.iriedance-theatre.org/#sthash.GGlEb8uw.dpuf) enabled young Black people in Britain to forge connections with the Caribbean and Africa (Ramdhanie, 2005).

Although Caribbean and African dance forms are connected, they have different evolutionary paths. Caribbean dance has inevitably been shaped by trans-Atlantic slave routes, incorporating different influences along the way and often signalling covert messages of resistance. Ramdhanie (2005, p. 27) writes about religious practices in the 'New World': 'Sango in Trinidad and Tobago, Kumina in Jamaica, Santeria in Cuba, Voodoo in Haiti [and] Candomblé in Brazil'. He describes the ways in which the African dance forms that accompanied these belief systems were suppressed and their followers punished. Yet slavery is not a key anchor point for traditional African dance and though undoubtedly infected by colonial encounters, is not defined by them (Adair & Burt, 2013). These different but connected histories are reflected in the development of Black dance in the UK.

The first Black dance company In Britain, Ballets Nègres was founded In 1939 by a Jamaican man who was taught to dance by the Maroons, the descendants of runaway slaves (http://www.vam.ac.uk/content/articles/h/history-of-black-dance-black-british-dance/). Other dance companies influenced by Caribbean heritage include the Delado Dance and Drumming Company founded in Liverpool in 1981 (http://www.communitydance.org.uk/DB/animated-library/african-peoples-dance-and-the-dare-project-in-live.html?ed=14046) and the Phoenix Dance Company, founded in 1982. The Phoenix Dance Company, one of the most successful companies in the UK was established by three young men from Leeds: Leo Hamilton, Donald Edwards and Villmore James who, though refusing to be compartmentalised as 'Black dance', gained much of their inspiration from the narratives of the migration of Caribbean elders to Britain (Kruczkowska, 2007; www.adad.org.uk/metadot/index.pl?id=24393&isa=Category). Dance companies in operation around the same time as the Abasindi Dancers and Drummers included Irie Dance Theatre in London (founded by Beverley Glean in 1984); Kantamantu in Manchester; Lanzel in Wolverhampton; Sankofa in Birmingham, and Ekome in Bristol (http://www.adad.org.uk/metadot/index.pl?id=22805&isa=Category&op=show). (For a short summary of the history of Black dance in Britain from the 1940s see Adair and Burt (2013).

What sets Abasindi apart from these groups is that we were never a professional dance company. We represented the cultural arm of a Black women's organisation that was engaged in serious political struggle against racism and gender oppression, issues that informed the songs we sang and our decisions about self-representation. For example, we were active supporters of the anti-apartheid movement and often concluded our sets with Nkosi Sikelel' iAfrika, the South African National Anthem (then the ANC anthem) and only ceased doing so once Nelson Mandela was released from prison. We were volunteers, who squeezed rehearsal time in between jobs, study and childcare and any Black woman could join the group regardless of talent or skill. The high standards we achieved, evident by numerous bookings for festivals and concerts, were due to our abundant enthusiasm and the dedication of the group's leader Abina who refused to settle for mediocrity. Although there were many highlights, up there at the top was the time we supported Ladysmith Black Mambazo at the Apollo Theatre in Manchester in the late 90s. Another memorable performance was at the National Theatre in Accra, Ghana as part of the Pan-African music festival, PANAFEST.

African dance has made a significant contribution to dance in Britain for over 75 years (www.adad.org.uk; http://www.vam.ac.uk/content/articles/h/history-of-black-dance-black-british-dance/) however it was no coincidence that Black dance groups burgeoned in the late 1970s and early 80s. Set against the upsurge in Black political awareness and reclamation of an African heritage following decades of disparagement and marginalisation, African and Caribbean culture provided a peaceful means of challenging racist representations. As Ramdhanie states, 'Psychologically, there was a new awakening in the definition of 'self' and an increased awareness and spiritual connectivity between Black people in the Caribbean, Africa and in the New World generally (2005, p. 31). This was a period marked by mass protests and riots against racial and economic disadvantage (see Chap. 7). Some people took to the streets for racial equality while others danced for racial pride—different coordinates on a shared political landscape.

Abasindi Dancers and Drummers performed at all kinds of events but its purpose within the local Black communities of inner city Manchester embedded African music within everyday social life in much the same way as in Africa. We danced and drummed for naming ceremonies, for Kwanzaa,[1] as part of carnival celebrations, for weddings, wakes, funerals, social gatherings and for Black History month. We opened conferences and we closed them. We were present to mark the milestones of many Black organisations, for instance we were part of the rituals for the land-turning ceremony when the Bibini Centre was built (Jones & Waul, 2005), at the opening of the Kath Locke Centre (www.kathlockecentre.co.uk) and at numerous events held by the West Indian Community Centres. For many years, we were a regular feature at International Women's Day celebrations, we performed at charity events, anti-deportation campaigns, anti-apartheid concerts and when one of

---

[1] Kwanzaa takes its name from a Swahili phrase 'matunda ya kwanza' which means 'first fruits of the harvest'. The seven-day end of year holiday was established in 1966 in the US by Maulana Karenga to celebrate African heritage. It has been adopted by several black communities in the UK and Europe (www.history.com/topics/holidays/kwanzaa-history).

the Abasindi women, Adele Jones was appointed a University Professor, we shook up the hallowed halls of that academic institution when we drummed at her inaugural lecture. Memorable for our audacity in setting free the stulti-fied air in this reified space, the audience spontaneously rose up from their seats and danced. Even the wooden robed White male 'Gods' of the institu-tion found some 'bootie' to shake that day—who knows what else we set free.

In the next section we reflect on the significance of our Diasporic connec-tions cemented through two of the festivals at which we performed: the Pan-African Festival of Music (PANAFEST) in Ghana and the Crop Over Festival in Barbados.

Diasporic Connections

PANAFEST is a 10-day festival of African dance and music held in Ghana every two years. 'Inspired back in 1992, by the late great Pan Africanist Efua Sutherland, PANAFEST has become a landmark festival in Ghana which gives Africans on the Continent and in the Diaspora a platform to address the most traumatic interruption that ever occurred in the natural evolution of African societies which, among other traumas, profoundly eroded the self-confidence and freedom for self-determination of a whole people' (https://panafestghana.org/) . Building on Ghana's unique contribution to the politics of African independence, the festival aims include the promotion Pan-Africanism and the development of the African continent.

The origins of Pan-Africanism lie in the slave rebellions and resistance of the nineteenth century (Abdul-Raheem, 1996) but the term seems to have first surfaced in 1900 when a Trinidadian barrister, Henry Sylvester Williams called a conference to challenge racial discrimination and British colonialism (ibid). Pan-Africanism was initially led by scholars from the Diaspora, most notable among them being W.E.B Du Bois who convened the first Pan-African Congress in Paris in 1919. Further congresses, each building on the scholar-ship and theory of Pan-Africanism followed: 1921 (London, Brussels, and Paris), 1923 (London and Lisbon), 1927 (New York) with the most significant being the 5th Congress held in Manchester in 1945. Ghanaian statesman Kwame Nkrumah was one of the key organisers and in 1957 he led Ghana to independence from Britain. The Manchester Congress was the first to include a large number of Africans from the African continent and is credited with providing 'impetus and momentum for the numerous post-war independence movements' (Pan-African Development Education and Advocacy Programme, n.d.). Woven throughout the political narrative of Pan-Africanism were intellectual discourses and cultural developments including: 'the Harlem Renaissance, Francophone philosophies of Negritude, Afrocentrism, Rastafarianism and Hip Hop… [while] Post-independence, a new generation of African writers – such as Chinua Achebe, Wole Soyinka, Bessie Head gave voice to issues that could be recognised throughout the Continent' (Pan-African Development Education and Advocacy Programme, n.d.).

Pan-Africanism is not without its detractors. Often criticised for an over-simplified analysis of causal and contributory factors to Africa's underdevelopment, scholars such as Obadina (1997) have drawn attention to the need for African nationalists to examine some of the internal constraints to progress:

> African ruling elites who have pillaged their people's wealth and held their nation's development to ransom are more culpable than Pan-Africanists acknowledge (Obadina, 1997, p. 316).

Perhaps one of the most important issues to blight the Pan-Africanist movement is its relative silence on the subordination of women and its failure to tackle patriarchal domination: '…The conditions which determine the African woman's state are imposed on her by a society which maintains rigid social-cultural values and practices against her' (ibid, 316). That the most significant Pan-African Congress should have taken place in Manchester, the birthplace of the Abasindi Cooperative, which was committed to ending women's subordination, is more than a symbolic link. The founders of Abasindi may have been influenced by Pan-Africanist thought but they were fiercely determined to ensure that women's liberation was stamped indelibly on any causes it supported. As we discuss elsewhere in this book, Abasindi grew out of the upsurge of activism against racial inequality and the celebration of Black pride that took place in the 1970s; mass movements which were sweeping the Diaspora. Pan-Africanism was reignited by this groundswell of popular action in a way that is unlikely to have been achieved by politicians or scholars alone, and within the small circles Abasindi operated in, we pushed against its gender barriers in many ways, including through the Drumming and Dance group.

Despite its limitations, Pan-Africanism remains an important force for political and academic debate and a vital platform for the cross-pollination of cultural ideas (Pan-African Development Education and Advocacy Programme, n.d.). As if to emphasise this, PANAFEST 2013, which coincided with the 50th birthday of the African Union (AU, formerly the OAU) and the 50th anniversary of the death of W.E.B Dubois, included several activities focused on the theme 'Pan-Africanism and the African Renaissance' (http://www.ghana.travel/events/panafest/). PANAFEST is also concerned with the re-memorying of slavery (beyond remembrance and somewhere between history and imagination, we use this term to symbolise a reflective process that seeks to connect the person to the history of slavery). Ghana served as a vital link in the trans-Atlantic slave trade and an estimated 12 million Africans are said to have been shipped to America and the Caribbean from the European forts and castles that dominate its coastal landscape (Kankpeyeng, 2009, p. 209).

> These forts and castles were designated as national monuments in 1972, and in 1979 the forts of Elmina and Cape Coast were inscribed on the UNESCO World Heritage list for their historic role in European – African interactions and the emergence of the globalised world. (Kankpeyeng, 2009, p. 209)

Diasporic Africans regard the slave forts of Elmina and Cape Coast as centres for spiritual veneration and their role as tourist sites have become a vital source of foreign exchange for the Ghanaian economy. One main event of the PANAFEST festival is a pilgrimage along the UNESCO-sponsored Slave Route.[2]

The Abasindi Drummers and Dancers participated in the PANAFEST festival of 1995; our 12-day tour enabling us to travel to different parts of Ghana conducting workshops, performing and taking part in jamming sessions with artists from around the world. One of the main performances took place at Elmina Castle (Fig. 4.11), possibly the most widely known slave fort in the world. We spent the day there before our performance in the evening; it was an emotionally charged experience for us all. The physical structure of the castle, with the ocean crashing against unassailable walls, is all the imagination needs to be transported to the herding, torture and trafficking of enslaved Africans. No artificial tricks or tourist gimmickry could do this—it really is the place itself. Its walls, two feet thick in places, its iron grills and its dank, dark cells exude utter misery. We wandered first as a group, becoming quieter and quieter—until we were almost silent. Then we drifted apart, each of us sinking into ourselves. It was impossible to escape our own thoughts—this was our history; we were connected to it in ways that recalled Hetty. Many years later, as we wrote this book, the memories were still vivid: we see the sun glistening from a shiny metal object, creating an iridescent pattern that is both beautiful and horrific—it is the ball and chain used to chain any errant slave, polished to a high shine by overuse and the passage of time; we see the balcony above the women's pen from which the White slave trader would pick

---

[2] The 2007 pilgrimage itinerary can be found at: http://www.info-ghana.com/joseph_project.htm/.

Fig. 4.11   Elmina Castle, Ghana

his rape victim for the night; we see the dark exit passageway that led from the castle to the ocean and the waiting ships. This last detail is perhaps the most distressing of all; the passageway is narrowed so as to allow only one person at a time to exit. When first built, the passageway was wide—to speed up the processing of transportation, but hundreds of Africans leapt from the ledge to their deaths, preferring to drown in the ocean than to endure as slaves. The traders could not afford this loss of 'property' and found it easier to prevent suicide by narrowing the gap.

We performed at Elmina Castle that night—possibly one of our best performances ever: we sang, drummed and danced in memory of our enslaved ancestors but afterwards we could not rid ourselves of the deep sadness we all felt—we talked until the early hours of the morning.

> *What for you is history captured in a book sealed paint on canvas*
> *Is the nightly wail of terror*
> *That wets our eyes each morning*
> *And for a moment*
> *The midst of dawn is tinged with sorrow*
> (From 'Memory', SuAndi, 2007)

If the Elmina performance had been emotional, the fact that we had been billed to perform at the National Theatre in Accra as part of the festival's finale was frankly intimidating. Ghana's National Theatre was built in 1990. Seating 1500 people in the main auditorium, the theatre is home to the National Dance Company, the National Symphony Orchestra, and the National Theatre Players. Anyone who has seen the National Dance Company of Ghana perform will understand our trepidation. Established in 1962 from artistic developments initiated by Kwame Nkrumah, the first President of the Republic of Ghana, the company, then with about 60 performers, had toured the world to rave reviews (http://www.ghanaculture.gov.gh/index1.php?linki d=331&page=2&sectionid=661) and we, the Abasindi Dancers and Drummers were just a small community group. It was not only the incredible skill of the performers that daunted us; F. Nii-Yartey who had been Artistic Director of the company since 1976, was well-known among the African dance circles in Britain of the 1980s and was credited as being the inspiration behind many of the groups we have mentioned earlier. The Abasindi Drummers and Dancers were a community group and only Abina, who was a popular jazz singer in Manchester, could be described as a professional performer; the rest of us made our living doing other things. We had fielded a group of twelve women but needed to fill a stage that was at least 60 feet across; our 12 foot square backcloth—a beautiful batik tapestry created with the help of a Sierra Leonean artist seemed insignificant and was instantly lost against the back curtain. We felt under-skilled and overwhelmed. We should not have worried—our hosts were beyond gracious. Our set was received with rapturous applause and the performers of the National Dance Ensemble all rose to give us a standing ovation. Our performance was not comparable with theirs, not in the slightest, this was immediately apparent when they took the stage, but we, a small group of Black women from an unknown area in Manchester, had given our all and the appreciation was palpable.

The second most significant of Abasindi's Diasporic connections was Barbados and the Crop Over festival. In Barbados, Emancipation Day is part of the annual 'Season of Emancipation' which includes the anniversary of the 1816 Slave Rebellion led by Bussa (a national hero), the International Day for the Remembrance of the Slave Trade and its Abolition and, the Crop Over festival. Crop Over in Barbados is one of several indigenous carnival festivals in the Caribbean. These differ from music festivals in that in addition to music and dance, they include masquerade and other performing arts. During slavery, crop over festivals were common across the region as they marked the end of the sugarcane harvest. Barbados was the Caribbean's largest sugar producer and Crop Over was a particularly significant event. The earliest reference to the festival in Barbados was in 1788 when the manager of Newton Plantation wrote to inform the estate's owner in England that he had held a "dinner and sober dance" for the slaves, saying: "twas a celebration of harvest time after the crop" http://www.bajanfuhlife.com/cropover/history_of_crop_over.html.

Crop Over (Fig. 4.12) provided an opportunity for the resurgence of African music and dance and was considered an indicator of the enslaved African's spirit of indomitability (Beckles, 2002). A major concern among slave owners at the time was that free time and socialisation bred rebellion. They were not wrong but crop over festivals persisted (Beckles, 2002). After the abolition of slavery, plantation life continued and the festival remained an important marker on the calendar. By 1940 however, the sugar industry had begun to decline and other sources of employment were developing. The end of plantation life brought an end to the festival. In 1974, Crop Over Barbados was revived to boost tourism and today it bears little relation to the festival it was during the time of slavery. Nevertheless there are still historical remnants, although these are only symbolic. The festival begins with the 'Ceremonial Delivery of the Last Canes' and the crowning of the King and Queen of the Festival—historic symbolism for the 'most productive male and female cane cutters of the season'. In Barbados, Crop Over is regarded as an 'extravaganza of music and masquerade, history and culture' and is a major feature on the regional tourism calendar.

Fig. 4.12 Masquerading (playing 'Mas) in the 'Crop Over' festival

The grand finale is the *Grand Kadooment*! This carnival parade features large bands with revellers dressed in elaborate costumes to depict various themes. Designers of these bands, compete for the coveted Designer of the Year prize while the revellers seem more intent on having a good time! The revellers make their way from the National Stadium to Spring Garden accompanied by the pulsating rhythm of calypso music. When they reach Spring Garden, the party continues with more fantastic music, lots of food and drink and, for some, a quick swim at the nearby beach. A grand end to a grand festival (http://www. bajanfuhlife.com/cropover/history_of_crop_over.html.)

In the early 90s, the Abasindi Dancers and Drummers travelled to Barbados to perform in several of the concerts given during the festival. In Ghana we had felt 'Like bats without radar, trying to find our way home' but Barbados reminded us that '...our ancestors once held hands in laughter' (SuAndi, 2007). If PANAFEST was homecoming and reconnection with our ancestors, Crop Over was the celebration of emancipation—fetters abandoned for joy. The group was privileged to perform in programmes and workshops that also featured Pinelands Creative Workshop, who specialise in carnival arts and with 'Dancing Africa', Barbados' own celebrated African dance company. We swam in the turquoise seas of the South Coast, soaked up some cold Banks beers and joined in the festival parades. Ghana had brought back reflections of slavery but we were not trapped in memory and in Barbados we celebrated for Hetty and other enslaved foremothers.

The Abasindi Drumming and Dance Group was a vehicle to rediscovering the value of African and Caribbean cultural heritage—our journey was historical, political and personal and though we shared everything we learned along the way, the greatest beneficiaries of our Ancestral Journey were ourselves.

5

Loving Body, Skin and Hair

Abstract 'Ain't I a woman…?' Not so much a question as an exclamation; this famous phrase, the axis around which Sojourner Truth constructed the speech she presented at a women's rights convention in Ohio in 1851 is the starting point for this chapter.

For over 150 years, Truth's words continue to provide valued currency for feminist discourses that at one and the same time seek to unify women and, crucially for Black women, to authorise the significance of difference. Donna Haraway (1992) suggests this is because in deconstructing the 'terrible edifice of "woman" in Western patriarchal language and systems of representation' (p. 92), Sojourner Truth challenges the idea of the Black woman as one who can never be a subject, who is only 'plot space, matrix, ground, screen for the act of man'. Historically, this 'act of man' has been concerned with the racialised and sexualised objectification of the Black woman to service the interests of male desire and white privilege while her exoticisation has ensured the marginalisation of her own versions of selfhood. This chapter is concerned with dominant representations of beauty and the ways in which Abasindi women redefined the concept of beauty in their own likeness. Taking the position that ethnocentric ideals that pervade constructions of beauty within a context of race and gender inequality are harmful to self-esteem and provide pervasive subliminal means of limiting women's power, reclaiming the Black self is not only vital for self-love, but also is in and of itself, a political act.

Keywords Sojourner Truth • Black women • Beauty • Ethnocentrism • Racism • Gender inequality

Stratifying Black Women

The stratification of Black people for the purposes of exploitation according to physical appearance, gender, age, skin colour, hair 'quality' and other characteristics has a long and terrible history and so too, has the stratification of women according to dominant tropes of beauty. To be determined 'unlovely', worse still, to be determined as never being able to attain the required standards of beauty is equivalent to being declared unworthy, un-womanly—less of a woman. Sojourner, with her Black body, skin and hair was so far removed from the idealised version of womanhood pertaining at the time, that she was not considered worthy of the right to vote, even as it was being extended to White women. "Ain't I a woman" begins an oration which demolished the notion of what a Black woman can and can't do, can and can't be and can and can't look like—Abasindi women simply followed her example (Fig. 5.1).

The social construction and appropriation of the visual imagery of Black people to fuel racism and feed sexual appetites is as much a contemporary issue as it is an historical one. The case of Saartjie Baartman however, an enslaved South African woman, who during the early part of the nineteenth century was objectified in the most literal sense vividly illustrates the point. Taken to Europe, Saartjie was presented in near nakedness to exhibit her distinctly un-European anatomy—large breasts and bottom and her enlarged labia (a presumed attribute since she refused to show her genitals) (Willis, 2010). These features, embodied within a Black skin gave her status as object a duality: given the historical, geographical and racially constructed space she occupied, it was assumed to be a 'fact' of nature that she should be a slave but it was as 'freak' of nature that her worth was measured. Worked to death in the fields might not have been preferable, but the alienation, isolation and ridicule she must have endured while exhibited as some alien being would have surely crushed the soul. Saartjie was gawped at, laughed at, and prodded; although she was ultimately able to buy her freedom, she had been trafficked for sexual exploitation and without any other mean of survival was forced to continue servicing the White man's desire—she died a destitute prostitute around the age of 25 (Willis, 2010).

Death bestowed no reprieve from indignity; Saartjie's body was dissected and bequeathed as trophy to the Museum of Natural History in Paris. Until as recently as the 1970s, visitors to the 'Museum of Man' could view her brain, skeleton and genitalia, although by then there was a groundswell of revulsion at her inhumane treatment and when Nelson Mandela became president of South Africa, he insisted that the French government release her remains. Born in 1789, and buried over 200 years later in 2002, Saartjie

I SELL THE SHADOW TO SUPPORT THE SUBSTANCE.
SOJOURNER TRUTH.

Randall

East Grand Circus Park,
DETROIT.

Fig. 5.1   Sojourner Truth

was finally laid to rest in the land from which she had been taken (Willis, 2010).

If in life the exploitation of Saartjie's body had taken a primarily sexualised form, in death it was distinctly racialised. The authorities had acceded to the museum's request to retain her corpse on grounds that it represented an interesting specimen of humanity, her body a 'rhetorical artefact' in furtherance of the pseudo-scientific determinism of the day with its preoccupation with proving the biological inferiority of Black people (Gilchrist & Thompson, 2012). As Gilchrist and Thompson point out 'Representations, definitions, and treatments of the body are inherently political statements because of what they communicate about the constitutive meanings, importance, obsessions, practices, and urgencies related to the body' (2012, p. 279). The racialised, sexualised and gendered politics of the flesh (body politics) that governs the meanings assigned to the relationship between biology and ideology is as much a feature of contemporary societies as it was in Baartman's time and perhaps even more so, given the universal reach of popular media (Spellers & Moffitt, 2010). Should one be in any doubt about the continuing pervasiveness and extent of racism in defining the concept of womanhood or in seeking to control the Black female body, one only has to refer to the case of Caster Semenya. Semenya, a Black female athlete, also from South Africa, first gained worldwide attention in 2009 when she competed in the 800 meters at the world championships in Berlin. Her speed and muscular physique caused questions to be raised by observers over whether she *really* was a woman. Semenya went on to win gold in Berlin but was subsequently subjected to a battery of dehumanising tests to determine whether she should be allowed to race as a woman in the future. According to the Telegraph Newspaper, Semenya, in an interview with HBO Real Sports said that track officials from the governing body "probably" thought she had a penis. "I told them, 'It's fine. I'm a female, I don't care. If you want to see I'm a woman, I will show you my vagina. Alright?'" (Associated Press, 2022). Semenya was eventually allowed to run again and went on to win gold in the 800 meters in the 2012 and 2016 Olympics. In 2018 however, the International Association of Athletics Federations (the IAAF) decided that runners with testosterone above a certain level must take medication to artificially lower it if they wished to compete against other female runners. Many commentators and Semenya herself believed that this action was specifically targeted towards her. She described the effect of being forced to take the medication as "torture": "It made me sick, made me gain weight, panic attacks, I don't know if I was ever going to have a heart attack… It's like stabbing yourself with a knife every day. But I had no choice". (Associated Press, 2022). Pagonis, in an interview about the treatment of Caster Semanya for Vox Magazine states, 'Certain bodies are never allowed to be female, are never allowed to be women, are never allowed to just be... What I think this comes down to is, Caster is faster than white girls and she made them cry'. Pagonis added: 'Had Caster been a gender-conforming, straight-identified white girl who just was faster than other people, they would have never invaded her body' by demanding testing (Pagonis, reported in North, 2019). To the present day, Semenya has continued to be the subject of relentless scrutiny and anatomical speculation by the media and by 'armchair' experts around the world—not because of her prowess as an athlete but because she does not subscribe to dominant notions of what it means to be a woman.

Forcing women to take medication to alter natural hormone levels in order to compete in sports is at the very least, medically unethical. It is also unsafe and unscientific. Tannenbaum and Bekker (2019) argue that the practice 'risks setting an unscientific precedent for other cases of genetic advantage'. They further point out that the medical profession 'does not define biological sex or physical function by serum testosterone levels alone'. Testosterone levels vary naturally in both men and women and Tannenbaum and Bekker highlight the fact there is a 'particular overlap among elite track and field athletes'. The IAAF's assumption of a causal association between testosterone levels and medal winning has no scientific basis since 'reproducible, valid laboratory tests to detect androgen sensitivity do not exist' (ibid). Tannenbaum and Bekker conclude their argument against the IAAF rules by stating 'The effect of these policies on individuals, societies, and even medical science has far reaching implications' (2019).

That this action was initiated with the direct intent of controlling the body and diminishing the performance of a Black female athlete is also both intrinsically racist and sexist—there are no testosterone limits in place for male athletes.

Many have compared Semenya's treatment to that of Saartjie Baartman, the Black woman from South Africa whose bodily integrity was publicly violated and whose circumstances we have discussed above. Pagonis agrees: 'Her [Saartjie Bartman's] body was put on display' for Europeans 'to look at it and to gawk at it,' and Semenya's treatment 'reeks of that legacy.' This is a chilling reminder of the ways in which discourses of genetic difference - in Baartman's case to prove inferiority and in Semenya's case, to deny her opportunity, have been used across centuries to dehumanize and control Black people and in particular, Black women. If those in positions of power have learned nothing else from the enslavement of Black people, surely they must know that policy, in whatever area of social life, that seeks to nullify genetic differences has dangerous precedence and is unsupportable without 'objective, rigorous, and reproducible data' (Tannenbaum & Bekker, 2019).

Semenya's story is far from over. Resilient and determined to re-establish principles of fairness and equal opportunity within athletics, she launched legal action against the IAAF testosterone regulations. Her central argument is that the way she has been treated is discriminatory. In July 2023, the European Court of Human Rights agreed with her. In a landmark legal victory, the ruling by the Strasbourg Court questioned the 'validity' of the IAAF regulations that required Semenya to medically reduce her natural hormone levels in order to compete and declared that her human rights had been violated (Associated Press, 2023). Semenya, like so many other Black women whose stories are reflected in this book, refused to accede to subjugation. We celebrate their resilience but we should also acknowledge the personal cost. Commenting on her legal victory, Semenya stated: "The hard work that I have put in to being the athlete I am, has been questioned. My rights violated. My career impacted. All of it so damaging. Mentally, emotionally, physically and financially. (BBC Sport, July 2023).

We should be reminded, as Jackson (2006) contends, that the interrogation of present-day Black body politics would be deficient without its historical context since some modern representations and imagery concerning the Black body can be regarded as 'contemporaneous with slavery' (p. 12), feeding off stereotypes imbued with meanings of emphasised sexuality, aggression, victimhood, dysfunction, intellectual inferiority and body physique that race constructions generate:

> Since the emergence of race as a social construct, Black bodies have become surfaces of racial meanings. So it is only logical that any attempt to divorce the concept of race from body politics leaves the analysis incomplete (Jackson, 2006, p. 12).

The exhibitions featuring Saartjie Baartman underscore the interplay between dominant conceptions of feminine beauty/ugliness and of racial inferiority. Along with the commoditisation of Black women's sexuality (hooks, 1997a, 1997b), these dynamics feed what Haraway refers to as the imperialist fantasies associated with colonial domination that are encoded within such 'taxidermic displays' (1989a, 1989b). As Cheng (2000) states:

> The works of Meg Armstrong, Emmanuel Eze, Henry Louis Gates, Sander L. Gilman, and Paul Gilroy, among others, have demonstrated the historic complicity between the philosophical discourse of aesthetic judgment and a metaphysics of racial difference since the Enlightenment. Aesthetic standards have often been deployed by thinkers from Immanuel Kant to Thomas Jefferson as literally the last moral ground on which to justify racist practices. (p. 192)

Baartman was not by any Eurocentric measure considered beautiful at all, even though she was once referred to as a 'striking African beauty' (cited in Willis, 2010) an on the contrary as Lovejoy states:

> … In the contested realm of Baartman's career, it was not a sense of "beauty" that was the main attraction, but her divergence from European conceptions of the female body, which effectively made her a "freak" suitable for public display, ridicule, and marvel. (2007, p. 3)

It is important to pause here and acknowledge that feminist scholars have produced an extensive body of work critiquing hegemonic concepts of beauty and their focus on the idealized and the imagined. These are coercive and exploitative of women and their ethnocentric biases construct aesthetic standards that are partial and exclusive (Cheng, 2000). The commoditisation of beauty, with its relentless mission to make the perceived unbeautiful beautiful, includes standards presented as incontestable that are marketed as pro woman. In actuality, this 'discourse of ideality' promotes and services patriarchal interests and this aversion to non-idealized femininities is anti-woman since it undermines self-representation. Beauty is at one and the same time, then, a discourse of the 'unlovely' as much as of the 'lovely' (Cheng, 2000) and both are used to feed sexual desires. While the idealised version of femininity may dominate the hegemonic porn culture, the woman who is deemed ugly, monstrous or different represents a different type of sexual conquest or adventure—to satisfy the fetishes of those whose interests may be considered deviant or perverse. This explains the fascination with Saartjie Baartman who, though considered the antithesis of beauty, symbolised a 'wild, untamed sexuality' (Holmes, 2007). The obsession with Saartjie's physical attributes was also a form of 'scientific pornography' (Holmes, 2007) since she was used not only to promulgate a 'primitive' Black sexuality for the titillation of White men but also to further the science that established that the place of the Black African was as link between man and ape in the evolution of Homo sapiens (Lovejoy, 2007). The dehumanization that resulted in Saartjie Baartman being reduced to her sexual parts was only made possible because of gendered and racist social constructions that positioned her as 'plot space'. Though at the centre of dominant Victorian discourse on the nature of the Black woman, Saartjie Baartman was entirely peripheral to it; she may have been physically present in the stories that circulated about her, but as a female African slave, her own voice was perpetually absent (Holmes, 2007; Willis, 2010).

If it were ever possible to reduce the Abasindi Cooperative to an *essence* this is the assertion we would make; that in the 200 years since Baartman's birth and the political, social and cultural activism in the wake of Sojourner Truth's historic speech, the Black woman has sought to position herself as subject rather than as backcloth to the tapestry of someone else's design. The Abasindi woman was plot, not plot space. And it is as plot that Abasindi asserted its own aesthetic standards of beauty. Sara Baartman's story reminds us that the attribution of meanings of beauty may reflect differential experiences for Black women than for White women since, as Cheng observed, Sara could not 'be made beautiful even in the imagination since her body is radically undisciplinable' (Cheng, 2000, p. 192). The celebration of skin, body and hair that surfaced within the context of the Abasindi Cooperative suggested a conscious act of insurgency—a political activism of sorts. But conscious or not, the championing of hair left natural and the perfecting of African hair styles (Fig. 5.2), the love of Black skin rather than its grading by shade and the assertion that the Black woman's body, however shaped, is unto itself beautiful; but more than this, is hers and hers alone, was undoubtedly an act of reclamation. Being part of Abasindi enabled the woman to reclaim for the self an aesthetic standard of choice and to celebrate, no, flaunt the joy of a female body that is undisciplinable.

Maga Women

Maga women
Strike poses in 6, 8, 10; sizes
Of sharp angled hips
Stomachs iron flat
And breast-less silhouettes
In clothed enviable perfection

But nakedness reveals
Knee bones protruding
Thighs calves forearms twinning
And arses hard to recognise.

These are the models
That sashay across our vision
As we purse our lips
In dismay disgust dejection

While our hands caress
The rise of belly
That folds into an apron of warm flesh

When we bend or breasts lead
Identical dancers in motion
The dimples of our elbows are deep

Fig. 5.2 Abina braiding hair

Our knees are satin cushions
Our lips cheek full
And when we turn to leave
Our hips are pivoting sensuality

But we are not stereotype caricatures of Africa
Maga women

Come in shades
Black and White
As do we
As do we
'Maga Women', SuAndi ©2014

Adele (Fig. 5.3) one of the Abasindi women reflects:

It was among Abasindi women that I made the decision to start wearing my hair in dreadlocks. Ask any black woman, or black man for that matter … 'locking'

Fig. 5.3 Adele Jones photographed by Bill Knight for the *Phenomenal Women* exhibition of UK Black female professors curated by Professor Nicola Rollock

one's hair is not simply a matter of choosing a hair style. For me, it was an act of reclamation – my locks were to become the symbol of self-love I needed to show to the world as I emerged from a childhood during which my skin and hair had largely attracted derision or ridicule.

That the beauty discourse has been used to control women's bodies was well understood within the organization but we did not accept that the idealization of particular notions of beauty which has been the source of much white feminist opposition, should necessarily speak in the same way to Black women, since we are excluded for different reasons.

> Much of what has been written about beauty's relationship to femininity speaks sometimes with and sometimes without self-consciousness to and from an exclusively middle-class White paradigm. And much of what has been written about beauty's relationship to racism has presumed that a racialised individual's relationship to gender discrimination is analogous to, if it does not simply double the burdens of racial oppression. But at the conjunction of racial and gender discriminations stands the woman of color, for whom "beauty" presents a vexing problem both as judgment and solution. That is, between a feminist critique of feminine beauty and a denial of non-white beauty according to racial stereotyping, where does this leave the woman of color? Can she or can she not be beautiful? Is her beauty (or potential for beauty) good or evil? It is unclear whether assenting to the prospect of a "beautiful woman of color" would be disruptive of racist discourse or complicit with gender stereotypes. (Cheng, 2000, p. 191)

Abasindi women, like Sojourner Truth and many women activists since, believed that reclaiming representations of blackness contained the potential to unsettle universalisms about dominant prescriptions of beauty which constrain all women—and also to confront racist ideologies within which these prescriptions are embedded and which constrain Black women in particular. For the Black woman, then, it is not only the fields, the workplace, the family, or the institutions that have been the site of her struggles but also her skin, her body, and her hair. It is not that the organization abandoned the call to sisterhood generated by feminist opposition to the idealisation of beauty, but because this was not grounded in shared positionings that incorporated race, culture or historical legacy, the Abasindi women constructed an alternative discursive tradition based on reclamation, self-representation, and the preservation of *their* versions of beauty. The theoretical anchor for this type of political activism is summed up thus:

> It is our task to make a place for this different social subject. In so doing we are less interested in joining the ranks of gendered femaleness than gaining the insurgent ground as female social subject. (Spillers cited in Li, 2006, p. 14)

And it was as female social subject that Sojourner Truth fought. Those familiar with her story will recall that a White male doctor protested the authenticity of her claim for equal rights and demanded that she prove she was a woman by showing her breasts. This was not simply an attempt to destroy agency by reducing the argument to anatomy, it was the exasperated outcry at the audacity that this physical manifestation of the black unlovely should apply to the claim for rights that the white lovely asserted. Truth owned rather than minimized her blackness—the discourse she engendered was for a 'collective humanity' that challenged the reification of whiteness and the whitening of blackness to make the Black presence more acceptable. She stepped out of her assigned role as plot space to centre herself as plot. Such a bold position was anathema to White patriarchal supremacists then and remains pertinent in the present. In recounting Truth's story, Haraway explains:

> Difference (understood as the divisive marks of authenticity) was reduced to anatomy; but even more to the point, the doctor's demand articulated the racist/sexist logic that made the very flesh of the black person in the New World indecipherable, doubtful, out of place, confounding. Remember that Trinh Minh-ha, from a different Diaspora over a hundred years later, wrote, "Perhaps, for those of us who have never known what life in a vernacular culture is/was and are unable to imagine what it can be/could have been, gender simply does not exist otherwise than grammatically in language." Truth's speech was out of place, dubious doubly; she was female and black; no, that's wrong she was a black female, a black woman, not a coherent substance with two or more attributes, but an oxymoronic singularity who stood for an entire excluded and dangerously promising humanity. The language of Sojourner Truth's body was as electrifying as the language of her speech. (1992, p. 92)

Although a free woman, Truth's skin, body and hair, like Baartman's, were the symbols of a status deemed so inferior as to justify the denial of her right to vote—she was not enough a human and even if *that* could be argued, she was not enough a woman to warrant it. Yet Truth claimed rather than minimised these attributes—her skin, body and hair were the voice she used to speak for Black women; the assertion 'ain't I a woman', though essentially a rebuttal of the notion that Black women should not be allowed the suffrage rights White women were fighting for also cut the heart out of the idea that feminine beauty equals white. With the vote established some 60 years before the birth of the Abasindi Cooperative and held firmly under the belts of its members, the aesthetic claims about Black skin, body and hair functioned as a symbol of resistance to the continued post-suffrage oppressions that many Black women in Britain faced.

Fig. 5.4 Atinuke (Tinu) and her resplendent headwrap

Armed with our Afros, cornrows, braids, locks and headwraps (Fig. 5.4), we were ready to do battle on several fronts and we organized around issues such as the lack of educational opportunity for Black women and children, domestic violence, the impact of immigration controls, the marginalization of Black art and the criminalization of Black young people (discussed later in the book).

Within a race conscious society such as Britain, black femininity cannot be taken for granted; however, the matter-of-factness of its existence among the Abasindi women and the loving of attributes associated with it: names, accents, art, body, skin and hair established its prominence within the communities of Manchester in ways that were political, oppositional and affirmational. Trinh Minh-ha suggests that those of us who inhabit Diasporic spaces live outside of vernacular cultures, yet the accounts of Abasindi women suggest that they created a vernacular culture of their own. This is illustrated in the reflection below from Yinka (Fig. 5.5) one of the Abasindi children.

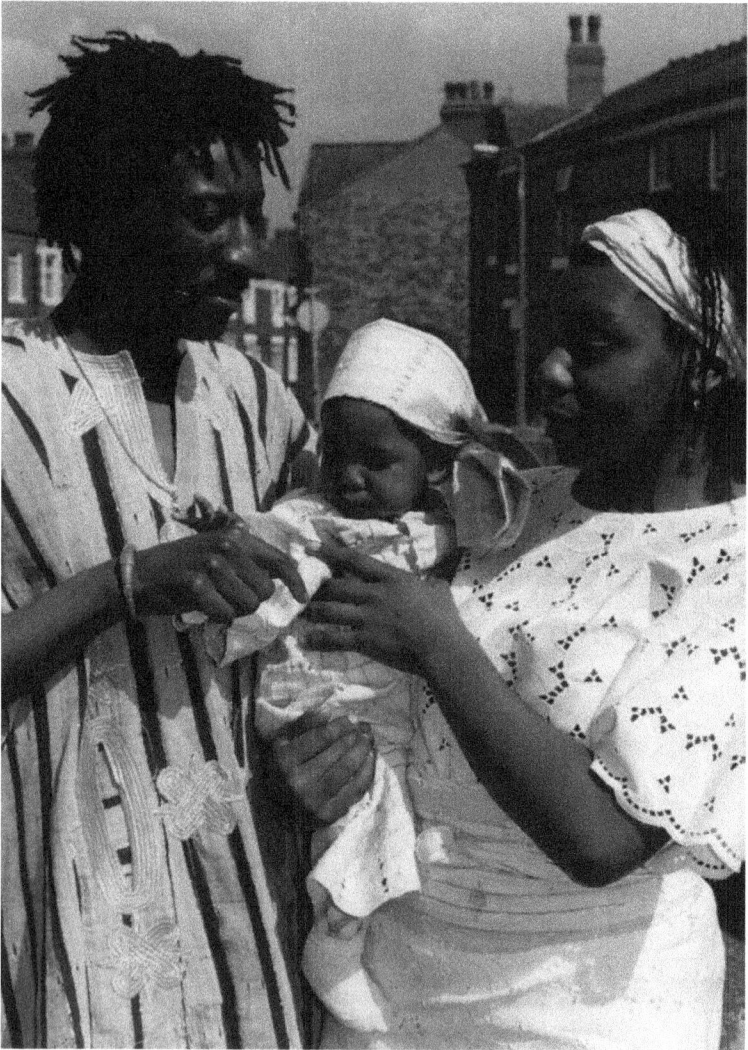

Fig. 5.5 Yinka with her parents, Leslie and Pauline, at her naming ceremony

My mother is one of the Abasindi women. This is a fact that I am proud of but do not often think about. The true impact of these women's history I haven't ever fully acknowledged … I have somewhat taken it for granted, this legacy I have inherited and become slightly blasé about. The beginnings of these relationships were so organic and embedded in my childhood that I am unaware of their inception. My mother had moved us back to London to be closer to our biological family by the time I was three, but many a school vacation was spent in Manchester. Abasindi morphed from its original home in a squat to various people's homes when the building threatened to collapse. I relished the opportunities I got to watch these women in action, and they always were in their element. As a girl I loved to just sit and listen to them reminisce and tell stories – these women are all my aunts and their children, my cousins. These occasions/moments were a major part of my development and pathologizing. I was provided with feminist opinions before I ever knew the terminology. By simply being in the company of Black women who were proud to be just that allowed me to love my Blackness in its totality, long before society at large had a chance to label me "other" and cause me to question the validity and value in my beauty. I think of those times as the sowing of seeds on very fertile ground. There was no definitive moment or conversation where I was told that being Black was a thing to be proud of. I do not remember being told to love my hair, complexion, shape, or any of the things I am instructed by society at large to be ashamed of. It just came with the territory I was in, the women of the proverbial village that my mother raised me in. These women came in various shades of blackness and body shapes, these were my norms. In a world that tends to pathologize Black women, Black women *were* my norm. Amazing! By virtue of the environment, I grew up in I have been very fortunate to have been able to avoid one of the major relationship pitfalls in the lives of many Black women – the one with her hair. For some reading this that may not be a particularly significant statement. But for others of you who have struggled with your hair and the relationship it inextricably has with your identity, never having been bound by these psychological issues is really a powerful thing. I am extremely thankful for this reprieve and can only hope and pray that more women experience this freedom and find genuine acceptance and love of natural hair. In saying all this, I was never very fond of my name, Yinka. Not due to it being African though. It has more to do with my being disappointed in my parents' lack of creativity in choosing one of the common Yoruba names for me and not even giving me a middle name to fall back on. Even in that choice I am reminded of what a bold statement was being made in selecting an African name while living in the Western world. It is so strange being in a new environment in which people are learning my name for the first time and how in awe of its "uniqueness" they are. However, this is nothing new. All my Abasindi cousins are mothered by Caribbean women who each made the decision to give them beautiful sounding names with even more melodious meanings. Our mothers are the women of Abasindi, what else would you expect? This is the nature of the women who comprised Abasindi the movement. It was not a movement in theory alone. These women were not donning African clothes for show and fashion. Their belief in and commitment to all things Abasindi in addition to the African and Caribbean culture ran deep. So much so that before people laughed *with* people's African accents and not *at* them, I was always secure in my dual heritage and there was never any separation between the two in my mind. Black is and always will be Black.

A note here about the use of the term 'blackness', which, for the purposes of this book functions as a shortcut for the myriad dimensions of the experiences and identities of Black people (Black being synonymous with the American expression, 'people of color'). These identities cut across historicised and contemporary considerations not only of race, but of gender, sexuality, ethnicity, nationality, language, religion, mixed heritage, and the intersection of these experiences. As illustrated in Yinka's account, for second, third or fourth generation Black people living in Britain, identity may also take a different form from that of their parents and grandparents. Abasindi did not hold with prescriptions of blackness and acknowledged that though identities are influenced by social context, Black people are not fixed within or defined by a 'static system of social locations' (Hill Collins, 1998). It is however, beyond the remit of this chapter to discuss identity and intersectionality in more depth and we refer the reader to the many excellent texts on the topic (for example, Hill Collins, 1998).

Participating in a collective whose ethos was political consciousness-raising and from which Abasindi women were able to derive positive affirmation of the Black and beautiful is not for all women, but at least this was available through the many grassroots Black and minority ethnic organisations that sprang up in Britain in the post-colonial years. Black children, however, have often lacked access to the places and spaces for affirmation of racial identity and their dependent status means that how they feel about themselves is usually contingent upon or influenced by values transmitted from the adults around them. Yinka's induction into Abasindi was as a young girl—this was neither accidental nor incidental since the Abasindi Cooperative had a deliberate strategy to foster self-love and to raise esteem, aspiration and achievement among Black children. This guided many of our activities and was given effect through the organisation's Saturday school, summer school (Fig. 5.6) and the teaching of African/Caribbean arts and crafts (Figs. 5.7 and 5.8).

We also involved children in drama, poetry and cultural activities and we contributed to children's political education (Fig. 5.9); they were with us when we discussed strategies to protect women and children from deportation; they came with us, in our bellies, in their pushchairs or strung together

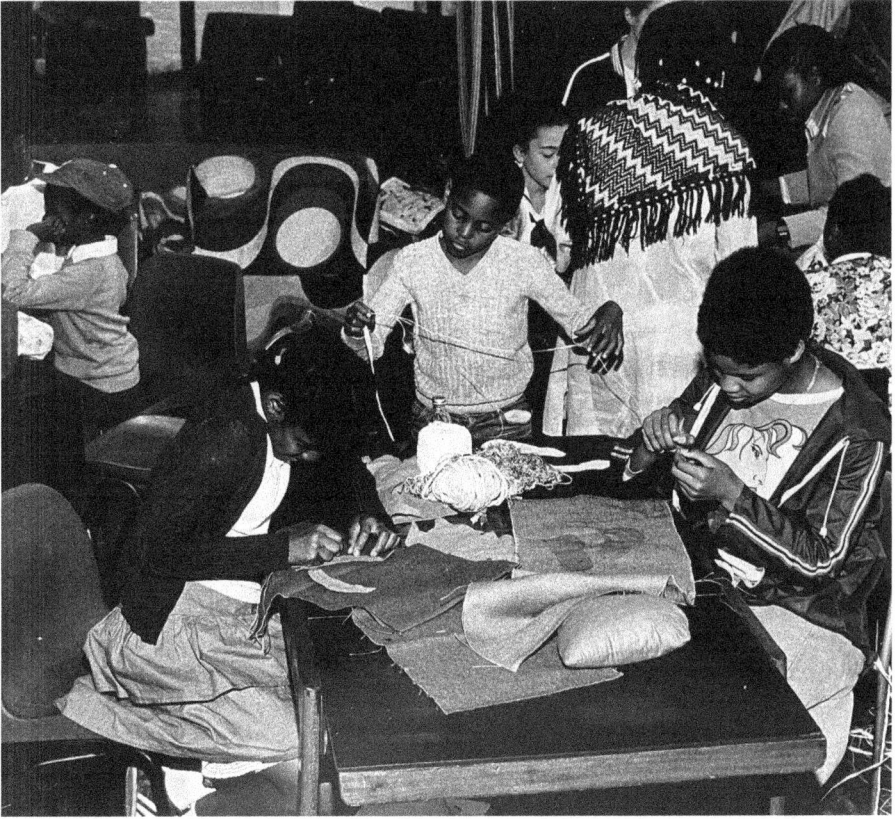

Fig. 5.6 Children involved in art and craftwork at the Abasindi Summer School

holding hands when we protested against apartheid, the proliferation of nuclear arms, the Israeli occupation of Gaza. And as they joined in the welcoming parties held for political activists fighting for liberation in countries such as South Africa, Nicaragua and Palestine, or to celebrate a visiting Black artist, they looked on perplexed at the different accents, names and cultural traditions our friends brought with them.

The most significant role Abasindi played in the lives of Black children was in the nurturing of a healthy and positive sense of identity. The importance of this cannot be overstated. Consider Pecola Breedlove, the young girl in Toni Morrison's first novel, *The Bluest Eye,* whose lot was to be born poor, Black and female and who desired nothing more than to have blue eyes. Denuded of the affirming benefits of being immersed in an environment in which being Black is as unremarkable, normative and esteemed as being White and where the markers of beauty and acceptance are not colour-coded, Pecola was

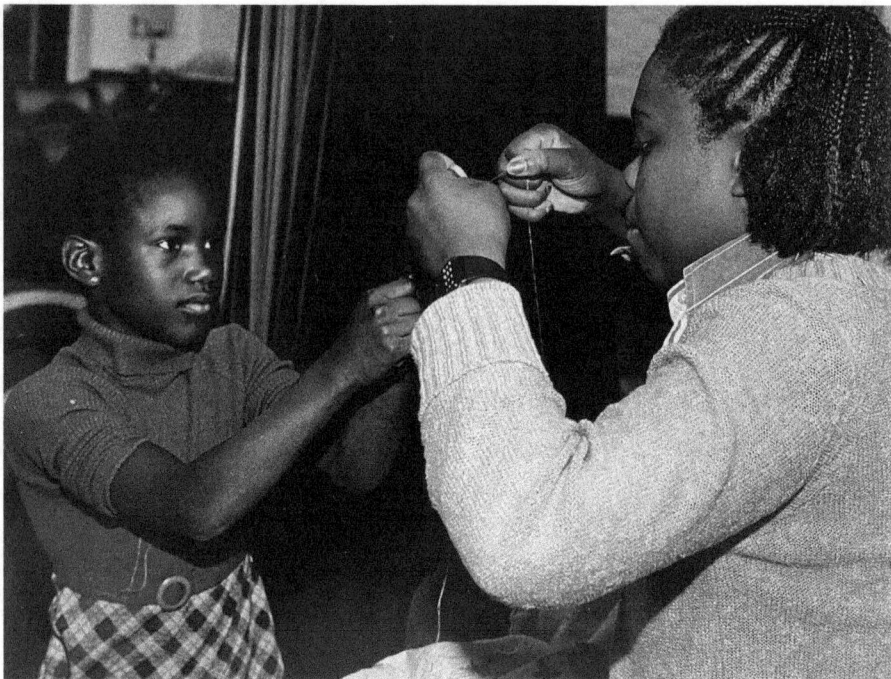

Fig. 5.7 Teaching children African/Caribbean crafts

Fig. 5.8 Women creating craft

Fig. 5.9 Children participate in the making of an educational film

convinced of her own ugliness and lack of worth. In a manner not uncon-
nected to the views about blackness that affected Saartjie Baartman over two
centuries earlier, Morrison's novel portrays a set of values predicated on the
aesthetic merits of whiteness and the intrinsic negativity of blackness; values
that can cause harm, confusion and distress to Black children.

For most Black children growing up in the UK, the Black people in their
lives, with all their strengths and failings: mothers, fathers, grandparents,
brothers and sisters as well as wider kinships provide a point of reference for
the formation of their own positive identities. However, Black children
denuded of Black family life may experience a sense of alienation from cultural, linguistic and religious heritage or they may try to construct an idealised
identity based on either fictional or pathological Black role models. One
group of Black children who are particularly vulnerable in this regard are
those who are brought up in local authority care. In the absence of alternative
representations, these children often internalise the derogatory messages
about blackness which are pervasive in the values and attitudes of those around
them, leading to feelings of rejection, self-deprecation, and distorted perceptions of self-image (Ung et al., 2012). Clearly, it is difficult to isolate the
internalization of negative beliefs about the self as a cause of children's emotional and psychological problems since children in care have usually

experienced a range of traumas, losses and disruptions that also generate these problems, but for some children this is a contributing factor. In his observations of the Black child in the British care system, Small argued four decades ago that a healthy personality requires that the psychic image the child has of herself must match her reality (Small, 1984). However, if the child is not to be 'engulfed and rendered impotent by such negative social images' to which Black children are often exposed, he or she must also be able to 'transcend reality' (Barn, 2000, p. 7). The fantasy of imagining herself with blue eyes was not evidence of Pecola's ability to escape her reality but the opposite; unable to transcend the reality of living in a world in which only little White girls could be beautiful, she internalized negative representations of blackness. Her search for blue eyes was in actuality a search for confirmatory signs of her own unloveliness and though the harm was initially felt only inside her, in time, the rage at the immutability of being Black led to a destructive rage that she began to externalize. Yet Picola grew up in the midst of her family; she was not taken into care, she did not grow up in a children's home, or a transracial foster or adoptive home. This tells us that immersion within a Black family may not of itself provide children with the emotional scaffolding to be able to transcend the reality of living in a racist environment if adults have themselves internalized negative portrayals of Black people and transmit these to their offspring. The creation of a healthy and positive identity over the lifespan is not about achieving congruence between perceptions of self and constructions of race (or of gender, sexual orientation, or any other aspects of identity) since, in environments in which destructive messages are prevalent, it is a transcendental imagination, the capacity such as that possessed by Sojourner Truth, to fashion oneself from a position of equal human value outside of the myopic lens of racism that is needed. Like many Black children in care, 'Pecola interprets poor treatment and abuse as her own fault. She believes that the way people observe her is more reliable than what she herself observes' (Morrison, 1994, p. 38); because her eyes are not blue she is inferior, unworthy and unlovable. Abasindi included several social workers and youth workers and we came across many Black children in the care system who were in search of blue eyes and who seemed to have few opportunities for the loving of blackness. Below, one of the Abasindi women who adopted a Black child who had suffered a series of failed White foster placements reflects on the silent transformation of the becoming black of her son:

My son came to me when he was six; he had last had contact with his father, who had been the only Black person in his life, when he was just a baby and had never been close to another Black man since. His distorted views of himself spilled out onto his drawings, he was the little White boy with yellow hair living in a little house with a White mum and dad. At first he gravitated to any and all Black men we met; it seemed to me as if he wanted to drink up their blackness. But this meant he was vulnerable; he would have gone off with anyone. I took him with me to Abasindi, to all the meetings we had, the music and dance sessions, the Saturday school and through the Black women he met there, he was introduced to their fathers, husbands, brothers, uncles, friends, and learned almost by osmosis who to trust and who to steer away from. Black people had been extraordinary to him and it was only when they became part of his everyday ordinariness that he could take his little Black self for granted. His early lessons about the beautiful kind of Black man he could and would become were learned at the feet of Black women.

Like other indicators of social inequality, Black children have long been disproportionately represented within the UK care system (Owen & Statham, 2009). This can be partly explained by the fact that among the myriad of factors that may lead to a child being received into care are those that particularly affect Black families such as poverty, social and economic disadvantage, poor housing, unemployment and parental ill-health (Pilkington, 2003). Children are also taken into care because they are the victims of abuse or neglect, because they have become separated from their families, as in the case of young asylum seekers, or because parents are unable to care for them. Figures have consistently shown that Black children are disproportionately represented in the care system than white children. In 2020, there were 80,080 children in care in England; White children were less likely to be in care (74%) and more likely to be adopted (83%) compared with their share of under-18 year olds (79%) while Black children were more likely to be in care (7%) and less likely to be adopted (2%) compared with their share of under-18 year old population (5%). The reasons for the persistence of such disparities include racism and structural inequalities (Barn & Kirton, 2012; Harker, 2012).

For more than half a century, local authorities have sought to resolve the problem of the disproportionate numbers of Black children in care by placing them in transracial placements. Transracial adoption and fostering refers to the placement of children across racial, religious and ethnic (and often geographic) boundaries and primarily involves White adults adopting or fostering non-White children. The practice is contentious, being ferociously defended by its proponents and severely criticized by those who consider this but another example of the domination and exploitation of one group by another (Ung et al., 2012). Our position as Black women was that the Black or minority ethnic child adopted into a family that lacks a reference point to their racial or cultural heritage is likely to be subjected to compounded forms of discrimination. Ung et al. (2012) state:

If this familial situation extends to the community and social holding environment of the adopted person, such that their genetic and visual racial group is not mirrored for them in their social environment, there is, according to the prevailing body of literature, little opportunity for her or him to acquire and achieve positive self-regard in relation to self and race, or reconciliation of racial conflict. (p. 76).

This issue seems to be little understood by those who hold the power to determine policy on Black children in care and from where they sit, to be in search of blue eyes may seem a small price to pay for life in a foster or adoptive family. The minimizing of the importance of racial, cultural, linguistic and familial heritage for Black children however, reflects some fundamental inequalities within the care system and, as Barn (2000) points out in relation to transracial placements, White children 'have not had to experience a similar [race/cultural] upheaval at a time of separation and loss from the birth family' (2008, p. 9). This determinedly colour-blind policy agenda has been employed by successive UK governments and masks an integrationist approach which fails to address the structural inequalities that impact Black children and families. Implicit in adoption discourses are deeply embedded notions of racial superiority and inferiority that position White, heteronormative and middle-class as best (Barn, 2000, p. 13). That these strategies should be implemented within the context of an intently race conscious society, in which the agenda of all political shades—from liberal to far-right is preoccupied with the 'foreign invasion', and the increasing control and surveillance of Black people is an irony that cuts deep. From the perspective of Black people, young people brought up in the care system have often reported a 'sense of isolation and alienation, of being 'dropped in a white sea', and of discrimination, lack of understanding or culturally insensitive provision [which] sadly remain a reality for some young Black and minority ethnic children in residential child care' (Voice for the Child in Care, 2004, p. 1).

In Abasindi there were women who had grown up in care themselves and who had sought out the group to help counter the effects of living one's childhood in a world impacted by racist constructions, and which at the same time was devoid of positive racial, cultural or linguistic anchor points. Other Abasindi women came into contact with Black children in care through their work as social workers and psychologists and some were the foster parents and adoptive mothers who looked after them. One of the Abasindi women wrote 'Letter to a Social Worker' which is included in a book on residential care. The letter seeks to unmask the collusion of professionals in a system established on the assumption of White as normative and Black as problematic in decisions about the placement of children. As the adoptive mother of a son, she was particularly concerned about the impact on him of the negative representations of blackness that had been part of his early care and found in Abasindi a route through which he could find a positive sense of himself (Fig. 5.10). The letter is written in the style of Audre Lorde ('An Open Letter to Mary Daly', Lorde, 1979).

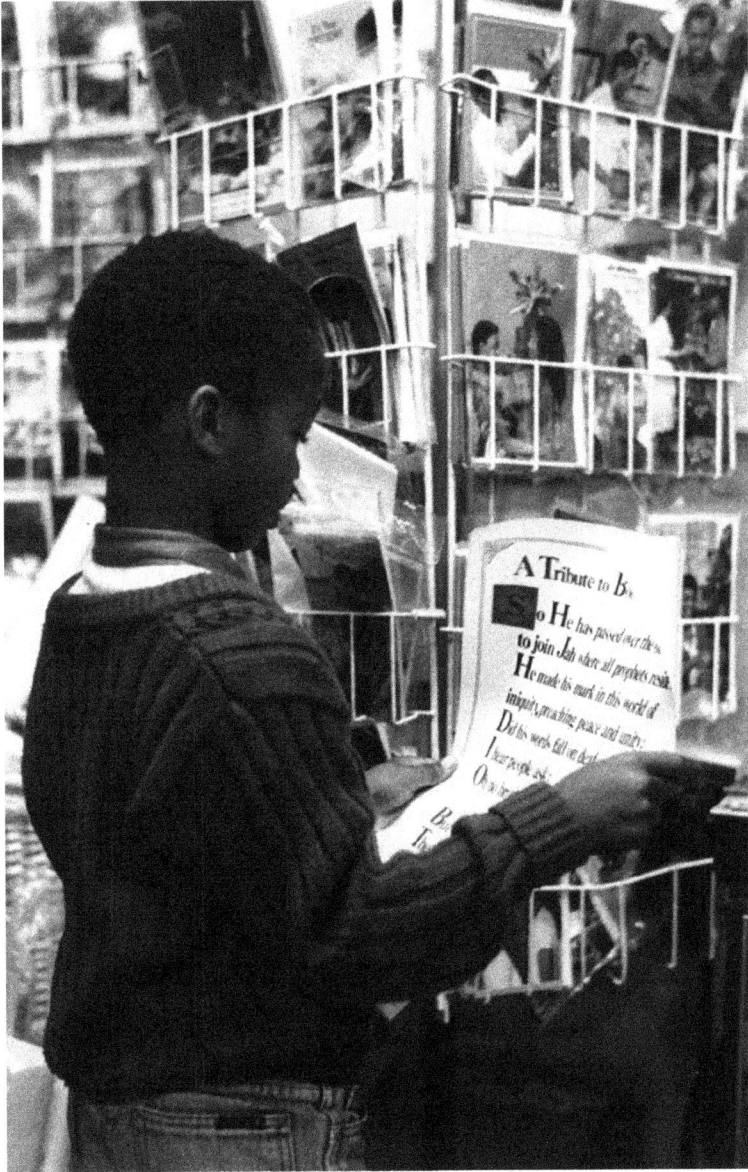

Fig. 5.10 A boy from the Abasindi Saturday School

Dear Social Worker

Identity is a complex, ever changing and multi-dimensional concept in which we are always becoming who we are. The most significant experiences in shaping who I am now are those to do with being a mother, although these are indivisible from my own experiences of having been mothered and indeed, my experiences of being a sister, a friend, a partner, a worker or the many other roles that give my life meaning. I came to mothering through adoption and it is as a Black adoptive mother that I write. I do not write for all Black mothers although I believe that what I have to say will resonate with many of them, and also with Black fathers too… Your decisions about race and who should and should not adopt Black children are set within the agenda of the government of the day. That you might, of course, consider questions of race in the placement of a White child is something you keep quiet about. Far from this being an irrelevant factor in the placement of White children, the silence in which you take refuge simply masks the fact that such is the depth and extent of consensus in assuming 'white' as normative that it does not even need to be stated. The assured, taken-for-granted status of 'whiteness' and its associated meanings informs adoptive assessment, approval and matching processes so pervasively and completely it is their lifeblood; what then, can there possibly be to question? This is a reminder to me that positions which benefit the dominant in society, unlike those of us struggling for recognition in the margins, rarely need to be defended and would never be subject to the charges of ideological radicalism those of us proclaiming the value of Black families have often faced. It also pointedly serves to under-score, should I be in any doubt, that my value to British society as a Black mother and my contribution to the lives of Black children is considered negli-gible at worst and minimal at best. Instead of simply accepting transracial place-ments as a solution to the placement needs of Black children, perhaps you should question why so much political energy is invested in supporting this position? Why is it that opposition is couched as extremism – what deeply held percep-tions of me as a Black woman could possibly demand or expect my acquies-cence? Perhaps you should think about the ways in which public research into the private lives of Black transracially placed children subverts the ways in which children are impacted by the internalization of racism and the distortion of self-image. Why it is that there are no similar public studies of the strengths of Black family life and the ways in which these can provide the protective, nourishing and empowering factors to achieve the outcomes you have subscribed to for children…Why is it that you want to play down difference when discussing these issues yet you are among those who have benefited from the negative rep-resentations of difference in wider society just as surely as Black children have not? Why is it that there are so many Black children in local authority care and what is it that the liberal among you are *really* saying when you assert that it is in support of Black children that so many are placed transracially? Can you con-ceive of the possibility that from where I am sitting, liberalism, despite benevolent intentions, may not look benign at all but may mask or perpetuate inequalities? And why must the lid be kept on racism, for this is what lies at the root of this discussion? I would like to see it raised up, so I can stamp on its head. And you, can it be that you are prepared to settle for avoiding discomfort rather than fighting for human rights and social equality that might attend to the needs of Black children and families? My comments are not about racial purity. I am not an advocate of clumsy experiments in colour or ethnicity matching and I am not the hostile voice of anti-White rebellion. It is simply that being denuded of the experience of growing and living among Black people is an impoverishing experience for Black children and for the Black people who have so much to give and to gain by becoming their parents. It adds the loss of racial and cultural context to the losses a child in care may already be dealing with (I make this point in the belief that people must not be reduced to definitive, static or homogenizing notions of race and culture and I also acknowledge that for many Black people, culture includes perceptions and experiences of Britishness and so on). It reduces Black children's opportunities for positive affirmation of themselves as Black people and for many Black children (this is the case regardless of the 'success' stories you remind me of) is often the source of distress and searching in later years. Perhaps when you have considered all of these questions, you will think about how you burden Black children with these weighty matters and also reflect on the messages you give to Black adults, for this may help to explain why it is that they may not be willing to come forward to offer themselves as parents to the children in your care. (adapted by the author from 'Letter to a Social Worker: Reflections on Mothering', in A. Douglas and T. Philpot (eds. 2003)

The manifestations of internalized racism include loathing of the physical characteristics associated with being black such as skin colour and hair texture, stereotyping, denial of heritage, beliefs about white superiority and black inferiority, and over-identification with people who derogate Black people. Black children may be subject to racial taunts, bullying, direct acts of discrimination, pervasive negative messages about Black people, or they may witness White children receiving preferential treatment. Cemented by structural inequalities and institutional racism, Black young people may come to view the lack of opportunity and the challenges in achieving aspirations as being attributable to their physical characteristics rather than to the social constructions spun around racial (and gendered) differences on which systems of domination and exclusion have been built:

It is now commonly recognized that black children face much greater difficulty in handling racism and clarifying their own sense of self if they are brought up in settings and neighbourhoods lacking positive role models. (Chakrabarti & Hill, 2000, p. 23)

Adults who are able to empathise with these experiences and provide explanations about the history and nature of racism can counteract the destructive force of these dynamics and prevent their translation into beliefs about low self-worth. Research by 'The Voice for the Child in Care' found that Black families may be the main, or even only, 'gateway' through which Black children in care can access their cultural and ethnic identity, whereas White children growing up in a predominantly White society have countless role models to draw upon. Where these protective factors are absent from the child's environment however, the internalization of racism may result in harmful behaviours being directed at the self or being externalized through anti-social acts, aggression, or bullying. These manifestations are the surface expressions of negative beliefs about the self that often reflect deeper psychological problems with implications for mental well-being and interpersonal relationships across the lifespan.

The extent and depth of the difficulties internalized racism can cause can never be known, but the physical neglect of the loving of blackness was often evident in the children in care that Abasindi women came across. Theirs was the hair left uncombed, un-oiled or cut short because it was simply too much trouble, and theirs was the Black skin left uncared for from lack of moisturizing cream so that, in the cold of Britain, they turned grey, ashen, dry, and mottled. These were the children who settled for being unlovely—since, like Pecola, they observed themselves through a prism of racial deprecation; a very subtle process which is all the more powerful for that fact. They were the Black boys first to be excluded from school and sent to pupil referral units for behavioural problems (Gillborn, 2004; Graham & Robinson, 2004) and they were the girls most likely to be sexually exploited by the older men who use gendered power and status to feed on their vulnerabilities (Jones & Jemmott, 2014).

Of course, there are many Black children in care who do well, who thrive regardless, or perhaps because of the care they have received and whose own family life would have been dismal but for intervention by the State. There are foster and adoptive parents, Black and White who have loved Black children beyond measure; indeed the colour of skin is no indicator of the capacity for parental love, as the countless number of Black children with 'mixed' (Black and White) parents can testify. But for the Black child removed from his/her birth family and who was then submerged in a world where colour, name, hair, religion, accent or nationality were the source of humour, derision or discrimination, Abasindi provided an opportunity for this child to feel good about him/herself. It was unsurprising therefore that of all the children brought to Abasindi to have their hair braided or styled in cornrows, several of them lived in children's homes or foster homes; the decision to positively embrace their hair was an act of self-affirmation and resilience as described by Melanie (Fig. 5.11).

Visualise proud beautiful Black women. Women of all ages, beautiful shades of the blue/black/brown hue and shapes and size. Each woman resplendent, everyone different, each has their own individual style. They ranged from beautiful to attractive and everything in between. Their eclectic mix of varying lengths in hairstyles and shapes. There were sisters wearing locks, plaits, threading, and cornrow. As I lovingly take care of my own natural hair, I give thanks and gratitude to the women who taught me to appreciate it. Hair was one of the things

Fig. 5.11 Melanie

Abasindi were famous for. As any number of women were seated in chairs around a huge table, talking, debating and arguing whilst being beautified. I would spend hours blending into the group as I waited my turn to take my seat in the chair, to have my hair cornrowed, I wondered what I would be transformed into, but I was never disappointed. The talking never stopped and there would be a number of conversations going on at once. They made cornrows fashionable in a time where Identity was an issue.

Historically, Black people's hair has been the most visible stigma of blackness, second only to skin (Mercer, 2000). For African people in the Diaspora, the emergence of the Afro in the 1960s represented a rejection of 'good' hair and its association with whiteness, acceptance and social status, and a celebration of hair that is naturally kinky and curly. Braiding, dreadlocks, and the Afro emerged as politicised statements of pride and empowerment (hooks, 1997a, 1997b; Weekes, 1997).

However, as bel hooks argued 'even during the most militant stages of the Black power movement, [women] had never really stopped allowing racist notions of beauty to define female desirability' (hooks, 1994, p. 177) and the natural look was for many simply a transient fad. Nyamnjoh et al. (2002) go further. In their exploration of the modernization of African hairstyles in Cameroon, they suggest that it was not so much politicization but the romanticization of an 'Africanist heritage' during the 60s, 70s and 80s which resulted in the popularization of the Afro, cornrows and beaded plaits (p. 107) and this, they argue, explains its ephemeral status. Nevertheless hair, however fashioned, has remained one of the defining characteristics of blackness.

For the last three decades at least, a global market of straighteners, weaves and wigs have fuelled consumption patterns that replicate Western aesthetic values. Nyamnjoh et al. (2002) suggest that consumption of these products this is not an abandonment of the traditional but the constant re-invention of self through aesthetic choices that reflect a distancing from the past and engagement with the modern. They argue that Black women use these goods out of economic and creative choice and that the styles they create, though influenced by socialization processes underpinned by hegemonic versions of beauty, do not emulate Western styles but are distinctive to Black women. Although the study by Nyamnjoh et al. (2002) is of African women in Cameroon, the insights generated are more widely applicable and demonstrate that between the forces of globalization and the aesthetic values generated from localized contexts, the use of 'shampoos and conditioners, straighteners and dyes, curlers and blow dryers create new spaces in which women make themselves neither according to conservative local structures nor in the exact image of the west' (p. 102). These Black women are not necessarily less politically astute than those who choose natural or traditional African hair styles but 'consumers living within the modernist aesthetic [who] constantly attempt to negotiate the rupture between creativity and (imaginative but co-opting) consumption' (Nyamnjoh et al., 2002, p. 101). Meaning making in relation to the adoption of false or straightened hair is therefore owned as much by the women who wear these styles as it is by those who dominate the reproduction of representations of beauty. These women may not be centre plot in the subject-object dynamic of representational body politics, but neither are they plot space—she is neither mime, nor counterfeit. Mercer explains:

> When hairstyling is critically evaluated as an aesthetic practice inscribed in everyday life, all black hairstyles are political in that they each articulate responses to the panoply of historical forces which have invested this element of the ethnic signifier with both symbolic meaning and significance. (Mercer, 1994, p. 104)

A woman who relaxes her hair, wears a wig or a weave does not do so in a political or cultural vacuum; indeed her agential choices, inimitably connected as these are to the underlying morass of a racialized aesthetic, may reflect a knowing subjectivity that traverses between the creative, the pragmatic and the self-representational. Modern day feminist theory must be able to embrace the idea that alongside the reclamation of Black natural hair, the bewigged versions of the Black aesthetic also contain possibilities for '…post-colonial, non-generic, and irredeemably specific figures of critical subjectivity, consciousness, and humanity—not in the sacred image of the same, but in the self-critical practice of difference' (Haraway, 1992, p. 87).

Hairstyles are associated with professional standing, occupation and prestige and are imbued with meaning about conformity, morality, wealth and social status. Thompson (2009) suggests that Black women may choose to wear false or chemically straightened hair because they are acutely aware of the potentially negative impact 'an authentically Black aesthetic will create' (p. 852). Thompson offers one explanation for the choices Black women make but she makes a larger point too—the discursive realm of Black hair is not simply a binary of polarised opposites between the 'natural', constituted as expression of political agency, and the 'unnatural', viewed as a surrender of sorts, but represents the entanglement of race, politics and history with popular culture and the subjective constructions of Black beauty within specific lived realities (Brown, 2014). Drawing on the work of Hill Collins, Brown (2014) argues that Black women have responded to hegemonic prescriptions of beauty by adopting a dual consciousness which enables them to both publicly embrace, and even adopt, the aesthetics arising out of relations of oppression, while in their private spaces and subjective standpoints they remain acutely oppositional to racist constructions (Brown, 2014, p. 10). As Marco (2012) states, 'positioning the Black self in this political culture is constant' (p. 30).

What this discussion highlights is that given the social conditioning of dominant representations of beauty, the internalization of racism which can lead to despising Black hair, the pathologizing of some natural styles and a socio-economic climate in which natural hairstyles may limit Black women's career and relationship prospects, the choice of the Afro, cornrow, plaits or dreadlocks represents both a personal choice and a political standpoint. And it is not only in relation to Black women that this matters; it matters to children too. In a UK landmark case, the High Court determined that a school's refusal to allow a Black boy to wear his hair in cornrow plaits was racial discrimination. The school had banned an 11-year-old African-Caribbean pupil because his hairstyle was said to breach the school's dress code and could be viewed as 'gang-related'. Although the Head teacher made it clear that he did not directly associate cornrow plaits with gang violence, he believed 'that allowing the wearing of any non-traditional haircut would lead to 'huge pressure' to unravel a strict policy which was 'a vital part' of the school's success in keeping out unwanted influences' (Daily Mail online, 18 June 2011). The question arises, how does a Black boy fashion himself in a society in which a traditional African hairstyle leads to his exclusion from education because he is an 'unwanted influence'. Though the judge ruled the school's action to be 'unlawful, indirect racial discrimination which is not justified' (Daily Mail online, 18 June 2011), the rallying cry in the school's defence was to draw attention to their excellent results and reputation, even among African Caribbean families. It was as if the acquiescence of Black children and parents to racism is the price to be exacted for a decent education. The Abasindi Cooperative offered a hairstyling service (Fig. 5.12) to women and children as a source of income but also in support of those who sought to challenge the pervasive imposition of white ethnocentric values that this case highlights.

For some Black children, the statement they make in choosing braids, cornrows or dreadlocks may indeed be reflective of the popular icons that have influenced them but for others, the statement is overtly political in its challenge to systems of domination. Like Black women, young people are bombarded by hegemonic images which seek to promulgate particular styles and they are the target for aggressive global marketing strategies for the consumption of products designed to promote universal representations of the popular and acceptable. But young people are the masters in the art of

Fig. 5.12 Braiding hair at Abasindi

weeding out norms masquerading as difference and whether they choose to weave or to 'Fro, these expressions of self-hood and imagination serve to 'deconstruct victimhood by reconstructing modernity, thus empowering those who would otherwise be disempowered in the end, both locally and by the giant compressors of global consumer capitalism' (Nyamnjoh et al., 2002, p. 102). As Nyamnjoh et al. (2002) argue, both women and youth are particularly positioned to exercise this imaginative capacity, which both 'liberates and captures' (p. 102).

Since the Abasindi Cooperative was first established, there has been a multiplicity of shifts in Black hairstyles (Figs. 5.13, 5.14 and 5.15) and there is a resurgent interest in natural hair (Brown, 2014). Brown (2014) utilised the social media site YouTube to examine the commentaries of Black women on natural hair styles. Established in 2005, YouTube, one of the most widely used websites, has been described as assisting in creating community and preserving culture, and Brown's study identified that the values transmitted within this virtual community embodied sensibilities of both the Black feminism of earlier periods and also the post-feminist feminisms of the present. She concluded that:

Fig. 5.13 Hyacinth

Fig. 5.14 Pauline

Fig. 5.15 Francia

Natural hair means *freedom*. For the women in YouTube's natural hair community naturally textured tresses mean liberation from the disparaging beliefs about Black hair that have been embedded in many of these women's psyches from birth by their family, communities and the aesthetic standards encouraged inside and outside of African American culture. (Brown, 2014, p. 78)

From the Abasindi standpoint, loving the Black body, loving Black skin and loving Black hair was indeed an expression of felt personal freedom but as a collective, in reconfiguring beauty in the image of the Black women we were, the adornment and fashioning of our bodies, skin and hair was the articulation of an urgent political insurgency. Our approach to Black beauty was not simply a response to the psychic threat of the internalization of the racial disparagement used to justify Saartjie Baartman's treatment and neither was it only emblematic of Sojourner Truth's act of non-compliance with structural locations that confine Black women, it was both. As Cheng (2000) points out, 'beauty as a process of identification registers her [the Black woman's] relationship to the education of beauty and to her history of negotiating that education – a negotiation of distances rather than an act only of internalization or compliance. Beauty as a question, as much as it may exclude her, also grants her an access to the intensities of its demands and its possibilities' (p. 209).

6

Sowing Seeds of Success

Abstract "Growing up as a Black child in Britain during the 70s and 80s was very disempowering" related one of the women we interviewed. Given the systemic failings and racism within the education system, this is unsurprising. In 1965, the Department of Education and Skills (DES) defined the task of educating the children of the Windrush Generation as 'the successful assimilation of immigrant children'. The focus on assimilation rather than on learning was further characterized by a series of ad hoc responses to the educational needs of immigrant pupils which included strategies designed to compensate for their assumed deficiencies while causing minimum disruption to the educational needs of White British children. One such strategy was to classify children with educational difficulties as 'Educationally Sub-normal,' a label that was disproportionately applied to Black children resulting in them being sent to special schools and receiving a substandard education, with consequences lasting into adulthood. This chapter explores how Abasindi dismantled the 'cultural deficit' assumptions about Black people and adopted a vision of education as taking place not only in the classroom but wherever people are. The children we came into contact with were exposed to a spectrum of positive black influences building up their proficiency not only in maths, the sciences and English, but also developing skills for self-care and raising self-esteem.

Keywords Black children • Black activism • Education • Systemic racism • Supplementary schools

© The Author(s), under exclusive license to Springer Nature Switzerland AG 2024
A. Jones, D. Watt, *Unsung Stories of Black Women's Activism in the UK*,
https://doi.org/10.1007/978-3-031-64201-2_6

Black Children's Educational Development

Bernard Coard's seminal publication of 1971 'How the West Indian Child is Made Educationally Sub-normal in the British Educational System' unearthed the scandalous neglect of Black children's educational development spanning decades and a BBC documentary (2021) shows its continued impact on Black lives. Coard's findings were directed towards the State but Black parents and community activists, only too aware that racism in the education system was destroying their children's life chances, took up the mantle and the Black Supplementary Schools movement was born. Black Supplementary Schools sprang up right across the country and in Manchester, it was the Abasindi Cooperative that responded to the call. As a Black women's organisation, Abasindi used a woman-centred model of schooling which focused on mathematics, English and science (areas in which teachers were failing Black children) and which was also concerned with children's emotional and cultural wellbeing. Coard had emphasised the importance of enabling Black children to develop 'tools to survive racism'; we agreed—many of the children we met had low self-esteem due to internalising racism they were subjected to and it was important to address this. We also recognised the importance of Black male teachers in unlocking the potential of Black boys (disproportionately disadvantaged within the British education system) and dispelling negative myths about Black masculinity and so we recruited Black university students, male and female as voluntary tutors. While acknowledging that self-help voluntary projects could not by themselves change the political and economic conditions of Black people, the Abasindi Co-op nevertheless recognized the need for Black women to organize projects aimed at identifying and responding to their particular needs and those of their families. As well as providing a social supportive base for Black women and a community resource centre, Abasindi was therefore also committed to the provision of supplementary and cultural educational activities for children and young people of African-Caribbean descent (Fig. 6.1).

The establishment of Abasindi Saturday Supplementary School was based on the disproportionate levels of educational underachievement of Black children, especially boys. The findings of Javed's research on the educational experiences of Black boys aged 13–16 in Manchester (2012) is evidence of the ongoing need for supplementary education, hence the involvement of Abasindi members in the development of the Louise Da-Cocodia Education Trust (https://www.dacocodiatrust.org.uk/). The chapter begins by looking chronologically at the racial and cultural issues which led to the establishment of Black Supplementary Schools. Discussion then focuses on the

Fig. 6.1 Abasindi women (Diana and Paula) teaching at Abasindi Supplementary School

development of the Abasindi Saturday Supplementary School during the 1980s and how this has in turn influenced current initiatives in the field of supplementary education.

Black Supplementary Schools

Chevannes and Reeves (1987) argue that the emergence of Black Saturday Supplementary Schools in the UK represents a collective response to the inadequate education available to Black children. The development of these schools was also directly linked to the experiences of migrant children during the period of assimilation. In 1965, the Department of Education and Skills (DES) defined the task of education as 'the successful assimilation of immigrant children'. This period of assimilation was further characterized by a series of ad hoc responses to the educational needs of immigrant pupils. These included strategies designed to compensate for their assumed deficiencies while causing minimum disruption to the educational needs of White British children. All this was taking place at a time when overtly racist attitudes towards Black people were commonplace and sanctioned by the State in implicit and explicit ways. The 1963 Conference on Communication, for example, concluded that Creole languages were a major area of deficiency. As speakers of 'sub-normal English', Black immigrant parents and their children were regarded as 'educationally sub-normal' and amongst those destined to occupy marginalized positions within British society (Dalphinis, 1978, p. 89).

The low educational performance of Black children at school was a constant concern for parents of the Windrush Generation. A study in 1963, by the London borough of Brent found that the performance of 'West Indian children' (*sic*) was, on average, much lower than that of White children in reading, mathematics and spelling and in 1965, research by Vernon, comparing students across London and Hertfordshire showed similar results (Rampton, 1981). In 1966 and 1968, Little's studies reported that Black children were performing less well at primary school than White children from the same socio-economic backgrounds (ibid) and a decade later, a study in Redbridge in 1978 (ibid), also showed considerable underachievement by Black children; things had not changed in 10 years. A School Leavers Survey in 1978/79 reported that the poor performance of Black children at primary and secondary school was also reflected in school leavers' attainments. The survey revealed that:

> In English 9% of West Indians scored higher grades compared with 21% of Asians (for many of whom English may have been a second language) and 29% of other leavers in these LEAs. In mathematics 5% of West Indians scored higher grades compared with 19% of other leavers. (Rampton, 1981, p. 7)

Despite the persistence of the problem, it took successive governments a long time to act. The 1967 Plowden Report was the first government report to draw attention to the low performance of Black children when compared to their White working class counterparts but it was six years later before the 1973 Select Committee on Race and Immigration established the Rampton

Committee to look into the matter. The terms of reference of the Rampton Committee, whose Interim Report was published in 1981 were to:

1. review in relation to schools, the educational needs and attainments of children from ethnic minority groups taking account, as necessary, of factors outside the formal education system relevant to school performance, including influences in early childhood and prospects for school leavers;
2. consider the potential value of instituting arrangements for keeping under review the educational performance of different ethnic minority groups, and what those arrangements might be;
3. consider the most effective use of resources for these purposes; and to make recommendations.

In carrying out its work, the Committee was required to 'give early and particular attention to the educational needs and attainments of pupils of West Indian origin and to make interim recommendations as soon as possible on action which might be taken in the interests of this group.' (Rampton, 1981, p. 6)

The government had been forced to act in response to the growing discontent amongst Black parents about the plight of their children in schools and the publication in 1971, of Bernard Coard's book *How the West Indian Child is Made Educationally Sub-normal in the British Educational System* which highlighted the disproportionate number of African-Caribbean pupils in Educationally Sub-Normal (ESN) schools or special units for disruptive pupils.

Coard's book has retained its significance for over half a century although there has been little government recognition of the long-term damage that was done to the children 'made educationally sub-normal' (*sic*). The practice Coard unearthed is described as 'one of the biggest scandals in the history of British education' and a 2021 BBC documentary '*Subnormal: A British Scandal*' (https://www.bbc.co.uk/programmes/m000w81h) shows just how deleterious its effects were. The documentary explores the impact from the perspective of a group of adults wrongly classified as ESN and who were consigned to special schools: they discuss the developmental, psychological and economic effects of their treatment and how these have continued to affect them into adulthood. The introductory text to the film reads:

In the 1960s, while young black adults were getting to grips with the struggle for black power and a long fightback against police abuse was starting, the majority of West Indian migrants were keeping their heads down. They were working hard and counting on providing better opportunities and education for their children. However, in a white-dominated country, where the politics were becoming increasingly racialised, there was a question of how society, and its teachers, saw these young black children. Before having a chance to develop intellectually, they were labelled as stupid, difficult and disruptive. The paradox is that many of the new migrants to Britain were in fact highly educated…At the same time, celebrity psychologists Hans Eysenck and Arthur Jensen were propounding theories that black people were genetically less intelligent than white people. These theories infiltrated teacher training and found their way into schools. IQ tests were then based on these theories with the odds horrendously stacked against children from the West Indies. (https://www.bbc.co.uk/programmes/m000w81h)

In 1981 the Rampton Committee released its interim report—the Committee had examined the practice Coard had unearthed, among other factors. The findings were prefaced with the statement: 'Virtually all these children [the Black children who had been included in the review] are British born. They are therefore in no way 'immigrants'. They are a permanent and integral part of our society which has a responsibility to ensure as satisfactory an education for them as for any other British child' (Rampton, 1981, p. 3). Though an important admission, there was no comfort in this formal recognition that the Black children being failed by the government were British and indeed, it made the lack of change over the previous two decades, all the more shameful for this fact. The Interim Report concluded that 'unintentional racism is widespread within the teaching profession and contributes, via the self-fulfilling prophecy, to the relative academic failure of West Indian children' (p. 7). Black parents knew this already, although they might have questioned the word 'unintentional'. However, the media, the government and mainstream society were outraged at the notion that schools and teachers could be deemed as racist at all—unintentional, or otherwise. The report was rubbished before it was even published; Anthony Rampton, Chair of the Committee was sacked and replaced by Michael Swann.

It was to be another four years before the Swann Committee released its findings. Meanwhile the failings of British education in respect of Black children were not only limited to schools, but they also translated into lower numbers of Black students in further education settings and, in the underemployment and unemployment of Black young people. These failings directly fed the frustrations of an increasingly disenfranchised Black youth and combined with other social and racial inequalities fuelled social unrest.

At the 1995 *Manchester Conference on 'Black Values versus State Education'* organized by Beresford Edwards (Nana Bonsu), political activist and Warden of the West Indian Centre in Manchester, Trevor Carter, keynote speaker stressed that the Rampton Inquiry was unique in that for the first time the State, as in the Department of Education and Science (DES) had acknowledged the existence of institutional racism. He argued that this acknowledgement was not a result of the actions of the handful of Black members on the committee nor was it based on evidence gathered from schools and communities across the country. According to Carter, it was largely due to the 1981 nation-wide disturbances by unemployed and disaffected young Black people. The 1981 disturbances in Moss Side and South London are said to have 'shattered the mirage of assimilation and ushered in multiculturalism' (Sallah & Howson, 2007, p. 30).

Carter had served on the Swann Committee of Inquiry—the Swann Report 'Education For All' was published by the DES in 1985. The report summed up the period of assimilation 'as one which gave recognition to the existence of a single cultural criterion, that which was 'White', 'Christian' and 'English speaking.' The language used reflected the values of this cultural criterion. It is therefore argued that schools serve as a vehicle through which the cultural capital and languages of subordinate classes are devalued (Bourdieu & Passerson, 1977). Stone (1981) writes of the pain of being 'Black in England,' and the shock and disappointment of parents who expected that their children born and brought up in the UK would not have to face the problems of settling in a new country and would have a greater opportunity to succeed. The fear of further disadvantaging their children's educational prospects led to some parents insisting that their British born children should only speak English at home. The concerns of parents was not unfounded. Some Black children although British by birth, spent many of their formative years in the Caribbean. On returning to England, they often found themselves in classes which did not reflect their ability based on a perception by teachers that they couldn't speak English properly.

I am one of the 50s children born in this country who was sent to Jamaica before I was a year old to be looked after by my grandparent. I was educated in Jamaica up to the age of 13 and then came back to England to join the secondary school system. I remember distinctively having to take a test which was all about the British experience. It was tailored towards their lifestyle and not a wider culture ... When we first started at the school, I felt a sense of strong injustice because both my sister and I were put into a lower class because of our dialect and not our academic ability. (Watt, 2002)

In his discussions on Caribbean languages, Dalphinis (1978) argues that although the languages of West and Sub Saharan Africa were taken to the Caribbean, the system of separating speakers of the same languages ensured the suppression of the various mother tongues. This strategy was aimed at inhibiting rebellion amongst the enslaved. They were punished for speaking their own African languages by whipping and sometimes death. During the 1950s, students in Kenya were punished for speaking in their mother tongue and made to wear a 'monitor' with an inscription aimed at shaming the wearer: 'I am stupid I was caught speaking my mother tongue'. Students in Kenya were still being ostracized for speaking indigenous languages into the 2000s; Wangari Maathai argues that this practice,

> … contributes to the trivialization of anything African and lays the foundation for a deeper sense of self-doubt and an inferiority complex. The reality is that mother tongues are extremely important as vehicles of communication and carriers of culture, knowledge wisdom and history. When they are maligned and educated people are encouraged to look down on them, people are robbed of a vital part of their heritage (2007, pp. 59–60).

Reflecting on her inability to speak the African languages of her ancestors, one of the Abasindi women commented:

> I spent much of my childhood in Sierra Leone, the birthplace of my father. Once when I was much older I asked him why he only spoke English and why he hadn't passed on his African language to me. He said that it had been "beaten" out of him. He recalled, from the age of four or five, being made to stand in front of elderly aunts and recite poetry in what he called "perfect Queen's English"; he couldn't have taught me his language, he didn't know it. (Adele)

Although each of the Caribbean languages was developed out of the language of the colonizers, they nevertheless maintained characteristics of speech which are directly associated with Africa (Dove, 1998). Louise Bennett (Fig. 6.2) was the first Jamaican poet formally to use Patois in her performances and her poem *Bans O'Killing* challenges perceived notions of language inferiority.

The late Victoria McKenzie, a member of Abasindi was amongst performing artists in Manchester who followed in Louise Bennett's footsteps and openly challenged the marginalization and disparagement of Caribbean languages.

> I'd asked a friend if she knew anyone who would be willing to teach me something about Jamaican Patois. It was the language my father had spoken, but he'd

Fig. 6.2   Louise Bennett (Miss Lou)

died when I was seven and to this day, whenever I hear it spoken round me, I'm reminded of him, so it was important to me to become more familiar with it. I teach Caribbean literature and I also wanted to be able to recognize words and structures of the language. The friend I asked was also a member of Abasindi Co-op and she told me that Victoria McKenzie, an active supporter of Abasindi was the person I should talk to. At the time, Vicky was in her eighties and had endured a lot of physical illness. She had suffered a great personal tragedy which had also taken its toll on her health. But as soon as I saw her, even though I met her on a day when she was unwell, I was struck by her inner vitality. This was a woman who could sparkle with enthusiasm and warmth. She welcomed me, a stranger, into her home and right from the start, she treated me as friend. As I got to know her I realized that Victoria McKenzie was one of the most prominent members of the Caribbean community here in Manchester. She was a writer, producing performance poetry and a community worker. She seemed to know everyone of Caribbean heritage in Manchester and had plenty of stories to tell. She had come to Britain while relatively young and had raised family here. She told me that it had been impossible in those early years for a Black woman to gain access to higher education or to find success as any kind of artist. She spoke of the obstacles she'd come up against, the racism she'd experienced, and the differences between generations; her generation had mostly been unable to fulfil their potential but she and others had made damn sure that subsequent generations would have the opportunities that had been denied to her. She spoke about the achievements of younger Black writers with pride, friends like Lemn Sissay and Pete Kalu, and never once displayed any kind of envy. All her energy went into supporting others, and although she did find success as a poet later in life, she never allowed that success or ambition to make her competitive or self-serving. She was someone who gave everything she could to further the education and the creative activities of the Caribbean community as a whole. One of Vicky's great successes was producing a book in Patois. She'd become aware that children who spoke Patois were disadvantaged in British schools and she worked to dispel the misapprehension that Patois characterized its speakers as unintelligent or uneducated. One of her main missions was to get Patois recognized as a language in its own right – it's not an inferior form of English or simply the language of the streets, it's a language that empowers its speakers and gives them the right to their own cultural, social and political identity. Vicky promoted Patois as all these things and went into schools and community projects to remind everyone of its value. In one of the calendars on Celebrating Black History in Trafford there is a wonderful photo of Vicky, her face alight with laughter, looking as if she's about to give a reading. Beneath this is her personal statement and, for me, this sums up the kind of person she was. She said 'We can achieve anything we want from the seeds our parents did plant'. (Jackie Roy).

Abasindi Saturday Supplementary School

Within the Black community, success is often linked to educational achievements. Parental influence, community projects and cultural activities were cited as contributing to the academic success of African-Caribbean people in the UK (Rhamie & Hallam, 2002). Coard's work was central to the development of Abasindi Saturday Supplementary School in Moss Side (Fig. 6.3). A high percentage of supplementary school programmes were organised by women. Hey (1998, p. 20) differentiates between male strategies for securing social resources, and female strategies for constructing social capital in order to develop effective community links as 'his and hers' approaches. Abasindi Saturday school was built on a 'her' version in the sense that it was mainly women that were responsible for its organisation, in the recruitment of Black university students, male and female as voluntary tutors and in the adoption of hooks (2003) vision of education as taking place not only in the classroom but wherever people.

In addition to the provision of supplementary teaching, especially in the areas of maths and English, the programme also focused on what Coard described as 'tools to survive racism'. This is in reference to Black children's

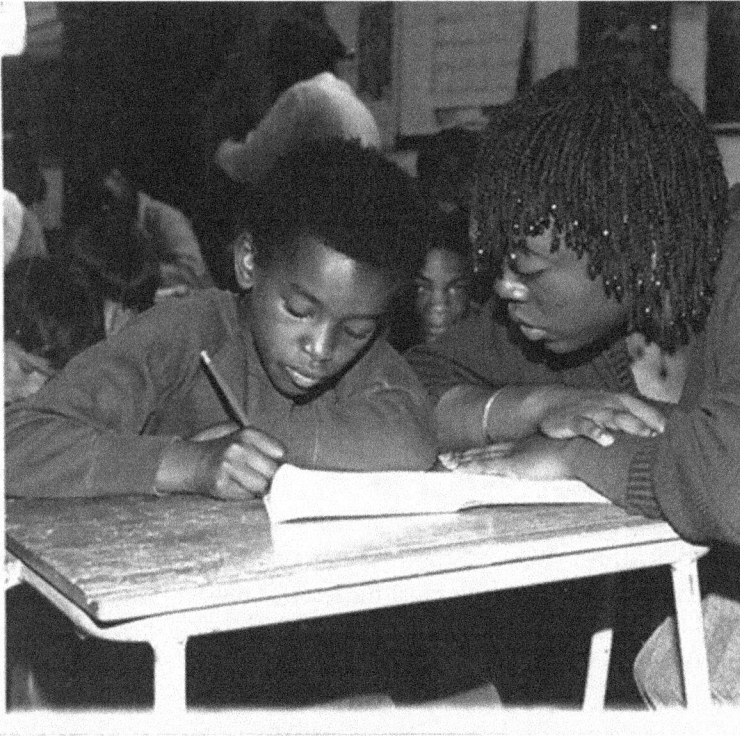

Fig. 6.3 Brenda teaching at the Abasindi Supplementary School

sense of identity, pride, and belonging (Andrews, 2013, p. 6). Clark and Clark (1939, 1947) demonstrated in their classic doll studies, that whereby 35 per cent of six year olds identified with the Black doll, 60 per cent expressed preference for White dolls and 59 per cent said that the Black doll 'looked bad'. Similar results were obtained in England and in his study of 7–10 year olds, Davey (1983) found that 86 per cent of White children regarded their own group more favourably than either African-Caribbean or Asian children. Less than half of the African-Caribbean and Asian children made 'own group choice'. Davey concluded that both minority and majority children saw the advantage of being White. Maxime (1986) described the case of a 12 year old black boy who from the age of six had lived with White foster parents in a very middle class area on the outskirts of London. A racial identity assessment revealed that he viewed Black people negatively and saw himself as someone who was trapped in the colour of his skin.

One of the most well-known models of black identity development is Cross's (1971) five-stage model of 'Nigresence', the psychological process individuals are thought to go through in their journey towards a secure and confident black identity. In the initial pre-encounter, Cross argues that a person's world view is white-oriented and, they are likely to deny the existence of racism. The encounter stage is linked to experiences or observations that bring the person face-to-face with racism and the realities of being black. The immersion-emersion stage involves critical exploration of issues of race and culture and the internalization stage represents a conscious move towards the development of a positive black identity. The final stage of the model is internalisation-commitment (Cross, 1971). Maxime (1986) found that students with high levels of black identification were more likely to participate in activities involving the Black community. The Abasindi Supplementary School turned this on its head—participating in activities involving the Black community helped Black children develop a positive sense of identity (Fig. 6.4).

At the 2005 *Black Perspective in Community and Youth Work* Conference in Manchester, Blackburn drew on the findings of her 2001 study to highlight the limitations of Cross's psychological nigrescence model. She argued that the DAISE model, a synthesis of Cross (1971), Parham (1989), and Phinney (1990), was far more relevant to understanding stages of black identity development. In the dormant stage of this cyclical model, black identity is not fully

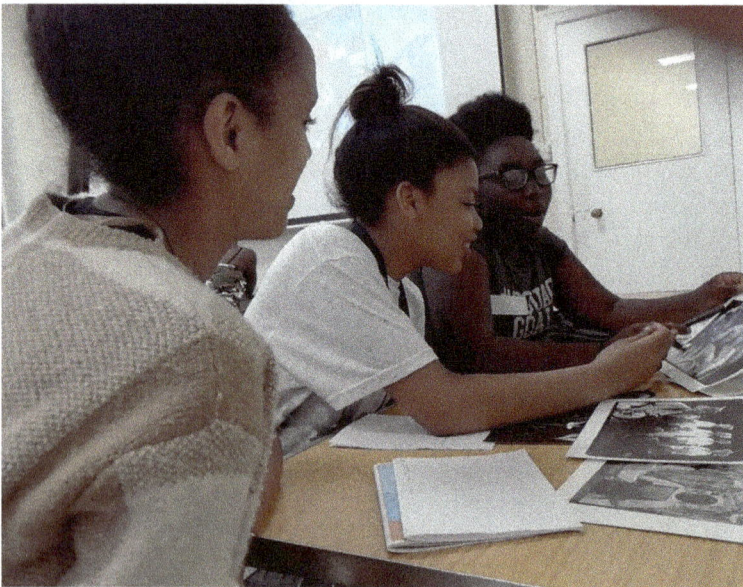

Fig. 6.4 Girls discussing positive images of African/Caribbean culture in one of the Abasindi classes

developed and there is a general tendency for the person to lack interest and knowledge about their cultural heritage. However, during the awakening stage of identity formation and consistent with the African proverb 'It Takes a Village to Raise a Child', Abasindi ensured that the organization provided a culturally supportive environment for the children and young people that attended the Saturday school.

> It was just like a huge family – everybody knew each other's kids, and if my mum wasn't around somebody was always there for me … Those are some of the things that I miss for my daughter because my mum lived in London, raising her has been lonely especially when I look back to those times in Abasindi when there were lots of aunties and uncles to nurture and make you feel safe. That is why as a Black woman I have always been proud of myself. (Anonymous – Abasindi Member)

The 'Awakening stage' is similar to Cross's (1971) 'Encounter stage', in relating to experiences of racism and children's sense of self. Most of the children who attended the Saturday school lived in areas with large numbers of Black residents: Moss Side, Hulme, Whalley Range, and Old Trafford. Pamela who lived elsewhere said that as well as her mother's involvement with Abasindi she was motivated to go to Saturday school because, unlike the predominantly White secondary school she attended, there was no racism.

> … I felt safe in Moss Side. At Saturday School I was with safe people. People that although they told you off, or told you to do things, it wasn't for their benefit it was more for yours. So they pushed you for you, rather than pushing you for them. I learnt a lot about culture and black history which made me stronger in Wythenshawe [a council estate in the suburbs with a predominantly White population]. If you know what I mean, it gave me that backbone for Wythenshawe, to stand up for my rights and to know that I was somebody. (Pamela)

Jennifer, who lived with her parents in North of England, said that her experiences of racism at infant school included dinner ladies ignoring children chanting 'black sambo' and also within the classroom. As the only Black child in the class she not only had to listen to 'golliwog stories' (Pool, 2009) but also the headmistress's version on the origins of Black people. In the words of the headmistress 'black people were black because when God made them, everybody had to run into the sea and black people could only put their hands and feet in the water'. When she told her parents about this incident her mother did not hesitate to "tell the teacher off."

Having failed in her attempt to get her secondary school to cater for her dietary needs, Doretta approached her headmistress regarding the wearing of white socks as part of the school uniform. She felt that in the school photograph the black girls looked as though they were wearing plaster casts. She showed the photograph to the headmistress and asked if it were possible for the girls to wear either black or brown socks. The headmistress agreed to raise the issue with the education department. Doretta said that in the meantime

> I decided to get other girls to back this petition and we rallied together but most of the girls laughed at me saying 'gosh you are such a Moss Side gal', but that didn't stop me. It must have been a few weeks later when the Head came back and said 'looks like you've won this one as from next term all girls will be able to wear brown, black or grey socks as part of their uniform'. I felt a sense of victory.

The stage of 'Internal Dialogue' in the DAISE model includes reflection and critical exploration of similarities and differences between personal cultural practices and those of the dominant group. Melanie observed that the Saturday school's replacement of meaningless Eurocentric nursery rhymes with powerful mantras such as 'we are the children of Mother Africa, you better clear the way let we pass', made her felt connected to her ancestors. The penultimate 'Self-Acceptance' stage of the DAISE model is similar to the last stage of Phinney's (1990) ethnic identity achievement. For the children at Abasindi Saturday school, this stage was represented by pride and a sense of belonging.

When Melanie at the age of nine, was told by a White boy at her primary school in Moss Side to "go back to her country" she took responsibility for organizing a 'Black Friday' protest, seeing it as a natural response to the racist comment. This was also an opportunity for her to share her knowledge of Africa with the other children and she felt proud and confident that she was being listened to. "I had a positive sense of self and I was not about to give it up, especially when told to go back to my country, knowing this is also my country". In her 2001 study, Blackburn identified age six to nine as the period when Black children become aware of their differences and are consciously involved in finding out more about their heritage. Externalization is the final stage of the DAISE model and Abasindi gave children and young people the space to develop the knowledge and skills that would enable them to engage confidently with their cultural heritage, both within the community and the wider society.

Doretta's decision that the West African dance routines which she learnt at Abasindi should form the basis of Black girls' performance in the school multicultural talent show is but one example of this confident engagement (Fig. 6.5). Although her friends thought she was crazy, she said that she wanted to bring the rhythms and beats of something that represented her as a Black girl.

The girls' contribution to this event was a great success and it was the talk of the school for months. It also opened the doors to other Black girls venturing into Moss Side and joining Abasindi (Fig. 6.6).

Christine Edwards, another Abasindi member who became associated with the organisation through its Saturday School reflects:

I can clearly recall the day my Auntie was having the conversation with my Mum about me attending Abasindi (Saturday School). I was a very shy and reserved child and had no wish to attend Saturday School. All I was told was that I would be attending the following Saturday, other Black children would be attending, and it would aid my education, end of conversation. Anyone who was a young person during the 70s/80s will remember we had no say in our parents' decision making. Do not get me wrong, we were loved but it was just that generation's way. But as a child I did find living in Britain and being a Black child confusing and challenging. It was decided I would go to Abasindi with my younger brothers. My parents were quite lenient with my brothers'

Fig. 6.5 Girls dancing

Fig. 6.6 Marsha White, Mellisa White and Beverley Hypolite- children of the Abasindi School

attendance, where I was made to attend religiously. I clearly remember the night before my first visit of being anxious and afraid. Being concerned and asking myself the questions would I fit in? Would the teachers be kind, would I understand the work let alone be able to complete it? My shyness made me so worried about having to mix with other young people. On arrival the teachers were welcoming and one of the first things I noticed was all the teachers were Black. Initially I hated going and resented the fact I had to give up my Saturday mornings. But I always ensured that I was obedient and worked hard and over time I did make several friendships and academically began to excel. Over time my feelings changed. Let me explain that the Abasindi lessons were delivered by strong, educated, and articulate Black women. Yet they were so caring, and patient and their knowledge was vast, yet they were still so humble, any egos were left at the Abasindi front door. I learnt the true importance of education, history and for me, the cornerstone being steadfast in who I am and what I believe. Attending Abasindi I was challenged academically, personally, and spiritually and I am so grateful for those experiences now, whereas at the time I thought I was being punished. The irony of it, ha ha! One of the fundamental things I drew from my experiences with these women was their nurturing and teaching gave me the confidence and ability to be proud of my Black history, thrive academically and most importantly to truly know myself. But on reflection attending the Abasindi has been one of the most powerful and empowering things I have experienced. Growing up as a child in Britain during the late 70s/80s was very disempowering. Black people were systematically marginalized, where being black you were made to feel like a second-class citizen and being a female to know your place, and that was fundamentally being in the home. My experience attending Abasindi showed me how to be strong, realize my dreams and not to let anyone dictate who I am. I am grateful and in debt to all these women who reached me and touched my life in so many ways. They took my hand and replaced my shyness with confidence. My fear of failure replaced with the belief I can succeed. Where I had self-doubt, they nurtured and gave me the ability to see I am one of God's children. They educated and taught me to be the strong confident woman that I am today. Looking back, just to think I thought I was getting a raw deal having to attend Abasindi while my brothers could opt out, on reflection I now understand it was my brothers who got the raw deal.

Abasindi and the Louise Da-Cocodia Education Trust

The late Louise Da-Cocodia declared that one of the reasons for her voluntary work in the community was to "help young Black people understand that this is their home, this is the society they live in, and that they have a part to play in developing it". Building on the early work of the Abasindi Cooperative, Abasindi women have taken a direct role in the organization and development of the Louise Da-Cocodia Education Trust Supplementary Education programme (https://www.dacocodiatrust.org.uk/). This entails a weekly Saturday

School and the 'Getting Ahead Cultural and Personal Development' programme (Fig. 6.7).

As a strategy for increasing representation, between 2000–2005 and funded by Cariocca Enterprise, the Trust administered a small grants programme for African-Caribbean heritage students who were enrolled on college and university courses in the areas of accountancy, science, engineering, information technology, business enterprise, occupational therapy, medicine, and dentistry. This work was extended and the pilot projects included Raising Education Study Skills Project (RESPECT), the Parenting Advocacy Support Service (PASS), Developing Inclusive Community Education (D.I.C.E), Raising Educational Attainment Cultural Heritage Project (REACH), our Moss Side Video Project, the Barriers Access and Gaps Project, and the RISE Project for Black boys at risk of exclusion from school.

The Louise Da-Cocodia Education Trust Saturday supplementary school was a direct outcome of the Edward-Kerr 2005 study on *Understanding the educational needs of African-Caribbean young men and developing pathways for action*. This study, of 93 Black pupils aged 12–15, from five Manchester

Fig. 6.7 Diane and girls from one of the Louise Da-Cocodia Educational Trust programmes

secondary schools, was undertaken in response to persistent under-achievement, school failure and disproportionate number of school exclusions among African-Caribbean heritage pupils, particularly boys. In comparison to other pupils, Black boys and girls of African-Caribbean heritage who participated in this study said they lacked a sense of 'belonging.' They nevertheless believed in the value of schooling in preparing them positively for the future. Twenty-six per cent of the children said they had been given fixed term exclusions and Black boys were more likely to be in detention than any of the other groups. Edwards-Kerr (2005) argued that this combination of exclusion and under attainment often meant that Black men who entered university did so at an older age and were likely to be under-represented in certain career areas and over-represented in community work courses.

The Louise Da Cocodia Education Trust Saturday Supplementary school focuses on providing a learning and teaching environment that encourages individual and team work, developing a 'can do' approach to new experiences in their students. In a survey to ascertain why parents sent their children to Saturday School, most said that it was to help with their children's school work and to prepare them for high school. One parent commented "We must be honest about things; our kids are failing when they get to high school. We need all the resources available to help them." Parents expressed relief that their children were in a safe and happy learning environment. Some of the parents were keen for their children to learn about African-Caribbean history and African-Caribbean cuisine as this would not only introduce the children to their cultural heritage but it would also enhance their sense of pride and self-worth. The routine and structure of attending the Trust Saturday school had also enhanced their children's self-discipline and encouraged rapport between children and their parents.

In the study on *Aspiration and Engagement Strategies for Working with Young Black Men* (Davis et al., 2012), young people, community workers, parent and youth workers in Moss Side and Hulme pointed to the important role of families and the home as a source of reinforcement, particularly in relation to educational opportunities. The importance of praise, encouragement, and the celebration of the achievements of young people was regarded as crucial to their development. However, some students faced a dilemma over balancing their parent's expectations with those of the school. One of the community workers gave an example of a boy whose parents wanted him to be an engineer whereas the school advised him to pursue a career in sports. This created a conflict between the school and the parent. The boy opted to go with the school's advice believing that the school was better placed to assess his abilities. Here the young person conforms to the traditional institutional stereotyping and to a belief in the school's better position to determine the future of its pupils. The widely held stereotypical view of Black pupils being good at sports rather than academic studies echoes the experiences of the poet Benjamin Zephaniah during the 1960s who stated that:

> … I don't know if it was just because of the colour of my skin or the fact that all black people are meant to be good at sport but they physically, literally forced me to play every sport in the school even like I never played cricket before, I got good, never played rugby before, I got good. (Benjamin Zephaniah)

Several parents observed that the Saturday School had exposed their children to an environment where there are Black teachers as role models to boost confidence and motivation. The *REACH* report (2007, p. 24) recommended that Black boys and their teachers be introduced to 'positive Black male role models who can engage, support and empower vulnerable Black boys and young Black men to turn their lives around …'.Defining a role model 'as someone you look up to and respect and someone who impacts your life in a positive way'. In Manchester, the *Strategy to Elevate People* (STEP) project and the City College Manchester Mentoring Programme were aimed at enabling inner city young people to identify with positive images of success beyond the entertainment industry and sports.

As a follow-up to Edwards-Kerr's study, the research on *Aspiration and Engagement Strategies for Working with Young Black Men* in 2012, focused on issues relating to young people's aspiration. The research was specifically linked to the work of the Louise Da-Cocodia Education Trust and other community and voluntary sector organisations in Moss Side and Hulme. A total of 17 young people and 16 adults took part in the research. The adults included youth and community workers, community activist, volunteers, and an adult education tutor. All the participants expressed the view that parents should be at the forefront of instilling an education mind-set in their children. The young people also acknowledged that they valued education as a result of values that were instilled in them at an early age. One woman said that she was actively involved with her son's education up to university level, and this included meeting with his lecturers from time to time. Although it was important for parents to understand the educational system, their expectations and attitude were regarded as equally important.

Evidence suggested that the careers services were not putting young people's aspirations at the centre of the decision making process. As such a number of young people are leaving school without attaining the necessary qualifications to fulfil their career aspiration. Similar to the findings of

Edwards-Kerr's 2005 study, a number of young people were doing courses that were not necessarily linked to their employment plans and personal development needs. One of the youth workers was of the opinion that,

> … nobody is actively listening to the young people and finding out what they are interested in. They are doing what they think is best for them, finding out what they are interested in and putting those into place might be a key element in education, employment and training and getting them involved (Davis et al., 2012, p. 19)

From discussions with the young people it was evident that they were investing a lot of time and effort in studying subjects that they felt were irrelevant to their future careers and existing employment opportunities. They were doing so in the belief that:

> The more qualifications you get the more you can put on your CV for experience. So if you are applying for any job it's what is on your CV that will get you that job. If you have loads of qualifications on the CV then you are most likely to get the job and that's what I'm interested in (Davis et al., 2012, p. 19)

The research further established that young Black men often have higher educational and career aspirations than some of their peers but aspirations are affected by changes in their lives that are often related to conditions around them. These include peer pressure and the lack of relevant services to meet their needs. However, the research also provided evidence that positive peer relationships contribute to young people continuing in further education. The young people in the study by Davis and colleagues, stated that it was this sense of camaraderie that helped them to remain engaged with their studies. Based on their classroom experiences, some of the boys in Javed's 2012 study echoed the views of parents that it was important to have more Black teachers in mainstream schools. Javed's study revealed that Black boys believed that Black teachers understood them and were less likely to treat them in a stereotypical manner. The Runnymede Trust 1987 found that 'African Caribbean students frequently experience relationships with White teachers that are characterised by relatively high degrees of control and criticism'. This finding has been replicated in infant and primary classrooms. Ironically, the percentage of teachers from Black and ethnic minority backgrounds, fell from 11.6 percent in 2008/9 to 11.2 per cent in 2009/10. Overall the teaching profession remains predominantly White. The Department for Education's School Workforce Survey (2011) found that 24 per cent of school age pupils in

England were of Black and ethnic minority heritage, but that there was serious under-representation of minority ethnic teachers in every sector (Hick et al., 2011).

Javed (2012, p. 14) found that despite experiences of racism, success and achievement for the boys in his study entailed 'having ambition, finishing school, getting good grades, being in a secure job and having the opportunity to support family'. In her discussion on 'spaces of possibility' bell hooks argued that:

> The academy is not a paradise, but learning is a place where paradise can be created. The classroom with all its limitations, remains a location of possibility. In that field of possibility we collectively imagine ways to move beyond boundaries, to transgress. This is education as the practice of freedom. (hooks, 1994, p. 207)

However, placing boys in lower sets because of their behaviour can adversely impact their future education and employment opportunities. '… I've got better marks than half the guys in the top set but they're like na: we, don't think you're ready and your behaviour needs to improve and that's rubbish'. The boys also spoke about their experiences of overt racism: 'There's this fat teacher who said to me that she might be fat but at least she's not Black' (Javed, 2012, pp. 41–44). A number of the boys in Javed's study openly acknowledged that they were viewed as rebels by their teachers: 'They would have seen us as rebels init because we're not following the school rules but if the school rule had an, if it had an explanation to why it was a rebellious thing or why it was wrong then alright, but if not then why not'. For these boys school was not viewed as a place of learning but rather a battleground to gain recognition. Sewell (1997) identifies four categories of black boys; conformists, innovators, retreatist, and rebels. The rebels are regarded as being opposed to the goals and means of schooling. This was not true of the boys in Javed's study and in accordance with Sewell's categories, they were retreatist in that they accepted the goals of schooling but were opposed to its means. They also acknowledged the significance of support from their teachers and family members. Rather than seeing children's poor performance as a failing of children, Majors considers it a call for self-improvement on the part of teachers and introduced a *Teacher Empathy Programme* designed to identify and develop those inter/intra-personal skills teachers need in order to create effective relationships with young people in a positive climate for learning.

Such skills include the ability to communicate effectively, raise attainment, manage difficult behaviour, find alternative solutions to punishments and exclusions and reduce stereotyping, and unfair treatment.

In their discussion on the role of family and kinship, Wright et al. (2010, p. 70) argue that the 'social and cultural capital of the Black family is often viewed by mainstream society as being weak and negative,' particularly in the case of single female-led households. This does not reflect the reality of the 25 year old who attributed his education and professional success to the women in his family. 'I come from a very strong matriarchal family that have instilled that strength in me … There were not many male figures around when I was growing up. As a child it was predominantly women and that's where I get my strength from'. Another young man also declared that his decision to go to university was very much influenced by a woman; his late mother, through the reflection on what Thomson et al. (2002) describe as 'critical moments.' He was referring to events seen as 'having important consequences' such as his desire to pay tribute to the memory of his late mother. Strand (2010) argues that African-Caribbean heritage young people start secondary school with aspirations of wanting to become doctors, pilots and lawyers. These aspirations are not static but dynamic and consequently young people often change aspirations in the light of new experiences, maturity, and sometimes parental influence.

Consistent with the aims of Saturday Supplementary Schools some members of Abasindi played a key role in organizing the 2009 Manchester Black Parents, Children and Young People Conference (Fig. 6.8).

The conference was aimed at building an alliance between parents, teachers and communities intended to address issues of low qualifications and disproportionate school exclusions amongst particular groups of Black and minority ethnic communities (Hick et al., 2011). The conference was organized in partnership with Manchester Metropolitan University and took place during Black history month. In addition to two keynote speakers, Richard Majors and Gus John, local organizations that took part included the West Indian Centre Saturday Supplementary School, Mothers Against Violence, the Black and Asian Police Association, the Chrysalis Family Support Project, and the founder of Universal Connection Soca Aerobic Ltd and Esther Furlonge Clarke, a member of Abasindi. This level of community engagement reflected an important ethos of Abasindi's work—the ability to translate 'papership' to 'partnership'.

Critchlow observed that for him, as a representative of the Black Police Association, the conference was an opportunity to work in partnership with

Fig. 6.8 Jumoke, Francia, Jennifer, and Veronica at the Manchester Black Parents, Children and Young People Conference

practitioners in the field of education and community development. His decision to facilitate the workshop on *Exclusion and the Criminal Justice System* was influenced by his concern about social justice. The importance of addressing issues that are likely to impact positively on the educational experiences of Black young people was evident in the workshops on '*Motivating Learning Through Students' Everyday Interests*' (Washington Alcott), '*Eagles That Soar'* – *Black Pupils Achieving Success* (Lorna Roberts) and *Space Exploration: Black Contributions to Aeronautics and the Space Programme* (Conway Mothobi). Omena Osivemu and Paul Lewis were two of the young people that facilitated workshops, *On the transition from Primary to Secondary school* and *Music - how they work together.* The workshop on building a culture of success offered participants,

> …insights and understandings about educationally 'successful' minority ethnic pupils – who are often ignored and overlooked within the prevalent concerns

with 'under-achievement'. Understanding academic success says a lot about under-achievement. The recognition and 'celebration of BME success provides an important challenge to the constant tirade of negative images and associations of BME young people as 'problem' and 'failing' pupils. Participants might be inspired to develop new, more positive ways of thinking about minority ethnic pupils, parents and issues of achievement. (Stirling, 2009)

The Manchester Black Parents, Children and Young People Conference had several outcomes. The Barriers, Access, Aspirations and Gaps project, a direct consequence, was undertaken in partnership with Zion Arts Centre (Z-Arts) and one of the local youth centres in Old Trafford. Here storytelling was viewed as an art form and of significance, not as mere entertainment. Several of the fifteen 15–25 year olds in the project found storytelling to be a valuable communication and motivational tool. The sessions gave them the opportunity to reflect upon their educational experiences and aspirations. One of these girls remarked that it was the first time she had given any thought to career and educational aspirations: "first time I've talked about the future, made me think about what I want to do in the future more seriously".

Engaging in a process which involved role play/poetry performances increased the confidence levels of some of the younger members of the group. The significance of informal educational sites as a source of information and knowledge was another emergent theme. The findings of this project challenged the assumption that the low participation in further and higher education of young people in the inner city Black communities of Manchester was due to lack of aspiration and confidence. From the discussions, it was apparent that the young people had high and varied aspirations and a number of them were knowledgeable about what was required to realize their ambitions, although most were not. Edwards-Kerr (2005) found that although Black pupils had high academic and professional aspirations and ambitions for the future, many of the young people were unclear as to the routes that were available for them or what was necessary to attain their career goals. She cited the case of the young person who wanted to be a solicitor but was instead enrolled on a travel and tourism course and another who wanted to do hairdressing but her college offered only drama and English.

At the 2013, conference *Making Education a Priority – Alternative Approaches,* keynote speaker, Diane Abbot MP, spoke about the benefits of having more Black male teachers in the classroom. The 2012 research project 'Race Equality in Teacher Education' was therefore aimed at exploring teacher educators' understanding of race in/equality issues within education and how teachers were addressing issues of race inequality within their practice. Abbot emphasised the importance of Black Supplementary Schools however, Andrews (2013, p. 52) argues that the 'politics in the supplementary school movement is not always quite as radical or tied into global issues of Black liberation' as it should be. Furthermore, John suggests that these schools do not represent a mass movement of Black people in education, nor have they inspired parents to take collective action (King, 2006). As well as developing a greater interest in education, Supplementary Schools can raise the aspirations of young people through their participation in this specific form of community based initiative (Pollard, 2011), a strategy which Mirza (2009, p. 57) argues has been 'used by parents to side-step the perpetual hum of racism'.

Education is a fundamental dimension of Black women's political activism and an 'important link between self, change and empowerment…' (Collins, 1990, p. 47). The everyday experiences of Abasindi women formed the basis of a culture of refusal and resistance by way of their engagement with all levels of the British educational system; the ongoing involvement of these women in a range of community based education programmes is a testament to women's commitment to the individual and the collective advancement of the Black community.

It is a source of enormous pride that against a backdrop characterised by racism in schools, the diversion of Black children towards sports and away from academic subjects, the disparagement of their languages, accents and dialects, the disinterest and dismissal of their cultural heritage, the reframing of resistance as rebellion, the all-too-ready labels of subnormal or anti-social and, the disavowal of State responsibility, that so many Black children have excelled. Though academic performance is not the only performance of merit and is not the only way to achieve success we, the authors, having worked for decades in higher education ourselves, recognise the importance of seeing Black graduates cross the podium to collect their awards (Figs. 6.9, 6.10, 6.11, 6.12, 6.13 and 6.14). These young people represent themselves primarily, but they also represent the families that struggled to help them get there and they represent the 'can do' spirit of Abasindi.

The Children are the Flowers of our Struggle and the Principal Reason for our Fight (Amilcar Cabral 1975).

Fig. 6.9 Zinzi

Fig. 6.10 Nkosi

Fig. 6.11   Dziko

Fig. 6.12 Abubakarr

Fig. 6.13 Yinka

Fig. 6.14   Thembi

7

The Politics of Sisterhood

Abstract This chapter explores the juncture of feminist and anti-racist struggle across several fronts that came to characterise the politics of sisterhood within the Abasindi Cooperative: domestic violence; immigration controls; police brutality, youth justice and the educational advancement of Black women and children. Reflections of the role of the organisation in social action on each of these areas are interwoven with a critical analysis of contemporary literature. The aim of the chapter is to highlight the ways in which the politics of sisterhood grew and morphed in response to the needs of the community in which Abasindi was located. As Gramsci and Hoare argued, theories of change must emerge from the everyday struggles that drive the need for social transformation (1978); we were Black women; we were Abasindi women and ours were the children we fought for. However, ours was not an activism that was solely concerned with local conditions; our education and influences came from international liberation struggles for social justice and this enabled us to connect with women from around the world; local activism within the context of a global vision.

Keywords Feminism • Anti-racism • Black women • Sisterhood • Liberation • Pan-Africanism

Sisterhood

The type of sisterhood Abasindi engendered in addressing the challenges which confronted Black women in the 80s and 90s meant that though we espoused feminist values, we did not always describe ourselves as a feminist organisation

Fig. 7.2 Members of Abasindi discuss the future and role of the organisation, from left to right: Carmen Robinson, Dorothy Kuya, Kath Locke and Ada Phillips

increasing recognition and respect within local and national settings and became known as a central hub for community activism. We were constantly developing, and this meant we were able to respond to the changing needs of the Black women we supported. Disinterested in establishing a reified version of Abasindi, or of sisterhood, feminism or of anti-racism, we took the position articulated by Lather:

> The task of counter-hegemonic groups is the development of counter-institutions, ideologies and cultures that provide an ethical alternative to the dominant hegemony (Lather 1984, cited in Weiler, 2009, p. 226).

I Am My Sister's Keeper—Combining the Personal, the Political *and* the Professional

As women of Abasindi we had our personal lives, our political lives and our professional lives and for many of us, the boundaries between these spheres of social life were permeable; we carried our roles and perspectives like rucksacks from one to the other. The Abasindi women who worked in the field of Immigration Advocacy were very likely to have someone in their family who was affected by immigration controls; the women who worked in higher education were there because they had witnessed, often in respect of their own children, the under-harvesting of ability among Black boys in the school system that would thwart their opportunities later on; the Psychologist, Social Worker or Counsellor who was a member of Abasindi is likely to have observed the over-representation of Black children in care, or of Black people in mental health institutions and those with law degrees often became the seekers of justice in racial harassment or criminal justice cases that blighted their neighbourhoods. For some of these women Abasindi had helped to charter their course to success and though there was no obligation, it became the way of things that one should offer whatever skills and knowledge one had acquired to support others.

It was the first request I'd received for social work support outside of my role as a professional social worker with a local authority. The family of four children was headed by a single-parent woman and lived in a cramped council flat in a socially deprived area notorious for high levels of crime; there was racism too - racist graffiti greeted them many mornings. The mother, Ayesha (not her real name) was a qualified accountant but hadn't been able to get work in her field and did two cleaning jobs; her eldest child aged 16 was also working to bring in some money. The family was from West Africa, but most of the children were born in the UK and, cooped up on the sixth floor, they were as rambunctious as any. The flat was clean and tidy but carried the hallmarks of poverty; mismatched carpet squares, over-washed school shirts with threadbare collars force-dried over radiators for wear again tomorrow, patched up wallpaper and curtains too thin to offer more than a pretence of privacy. It was home. I was from a West African family myself and had spent part of my childhood in a council maisonette; this could have been my home and what bound me to them was the fact that like us, the family was determinedly father-less. The mother of these children had lived for a very long time as a victim of her husband's violence, and so had mine. Bruised eyes, dark glasses, blood and broken bones were the physical manifestations of a psychological terror we lived with all the time, that he could and would erupt without notice or provocation – as children, we learned to creep about like Jack, silently so as not to waken this fearsome giant. The emotional tension was so intense that it was almost with a sense of relief we ran to hide when he did start to hit out, under beds, in cupboards or squashed thin against the wall, holding your breath to make yourself invisible. The relief quickly gave way to a pounding terror, as the sounds and sights of mum being punched and kicked pervaded the house – there was no way to hide from this. To this day, some 50 years later the memory invokes the rising vomit I had to fight to hold back as a small child. Ayesha's family, like ours, had finally escaped the violence and were now father-less. We never thought about the good a father might bring to his children, we had no experience of this; for us being without a father simply meant being without his violence and as I sat in the council flat on that first meeting, I felt the sanctity of the safety of this cramped little place as keenly as I had in our maisonette. The family had been housed from a women's refuge by the council, Ayesha's husband did not know where they were living and it was crucial he didn't find out. And this is where our narratives take a different shape. Leaving my father meant my mother could raise her children in relative peace but for Ayesha, leaving a violent husband had catapulted her into virtual statelessness and this created a whole set of different threats for her and her children. Despite having lived in the UK for over 14 years she was not a citizen and her right to stay was tied to her status as the wife of someone with a British passport. She divorced her husband and he reported her to the Home Office. Shortly after, she was issued with a Deportation Order. The Home Office (now UK Borders Agency) was merciless; she was directed to leave the UK. Her council flat was taken as evidence of her dependency on the state and it was assumed that she would be a long-term drain on the welfare system should she be allowed to remain in the UK. The Deportation Order would have the effect of enforced separation from her children, five of whom were British citizens and could remain. (Adele).

This was the 1980s and people subject to immigration controls were not officially restricted from accessing welfare support. However, since the 1960s social security officers had been under 'secret internal instructions' to restrict benefits to 'any claimant who appears to come from abroad' (Kundnani, 2007a, 2007b, p. 75). By 1988, new income support regulations had all but formally embedded immigration control and surveillance as part of the Welfare State and accessing benefits was tantamount to signing one's own deportation papers. Had Ayesha remained within a violent marriage, the family would have been entitled to apply for benefits if they had been destitute but as a Black single mother of four children, *without the right to live in the UK*, when she left her husband she faced a form of institutionalised destitution as she could not claim benefits. The use of the welfare system as a surveillance tool was later reinforced by the Asylum and Immigration Appeals Act 1993 which placed a duty on local authorities to investigate the immigration status of benefit claimants suspected of being asylum seekers and to pass the information on to the Home Office (Kundnani, 2007a, 2007b).

Ayesha could not leave her children, and left with few choices she decided to claim asylum.[1] She claimed that forcing her to leave would be in breach of

---

[1] Immigration rules subsequently changed to make it all but impossible to claim asylum once a person has entered the country.

rights laid down in the 1950 European Convention on Human Rights (ECHR). Her application was rejected. Ayesha had six children, five of whom were British citizens, a fact that was simply swept aside. Should Ayesha decide to leave them in England then they would be taken into local authority care. With staggering disregard for the best interests of the children, the Home Office contacted the Local Authority to alert them that a placement might be needed. It was at this stage that Ayesha came to Abasindi. Known for its social and political activism against injustice to Black women, Ayesha's situation represented two of the most pressing issues of the eighties with which the organisation was grappling: domestic violence and immigration control. Over three decades later, the political and economic landscape may have changed but the double danger Black women face when they are caught up within violent relationships and subject to immigration control has not diminished. As it had done on behalf of many other women, Abasindi launched an anti-deportation campaign for Ayesha.

Ayesha's eldest daughter, who became an active member of Abasindi when she was older reflects on her family's experience:

> Hope you're well and thanks for the opportunity to speak my voice.
>
> My family arrived from hot Nigeria to a cold January in 1984. As a child, I had never seen snow. Everything was different. The way people spoke, dressed, food etc. I was relentlessly bullied when I began secondary school. The quiet African girl. I didn't know children could be so vicious. I hated going to school. When I complained to my parents, they always advised me not to fight back. I became a target. After some years, my parents' marriage broke down but although I was the eldest child I didn't quite get what was happening. I do however remember mum saying we had to go back to Nigeria because the Government had said so. By now although we didn't have family here we had made a few friends. I do remember spending lots of time at the Ascension Church in Hulme during the Viraj Mendis anti-deportation campaign. I didn't know; I actually don't know how my mum was introduced to the Abasindi women. What I do remember was meeting all these new Aunties. These women with their welcoming personalities. These Black women became very prominent in our lives as they became the front line soldiers in our anti-deportation campaign. I remember going to their base (St Mary's Centre). I was empowered to see posters on the walls of activists and positive Black images. These images went on to give me a sense of pride. We eventually went to win our anti-deportation campaign but remained forever entwined with our new Abasindi family. (Anonymous – Abasindi member).

It was to be a long battle and though Ayesha eventually won the right to remain in the UK, the chronic stress and anxiety she suffered over the years it took, exacted a huge toll on her health. Abasindi helped Ayesha to access free legal advice through one of its members, whose expertise on the subject led to her employment as an Advice Worker with an Immigration Rights agency, while in my role as Social Worker, I provided evidence in support of the needs and rights of the children to remain with their mother. Abasindi women collected petition signatures outside shopping and community centres, they engaged religious leaders, enlisted the support from the schools the children attended, leafleted government departments, harangued politicians, and they held fund-raising events to generate income for the family. (Adele).

Simultaneous, Multiple and Interlocking Oppressions: Domestic Violence, Immigration Controls and Poverty

Ayesha was much more than the sum of her experiences: she was resourceful, well-educated, ambitious and multi-skilled and she did not fit the wounded and disempowered image of the battered woman that pervades much of the domestic violence literature. Yet subject to 'simultaneous, multiple and inter-locking oppressions' (Mann & Grimes, 2001, p. 8), these intersecting factors fed into a construction of an identity that demeaned these strengths: she was a poor, Black woman and what is more, as an African woman without resident status in the UK, she was classed as an alien subject and subsequently had to endure the dehumanising surveillance of the Home Office. In the UK, violence against women and girls is widely understood to affect Black and minority ethnic women (including migrant women) disproportionately (IMKAAN, 2017).

> This relates to the ways in which the risk factors that precipitate gender-based violence intensify as well as how women face more complex barriers to safe dis-closure and reporting. In the context of the hostile environment for migrant women in the UK, the threat of destitution, detention and/or deportation looms large over them, especially when their immigration status is insecure and when they have 'No Recourse to Public Funds' (McIlwaine et al., 2019, p. 4)

Though domestic violence is a universal problem, levels of risk are not universal; poor Black women 'are more likely to be in both dangerous intimate relationships and dangerous social positions' (Richie, 2000, p. 1136) and women with temporary immigration status are particularly vulnerable as they are often unable to access welfare support that might facilitate their escape. Their immigration status might prevent them taking action against their partners in case they lose their right to remain in the UK (Gower, 2013). The common thread that runs through the wealth of research and literature on domestic violence is the recognition that this problem cuts across, race, class, religion and nationality. Increasingly however, scholars have questioned the ways in which the levelling out of differential experiences masked by universalising statements such as this, contributes to the marginalisation of some women (Richie, 2000; Ristock, 2002; Russo & Pirlott, 2006). Abasindi's politics of sisterhood and the social action it spawned were based on a race and class analysis of violence against women which enabled differential risks and circumstances to surface.

Yes, domestic violence occurs in all settings but Ayesha's experiences were impacted by cultural and structural factors that meant she was exposed to threats that do not affect all women. Though there are high levels of domestic violence in many countries, Ayesha originated from a country in which domestic violence has long been viewed as a culturally rooted problem that is either too complex or not severe enough to warrant attention (International Rescue Committee, 2012). A 2014 article in 'Think Africa Press' reported:

Between half and two thirds of Nigerian women are subject to domestic violence in their homes. This trend occurs across much of the world, but Nigeria's discriminatory laws and dismissive police compound its particularly high rates of domestic violence. Most potently, its prevalent culture of silence and stigma for the victims of domestic violence hinders public acknowledgement of the problem... In general, domestic violence is seen as a 'private' matter to be dealt with by the family, typically a domain of male authority. Nigerian women are expected to behave with subservience to their husbands, and domestic violence is often accepted as a part of marriage. According to Amnesty International, many believe that a woman is "expected to endure whatever she meets in her matrimonial home", and to provide "sex and obedience" to her husband, who has the right to violate and batter her if she fails to meet her marital duties... Domestic violence in Nigeria is often viewed as a necessary corrective tool for women, at best a part and parcel of married life. (October 11, 2014, http://thinkafricapress.com/nigeria/domestic-violence-problem-pervading)

Though this article reports on Nigeria, it reflects cultural values that constrain women's agency and forces them into acquiescence with patriarchal domination that have existed throughout history and in most other countries too. Ayesha did not escape cultural constraints when she moved to live in the UK, and leaving her husband, though an act of resilience essential to her wellbeing, is likely to have led head-on into her having to confront other ways in which discourses of culture and the behaviours they engender can further bind women. Writing about the trauma of domestic violence, Nixon and Humphreys (2010) suggest that:

> To hold traumatic reality in consciousness requires a social context that affirms and protects the victim and that joins victim and witness in common alliance. For the individual victim, this social context is created by relationships with friends, lovers, and family. (2010, p. 137)

What is missing from this statement is the recognition that the common alliance may be severed if the victim takes a stand against oppressive cultural values that are part of the social context. Leaving a violent husband can result in a woman literally being jettisoned into cultural and social isolation, especially if she is viewed as having betrayed the conventions of domesticity to which the family and community subscribe. Nixon and Humphreys (2010, p. 138) go on to say that at the societal level the social context is created by 'political movements that give voice to the disempowered', but these movements can only be effective if their analysis of domestic violence also focuses on its cultural as well as structural underpinnings. Abasindi women were acutely aware that, as Sokoloff and Dupont (2005) point out, the manifestations of domestic violence may differ according to cultural context. After all, the community in which the organisation was located is one of the most diverse in the region with over 78 languages spoken in its schools (Day Care Trust, 2011). Abasindi was equally vociferous however, in its rebuttal of the ready supply of simplistic and reductionist cultural arguments that, under the guise of 'culturally sensitivity', too often resulted in women being abandoned to their fate.

Discourses of culture; the embedded, and often implicit or tacit beliefs about what is normal or acceptable behaviour and ideas in a particular reference group (Fook & Askeland, 2007, p. 3) and about which, considerable has been written (see for example the rich body of work by cultural theorist, Stuart Hall) suffer from a dualism of objectivism and constructivism. On the one hand, the term is imbued with concretised notions of exotic artefact, behaviour or tradition and on the other, these 'objects' of culture are dependent upon subjective interpretation of meaning. When culture is served up as explanation for oppression or as justification for not intervening when women or children are at risk, the ambiguity generated by this dualism is appropriated, inadvertently or not, to suppress the needs of marginalised communities. Though Ayesha *did* receive the support of a women's refuge, as a woman from a minoritised ethnic group, this is not something she could have taken for granted. A 2014 study of domestic violence survivors among minoritised ethnic women in the UK found that they often had restricted access to services because of racism and cultural assumptions:

> Discourses of both cultural specificity and generality/commonality are shown to intersect to effectively exclude minority ethnic women from such services. Domestic violence emerges as something that can be overlooked or even excused for 'cultural reasons', as a homogenized absence; or alternatively as a pathologized presence, producing heightened visibility of minoritized women both within and outside their communities – since domestic violence brings them and their communities under particular scrutiny. (Burman et al., 2004, p. 332)

We do not argue here for the isolation of cultural factors in explaining domestic violence or in examining the responses of agencies; such an approach would limit understandings of diversity to privileged spheres of knowledge (Andersen & Collins, 2001). Neither do we agree that gender should be the primary basis of analysis. Instead we support the views of scholars such as Sokoloff and Dupont (2005), who have called for the examination of how 'other forms of inequality and oppression, such as racism, ethnocentrism, class privilege and heterosexism, intersect with gender oppression (2005, p. 39). Such analysis should include the critical scrutiny of culture, not as exoticised characterisation of the other but of the ways in which discourses of culture are used to sustain hierarchies of interests and needs (Andersen & Collins, 2001). This might help to explain why Black and minoritised ethnic women in the UK who are subject to domestic violence are rendered less visible, their experiences explained away for cultural reasons (Burman et al., 2004).

In 1989, around the same time as Ayesha won her right to remain in the UK, Amina Mama published her research on the statutory and voluntary sector responses to domestic violence against Black women. 'The Hidden Struggle: Statutory and Voluntary Sector Responses to Violence Against Black Women in the Home' turned the spotlight onto the institutions and structures that were designed to help: the criminal justice system, housing services, police and social services, refuges and voluntary organisations. Mama's research revealed extensive policy and practice failings and demonstrated the ways in which entrenched structural inequalities compounded problems for women escaping violence if they were Black. The strategy adopted by Abasindi in its support of such women involved building anti-violence coalitions based on an intersectional analysis of violence that recognised these inequalities (Collins, 1998).

Though the organisation took a general stand on violence against women, we saw that women were not equally affected by violence. For example, had

Ayesha been a Black British or White woman, leaving a violent husband would not have resulted with her facing forced removal from the country or separation from her children. Intersectional analysis also reveals that poor women are at greater risk of violence in the home because they have fewer resources to draw on to ensure their safety. And Black women are more likely to be in poverty than White women (except for women from traveler communities who also experience disproportionate poverty and structural disadvantage) (IRR, 2013). Families from Black and minoritised ethnic groups on average live on less than 60 per cent of the median UK household income (IRR, 2013). Had Ayesha been a woman of Caribbean descent escaping domestic violence, she might have been among the 30 per cent classified as income poor, a better position than women of African descent, for whom the rate is 45 per cent and significantly better than had she been Pakistani (55 per cent) or Bangladeshi (65 per cent) (these figures compare to the lowest rates of income poverty among White British people of 20 per cent) (Palmer & Kenway, 2007).

As a lone parent family (a more prevalent family type in African and Caribbean communities in the UK), a Black woman's risks of poverty increase considerably and as an asylum-seeking family, the policy of enforced destitution that is a feature of immigration policy may do exactly that, force them into destitution. One third of people who apply for asylum in the UK each year are women. This number has remained fairly constant for the past decade and in 2010, for example, 5329 women claimed asylum compared to 12,571 men.[2] The vast majority of asylum seekers live in poverty as they are unable to seek permission to work unless they have waited more than 12 months for a decision on their application, and during this time they do not have access to the social welfare system. Asylum seekers *can* apply for asylum support from the UK Border Agency, but the money they receive if they can prove destitution is set below subsistence level. Around 70 per cent of women's asylum claims are rejected and the situation for these women is particularly acute as they have no entitlements at all. Women subject to immigration controls are among the most disempowered of all groups in the UK. Their movement and civil liberties are controlled by the State and though unable to access welfare support, the immigration system actually creates and enforces their dependence on the State (Cohen, 2006; Dumper, 2005). Before the Deportation Order, Ayesha was working and supporting her family but as a 'failed asylum seeker' she was not permitted to work and her limited access to benefits meant

---

[2] Home Office, Immigration Statistics, April to June 2011: Asylum, Table as.03: Asylum applications from main applicants by age, sex and country of nationality.

the family had to live at below national subsistence levels. These differences show that it is not just race, class and gender that determine women's oppression, but institutional structures and equity of access to support.

Abasindi's political position was to take social action beyond the boundaries of culture, race, gender and class by confronting and even circumventing the systems which sustain these inequalities. For example, with women who were subject to immigration controls, one of our members helped them access one of the best free legal services available, through the Greater Manchester Immigration Advice Unit. Good legal advice is essential for the protection of human rights and has long been a cornerstone of asylum advocacy work, yet cuts in services, alongside legal aid reforms have led to a drastic reduction in the number and quality of immigration specialists. In 2010 Refugee and Migrant Justice was shut down and in 2011, the Immigration Advisory Service was closed. The GMIAU, one of the oldest legal advice services in the country, and which incidentally was the agency which supported Ayesha in the 80s, had a 70 percent cut in funding for its legal aid work (IRR, 2013, p. 4). Together with cuts in services, legislative and policy changes have curtailed people's access to effective legal representation and though legal aid funding can still be obtained in asylum cases, general immigration work has been removed from the scope of legal aid. Cuts in services have differential impacts and as women's immigration cases tend to be especially complex, women are disproportionately affected by these changes. The Institute of Race Relations summarises the impact of these changes:

> … the effects of the changes are injustice, destitution, illegal working, frustration, loss of faith in the justice system, desperation and exploitation. Many law firms have pulled out of asylum and immigration work altogether or have significantly reduced the amount of work they are able to take on. (IRR, 2013, p. 3)

Alongside these challenges there have been some important advancements in respect of women's rights. For example, the combined efforts of anti-violence and asylum advocacy campaigns resulted in changes to the Immigration Rules so that the spouse or partner of a person with British citizenship or resident status can now apply to stay in the UK permanently if she is a victim of domestic violence. In the past, the 'no recourse to public funds' rule prevented victims of domestic violence from accessing housing or welfare benefits until they had an immigration status which entitled them to public funds, such as Indefinite Leave to Remain. As few refuges would accept people without access to benefits, women often had no choice but to remain in the violent situation. In April 2012 however, a new policy concession was announced to enable women to apply for a temporary immigration status and this gives access to public funds while they are waiting for a decision on their application for indefinite leave under the domestic violence rules. An important caveat to note however, is that this provision—the Destitute Domestic Violence Concession (DDVC) is only available to women who enter Britain on a 'spousal visa'.

Despite this change, women like Ayesha still cannot access legal aid for representation if they have been issued with instructions that mean they must leave the UK and their children behind, or if their immigration status puts them at risk of being returned to a situation of violence or abuse. In this respect, things are worse now than they were 30 years ago. The government position '…immigration is a matter of choice, so that those seeking to enter or stay should fund their own legal appeals' (IRR, 2013, p. 7) fails to take into account the specific risks that women face and ignores repeated calls for a gender-sensitive approach to immigration support (Dumper, 2005; Women's Aid, 2019).

We met Ayesha in the early 1980s but domestic violence, poverty and immigration controls continue to restrict women's rights and freedoms today. Abasindi was one of the first organisations in the UK to address immigration controls, domestic violence and poverty as an interconnected human rights issue, an approach subsequently adopted by organisations such as 'Safety4Sisters' (https://www.safety4sisters.org/), which points out on its website that 'a good service can be measured by its capacity to fulfil the needs of the most marginalised and vulnerable groups'. Like Abasindi, Safety4Sisters has long campaigned for the rights of Black and minoritised ethnic women subject to immigration controls and who also face violence. The organisation sums up its concerns thus: 'Women with insecure immigration status are excluded, disadvantaged, and increasingly unpopular. Their existence in society has been considered illegitimate, and accordingly the violence against them has been disregarded and their access to justice and safety denied.' (2016). During the 2020–22 Covid-19 pandemic, the incidence of violence against women increased while at the same time access to support services for Black and migrant women was even more restricted (Davies, 2020; IMKAAN, 2020). In the report 'Locked in Abuse, Locked out of Safety' based on qualitative research with women impacted by the pandemic, Safety4Sisters reported:

- Referrals and caseloads doubled
- All the women supported were without recourse to public funds
- Many were in need of immediate safe accommodation or a refuge space, yet 100 per cent per cent of women referred who had sought a refuge space

were initially refused due to the NRPF (no recourse to public funds) requirement.

- In addition to a need for safety, women faced worsening physical health, mental health, poverty and racism.
- Migrant women and their children were being left in high risk situations with violent perpetrators, often with inadequate explanations offered as to why accommodation and safety could not be provided by statutory services
- While some women received support from statutory services it was often not enough to get them to safety (Safety4Sisters, 2021, p. 5)

Among the reports' recommendations was the request to government to remedy two of the most significant barriers to Black women's safety: an end to discriminatory policies which place migrant survivors of abuse at further harm including the removal of the 'no recourse to public funds' condition and, the reinstatement of legal aid for immigration matters (Safety4Sisters, 2021). These were the policies and practices that had most disadvantaged Ayesha. In the final analysis, we have to conclude that despite the two decades of campaigning for change by Abasindi and other women's organisations, little has been achieved in protecting Black women who are migrants, from abuse and exploitation. Black women are, however, nothing if not resilient and Abasindi has spawned several other organisations that continue its work. One such organisation is 'Afrocats' founded in 2003 by Abasindi member Magdalen Bartlett (Fig. 7.3).

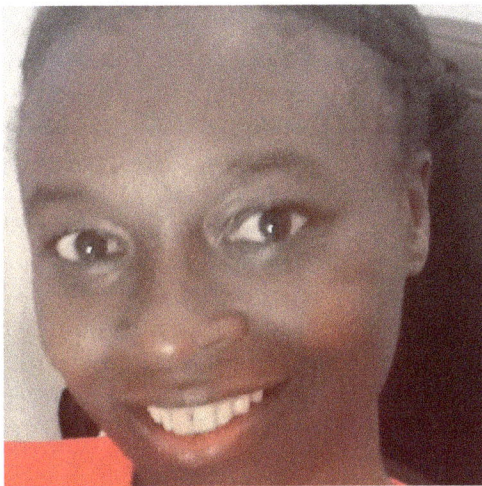

Fig. 7.3   Magdalen Bartlett; Abasindi member and founder of Afrocats, Manchester

Afrocats is a female-led charity that works with women refugees and asylum seekers to dismantle inequality and create inspiring experiences and opportunities that build resilience among marginalised and socially excluded women and children.

I arrived in the UK from Barbados in December 1988 when I was 12. My family lived in London for a year where I attended school and for the first time I experienced what it was like to be an ethnic and cultural minority. We moved to Moss Side in Manchester, where the majority Black community faced stigma and frequent stereotyping in the media. My parents lived in council housing which often placed Black people in segregated pockets leading to postcode discrimination, isolated communities and low employment aspirations. My mother was active in cultural activities and recognised their importance for forming identity and confidence. She enrolled us both in a local all-female Afro-Caribbean group called Abasindi, which had held performances around the UK since the 1970s and had a good following. Abasindi provided me with an important platform to embrace and celebrate my cultural heritage in my new country. I was able to travel around England performing as a dancer and delivering workshops from the age of 14 which was hugely important for me. I had been very shy when I arrived in the UK and this opportunity allowed me to develop my confidence, my abilities and my sense of self. A few years later my family was threatened with deportation and we fought this with the aid of our local community. Our campaign was high profile and featured in newspapers and local television in Manchester and beyond. I attended university in Bedford during this time to study dance and drama and promoted our campaign there, gaining further support from students and locals. Our campaign has since been archived in the Ahmed Iqbal Centre at Manchester Central Library and appeared in books. We won our appeal to stay but the whole process was protracted and highly stressful for my family. I successfully graduated from both college and university; however I was always very aware of being a minority throughout and was often the sole Black person, an isolating experience. Throughout my career in the creative industries I have found that there is a racial disparity between those who lead events and the participants, with people of colour largely fulfilling the latter role. Frequently in my professional career I find myself in spaces where again I am the only Black person. After finding it difficult to get a management-level position I decided to create an opportunity for both myself, and the people I work with by setting up Afrocats. This allowed me to move from being an artist to working as an arts project manager and then as a community engagement consultant. I find it very fulfilling to use my skills and experience to help others who struggle to navigate the necessary social hurdles for progression. (Magdalen Bartlett; https://www.afrocats.org.uk/)

Marginalisation of Black Young People

Although set up primarily to support Black women, the Abasindi Cooperative acknowledged that alongside the specific concerns of women, marginalisation and vulnerability were problems that affected the community more widely. In the 80s, young Black people were being made increasingly vulnerable to long term economic disadvantage and under-employment by an education system that was largely failing them (see Chap. 6) and a resurgence in racism alongside the economic policies of the Thatcher Conservative government added to their marginalisation. The UK had suffered a series of economic crises in the 1970s and by the time Margaret Thatcher came to power in 1979, the country had joined the list of recession-hit countries in the economically developed world. Inflation was about 10 per cent and unemployment, which had been steadily increasing since the mid-60s reached record levels. By 1982, the number of unemployed had exceeded three 3 million, with people out of work being referred to as "Maggie's millions" (BBC January 26, 1982). The policy view at the time, that the macroeconomic benefits of high unemployment outweigh its economic and social costs (Politics.Co.UK, n.d.) seemed simply to consign young people in deprived areas to a future without hope (Lea & Young, 1982). It was only a matter of time before the simmering resentment and frustration that many people felt was to boil over; this was the backcloth to the 1981 uprisings (riots). In the next section we turn our attention to these topics.

Supporting a Community on Fire

While Ayesha was battling violence in the home, violence erupted on the streets just a stone's throw away from where she lived. Abasindi Cooperative was housed in an old church building in the heart of Manchester's Moss Side community, an area with a high number of Black people (just over 50 percent of the population are from Black or minoritised ethnic groups) and where unemployment and deprivation were high. Evidence submitted to the Scarman Tribunal in the wake of the Brixton disturbances that preceded the eruption in Moss Side revealed that at the time Black young people encountered employment discrimination which thwarted their aspirations even when they had the qualifications for better jobs (Cross, n.d.). In 2017, a Joseph Rowntree report stated that 48.1% of households in Moss Side were found to be in poverty compared with the national average (Joseph

Rowntree Foundation, 2017). Ten years before this; in 2007, the average unemployment rate in Moss Side was reported at 17 per cent, well above the 9% average for the city as a whole, and among the Somali community, unemployment was as high as 47%. The high rate of unemployment among the Somali population of Moss Side was partly due to the fact many are asylum seekers and are unable to work until their asylum application has been decided (Phillips et al., 2007).

Back in 1981, it was 'Thatcher's Britain' and many young people felt disenfranchised, isolated and neglected. There was growing racial tension across the country fuelled by experiences of police harassment and the controversial 'sus' (Stop and Search) laws. The overt racism in the 50s and 60s had led to the growth of cultural and political resistance in the 1970s as ideas of Black consciousness and Black power gained increasing popularity. Yet despite concerted anti-racist action and alliances, racism seemed not to be declining but actually increasing. With this as the backcloth, the 1980s generation of Black young people in inner cities, trapped in worsening poverty, under-education and poor employment prospects were ripe for protest.

In the early hours of Sunday 18 January 1981, a 16th birthday party in New Cross, South London ended in tragedy when the house was gutted by fire. Thirteen young Black people lost their lives in the fire (another later died in hospital) and a further 26 suffered serious injuries. At the time, and given the increase in racist hostilities, the fire was believed to have been the result of racially motivated arson. The government response at the time seemed to indicate an indifference to the loss of Black life and this was exacerbated by a general belief that the police did not take seriously the possibility that the fire may have been caused by a racist firebombing. Later reports indicate that the fire had been caused by a faulty paraffin heater but at the time, the rise of racism and the increasing number of racist attacks, pointed to racial hatred as the cause. When the focus of the investigation turned towards blaming the young people who had been at the party, there was outrage among the victims' families and local communities (La Rose et al., 2011). A Black People's Day of Action was called. On March 2, 1981, around 25,000 people turned out on the streets of London to demonstrate against the general rise in racism and especially within policing practice (Fig. 7.4).

Over the next few months, the tensions mounted, and violent unrest erupted right across the country, beginning in Brixton. By the end of the summer, there had been disturbances in Leicester, Birmingham, Preston, Blackburn, Sheffield, Newcastle, Luton, Wolverhampton, Stockport, Ellesmere Port, Liverpool, Chester and Manchester (La Rose et al., 2011). In Manchester's Moss Side, both Black young people and White rioted, suggesting that it was not just racism, but inner city deprivation, that had fuelled the

Fig. 7.4 New Cross Fire protest

disorder. Reflecting on the events 30 years ago, people present at the time reported:

> Buildings were being stoned and glass windows were falling apart. Buildings were burning. People were shouting and screaming. It was a cacophony of all those things.
>
> … It was deeply concerning. There were particular concerns for the young people on the streets and the older people running around trying to find their children. The riots were eventually brought under control but the conduct of some officers was heavily criticised. People who had done nothing wrong were indiscriminately arrested and assaulted… (Manchester Evening News July 9, 2011   http://www.manchestereveningnews.co.uk/news/greater-manchester-news/moss-side-riots-the-night-years-864536

The state of relations between the police and Black communities at the time could hardly have been worse. Academic John Rex observed that to 'catch each criminal youth it became normal practice to interview up to fifty others who by virtue of their blackness, their cultural symbols or suspicious behaviour, were thought to be possible criminals' (1983, p. 101). Rex's comment might have been based largely on anecdotal evidence but statistics on the ratio of arrests and searches to actual convictions, and the rates of stop and search among different groups reveal that then, as now, criminogenic constructions continue to be influenced by racial stereotypes (Kundnani, 2007a, 2007b). That policing practices were a key factor in the Moss Side riots perhaps explains why, during the height of the violence, the police station was besieged by angry crowds for three days. Father Phil Sumner, a Catholic priest who was to spend over 25 years working in Moss Side recalled:

> "I turned the corner onto Quinney Crescent and there were hundreds of young Black people on one side and the police with their riot shields on the other," he said. "The next thing was a brick bounced off the bonnet and hit the windscreen."…"I remember standing there talking when the police launched a baton charge into the crowd. "We headed down what is now Raby Street, past Our Lady's Church, and at the gate was a burning barricade." At the time, unemployment among young Black men in Moss Side had reached 80% and few stood a chance of finding a job. But it was the use of "stop and search" by police that left many people in Moss Side "waiting for something to happen". "The whole Black community - not just the young people - felt such anger towards the police," Father Sumner said. "So there was a real breakdown in that relationship." A memorable piece of graffiti at the time – "Help the police, beat yourself up" - summed up the mood of many. (BBC online, 8 July 2011 'Hope and despair' 30 years after the Moss Side riots http://www.bbc.co.uk/news/uk-england-manchester-14047491)

A local White physician, Donald Bodey gave evidence to the Hytner Inquiry that followed the Moss Side riots. He told the inquiry that he was outraged at having to treat injuries caused by police brutality, injuries consistent with beatings such as suspected fractured ribs, bruises and cuts on the face, legs, and arms, and blood-filled cavities under the skin and which he had "never expected to see in England" (*New York Times*, July 22, 1981). Speaking out was however to exact a cost for Bodey and his wife as they subsequently became a target for racist extremists—"We were also sent hate mail with razor blades in from far-right extremists", Carol Bodey told the *Manchester Evening News* (July 6, 2011).

Gender, Race, Class and Protest

Variously called 'riots', 'protests', 'disturbances' and 'uprisings', depending upon one's political perspective, these events were the subject of numerous media reports, scholarly articles, books and government inquiry reports (the

Hytner Report, 1981 and the Scarman Report,1981). Reading archive material from the times, one might be forgiven for thinking that gender was not a significant factor in the riots, that all the protagonists were male, and all the women absent. The fact that the outward face of the violence was male is undisputable, evident by the young Black men with their stones and bottles gathered on one side of the road and of the police officers with their riot shields and truncheons on the other (Fig. 7.5).

But women were present. We were the mothers, sisters, girlfriends, and grandmothers of the young men who had been failed by their second-rate education. We knew too many who had been shoehorned into unsatisfactory work training schemes which offered no entry to 'the anterooms of employment' (Rex, 1982, p. 108) and, on the contrary, which only compounded their simmering frustration. Women had been the ones to caution a respectful attitude to the police, the advice most Black inner-city parents issued to their children in the hope that this would prevent them being targeted. We had witnessed young Black people turn their discontent to the self-destructive pursuit of drug dealing and addiction: we were witness when they turned against one another in the violent gangs that troubled our neighborhoods, and we had witnessed the ways in which systematic neglect by the State had contributed to all of these problems. During the uprisings we saw evidence of the expression of masculinities that reified physical prowess and domination (Baker, 2009) and which disturbed us deeply. And through all our witnessing

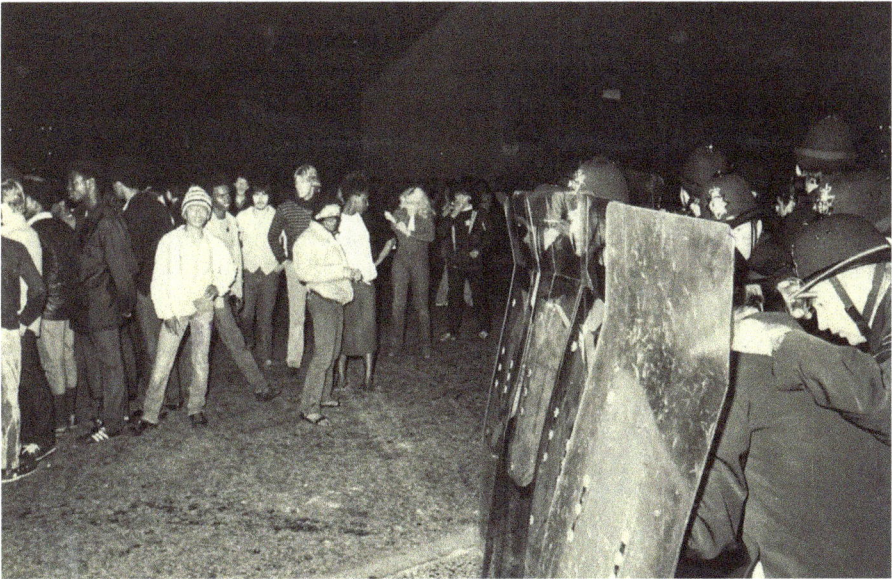

Fig. 7.5 Young people gather to protest against police brutality

we had observed the Black young men and women of our communities who had risen above their adversities and were a credit to us all. Our witness was not passive but political. In a similar vein to that great American writer James Baldwin who declared himself 'witness to the truth' and who wrote—"All over Harlem, Negro boys and girls are growing into stunted maturity, trying desperately to find a place to stand; and the wonder is not that so many are ruined but that so many survive" (Baldwin cited in Blair, 2007, p. 178), we felt much the same about the young people in Moss Side.

Despite our presence, noticeably absent from any of the articles about the riots were any observations about the role of Black women; a powerful lesson to us, that Black women must be their own historians. The lack of a rigorous gender analysis does not mean however, that discourses on the role of women (as mothers) or men (as fathers) did not surface in the postmortem that followed. The hegemonic narrative that emerged, then, as now, linked criminality with the deficits of parenthood and family. Female-headed single-parent households were held culpable for anti-government disorderly behaviour of young people, even in the face of glaring evidence about the extent of inequalities and social exclusion that such families experience (Ashe, 2014). Implicit in these discourses on single motherhood is another discourse, that of the missing father, the 'phantom' of Black family research who has been studied more for his absence than his presence (Hill, 2003).

> A range of conservative commentators suggested that the aggression expressed by young men during the civil disorder was a product of absent fathers. Young men, they contended, need fathers to have a presence in their lives to reduce this kind of antisocial behaviour. These narratives depoliticised the causes of the civil disorder by depoliticising the constitution of the identities of those young men who participated in rioting and looting. They operated to sideline the role of socio-economic factors, including gender power relationships, in the production of young men's identities. Additionally, the depoliticisation of the riots through the narrative of the absent father framed the lone mother family as a failing family form. (Ashe, 2014, p. 654)

These observations, written in the aftermath of the disturbances of 2011, were also a feature of the analysis of the 1981 riots. However, those of 1981, despite negative press to the contrary, were not about single parent families or the lawlessness of young people and Black communities. They were a reaction to the entrenched neglect of inner-city communities, a neglect institutionalised through government economic policy and a reaction to attempts to construct Black people as aliens swamping the land in order to live off its welfare system (the irony being that the welfare system would have collapsed without Black people's taxes and labour). The construction of the 'alien other' to serve nationalist and racist ideologies is a process that is institutionalized within societal structures at all levels. A group within the Conservative Party (The Monday Club) for example, published a pamphlet in 1981 which called for the repatriation of 50,000 immigrants each year, the abolition of the Commission for Racial Equality and the repeal of all race relations legislation. Harvey Proctor MP stated, the "indigenous population' would only be reassured 'that they are not, in the words of the Prime Minister, going to be swamped' if the size of the 'ethnic population' was reduced to zero" (http://www.runnymedetrust.org/histories/race-equality/83/repatriation-demand.html). What Proctor and his bedfellows failed to appreciate was that the majority of the 'ethnic population' were British citizens, as were most of the people who had revolted against the rise of racist ideas such as this.

If the face of the violence in the events of 1981 was that of the young Black man, this too was understandable. The disturbances were fired by the racist and classist bias of the British education system which particularly disadvantaged Black boys, and by policing practices that deliberately targeted and criminalized Black young men. There were multiple layers of structural disadvantage and though they concerned both Black and White people, Black youth were at the nexus and felt the oppression especially keenly. As Frost and Phillips (2011) put it, Black youth were not starting a fight, they were fighting back. In August 2011, trouble again broke out across the UK and the scale of the disorder was far greater than in 1981: the disturbances spread to 66 locations across the country, involved around 15,000 people, led to 4000 arrests and cost five lives and an estimated half a billion pounds (Newburn et al., 2011; Bridges, 2012). The social context was also somewhat different (Newburn, 2012). Though the spark for the initial 2011 protest in London was the killing of Mark Duggan, a Black man, shot by a policeman, the antagonism that underpinned the disturbances that sprang up in other parts of the country was less about racism and more the result of generalised discontent.

The riots of 2011 differed from 1981 in other ways too; for example, they contained inflections of the consumerist preoccupations of British society, a factor not identified as a feature of the earlier uprisings. Furthermore, the instancy of the mobilisation power of communication technology spread the unrest in ways that were not possible 30 years earlier. The disaffected were mobilised in days, whereas in 1981, there were three months between the initial incidents in Brixton and the protests in Moss Side. Mobile phones had served as a conduit for not only legitimate protest, but also for opportunism—some people seemed to join the fray not because of disadvantage but to take advantage of the chaos. The disturbances in the summer of 2011 became a 'mix of violence, protest, looting and pleasure' (Ashe, 2014, p. 652) but the profusion of explanations that followed again suggested their cause was the dysfunctionality of the single-parent family. However, this time 'moral vacuity, greed and popular culture' were also highlighted (Ashe, 2014, p. 654). Platts-Fowler (2013, p. 18) observed: 'The usual culprits cited as responsible for this breakdown were feral children whose parents had failed in their duty to socialise them, and criminal gangs' echoing views such as those espoused by Carroll (2012), that the disturbances were symptomatic of a 'spoilt brat mentality' linked to welfare dependency (Carroll, 2012 cited in Platts-Fowler, 2013, p. 18).

These explanations masked an inconvenient truth; that as in 1981, the history underlying the 2011 disturbances was the longstanding deprivation and neglect of certain sections of the population (Lea & Hallsworth, 2012; Wain & Joyce, 2012). Milburn's (2012, p. 402) argument that the riots emerged from a 'context of crisis and austerity' was supported by the fact that seventy per cent of those later brought before the courts were reported to have been from the 30 per cent most deprived areas in the UK (Ashe, 2014, p. 656).

> Young people, representing approximately half of riot participants (Ministry of Justice, 2012), had already been hit particularly hard by economic decline and austerity measures. Youth unemployment had reached record levels, and cuts to youth provision had left some young people with little to do… (Platts-Fowler, 2013, p. 18)

The disturbances of 1981 were sparked by entrenched institutionalised racism plus structural disadvantage. In 2011, the most significant contextual factor seems to have been the demise of the Welfare State and the harsh realities of neoliberalist policies (Kundnani, 2007a, 2007b; La Rose et al., 2011; Lea & Hallsworth, 2012; Milburn, 2012) which, not coincidentally, had their genesis in the period leading up to the 1981 events. Though less a protest about racism, what happened in 2011 revealed that racism in the police force was still a major concern (Solomos, 2011). Black people who had taken part in the riots reported unfair treatment at the hands of the police (Muir & Adegoke, 2011) and though there had been changes to the stop and search rules over the years, Black young people were still disproportionately targeted (Prasad, 2011). The police shooting of Mark Duggan which had provoked the initial protest—a small and peaceful gathering of about 50 people outside Tottenham Police Station, revealed similar concerns about racist profiling within policing practice that had contributed to those earlier disturbances.

There were also important gender considerations. In her analysis of riots that took place in 1991, Campbell (1993) highlighted the differential impacts of economic marginalisation on men and women, while research into the 2011 riots by *The Guardian* and the London School of Economics revealed that gender was a factor in the shape and forms of disorder (2011). We suggest that an analysis which explores the intersectionality of gender, class and race may reveal dynamics in the politics of resistance that might not be made visible by unitary approaches alone. For example, Ashe (2014) describes the violation to the sense of self that stop and search practices can evoke in young men who experience socio-economic exclusion (2013). Drawing on work by Messerschmidt (2000), Ashe posits that stop and search could be viewed as a 'very public form of emasculation' of one group of men by another more powerful group (Ashe, 2014, p. 659).

> Stop and search is not just an attack on the rights of the community; it is a technology that attacks the integrity of young men's identification with certain ideals of masculinities by invading their bodily space, discarding as irrelevant the traditional boundaries of male autonomy in the interests of surveillance. The issue of policing not only connects to class or racial politics but also incorporates a gender body politics. (Ashe, 2014, p. 659)

Given the dominance of repertoires of violence within discourses of masculinity (Barker, 2005), it is unsurprising that young men who believe they are victimised and marginalised use violence in their protests. After all, the behaviour of male police officers against which they are reacting draws on these same repertoires of violence. While young men often resort to expressions of violence, Campbell (1993) noted that women are more likely respond to their economic conditions by building community support. This too is hardly surprising. While violence is not necessarily a trait of masculinity, or peace of femininity, male violence is endemic within British society (Connell & Messerschmidt, 2005). Whether confronting police violence against their sons, or the gang violence that beset the Moss Side community for many years or, as we saw in the case of Ayesha, confronting domestic violence perpetrated against women by men, the Abasindi Cooperative had a long history of tackling violence, and had no appetite for more. The Abasindi strategy tended towards justice, support and strengthening community, rather than combat. This was the primary role adopted by Abasindi in the Moss Side riots of 1981. For example, the organisation played an active part in supporting the Moss Side Defence Committee, which helped young people access legal advice and challenged the distortions in the media and police accounts of what had taken place. This spirit of solidarity was reflected right across the district as community services opened their doors to support young people in the area. Under the leadership of community activists such as Charlie Moore, Hartley Hanley, Gus John, Beresford Edwards (Nana Bonsu), Paul Okojie, Ken McIntyre and others, support was provided to hundreds of young people, with two notable places of refuge being the Moss Side Youth Club and Hideaway, another youth centre. As the fire raged though, it was Abasindi to whom the people turned. Unlike State-funded organisations ordered to shut down, we were financially autonomous and no one could order us around - we kept our doors open. We were the place to which the injured were taken and our women became the nurses and providers of care (Fig. 7.6).

'…community worker Elouise Edwards was helping to set up a makeshift hospital at the Abasindi centre to treat the injured. "It was a terrible time," she said. "It was so frightening. One young White lad came in, he had been beaten up. He was an apprentice baker just coming home from his job; he didn't know what was going on. We took him to the hospital because his injuries were too big for us. We were Black people taking this young White man to hospital – we could have left him on the street – and he said something that has stuck with me forever. He said, "But you were the people they taught us to hate". (*Manchester Evening News* July 9, 2011)

1981 Abasindi
The day was not normal
For days
The air was static with tension
It was feared expected and rejected as easily as breathing
Hair weaves continued
Cornrowing and stock checking
African fabric and outfits
Amongst the drums ready for rehearsals

No Facebook or twitter existed to newsflash
But everyone knew it
Heard it
Smelt the fear felt the anger
When all exploded at 2am

This space
This haven for women and children
Now opened its arms to refugees
Of local not global despair
Welcomed the injured
The frightened
This space gave solace and protection exactly when needed

Fig. 7.6   The Abasindi building: a makeshift hospital

One day, July 8th 24 hours
2 days July 9th 48 hours
1981 Abasindi never closed its doors
To anyone
'1981 Abasindi', SuAndi ©2014

One of the responses to the disturbances of 1981 was to increase opportunities for Black people to enter further and higher education institutions through the establishment of access courses. In the next section we discuss the contribution of the Manchester Black Access Course to the politicisation of Black women.

Accessing Higher Education

Although there have been improvements in the gender balance in higher education in that women now represent 44 per cent of academics in UK universities, the percentage of Black people remains disproportionately low at 1.6 per cent (2011/12 HESA Staff Record).

At a recent public talk at University College London, titled "Why Isn't My Professor Black?", black scholars claimed that insidious forms of racism may explain why just 85 of the UK's 18,500 professors are black, and only 17 are black women. (*Times Higher Education*, April 6, 2014)

The racial inequalities these figures reflect have been the subject of research and policy concerns stemming back to the riots of 1981 and even before. In 2009, the National Union of Students conducted a study of the gaps between the attainments of Black and White Students. The survey of 938 respondents demonstrated that one's experience of school and college had a direct impact on how a student performed in further and higher education settings and that coming from a poor socio-economic background, which was the experience for many Black people, had reduced their access to education during formative years of a standard that would equip them for adult learning. The report concluded that the attainment gaps would only be addressed through changing the organisational nature of institutions and tackling institutional racism, which they defined as:

> The collective failure of an organisation to provide an appropriate and professional service to people because of their colour, culture, or ethnic origin. It can be seen or detected in processes, attitudes and behaviour which amount to discrimination through unwitting prejudice, ignorance, thoughtlessness and racist stereotyping which disadvantage minority ethnic people. (The Macpherson Report 1999 cited in NUS, 2010, p. 56)

Alongside the need to tackle structural inequalities, some scholars believe there is also need to establish accredited Black studies programmes within UK institutions. They point to way the growth of women's studies over the last 30 years has contributed to knowledge on gender inequality and increased the visibility of feminist academics. It is argued that academia, while generating an impression that the production of knowledge is a neutral endeavour, is dominated by a Eurocentricity that marginalises Black people's experiences and downplays the contributions of scholarship arising from the analysis of racial disadvantage. Gil Robinson claims that: "Establishing black studies programmes will increase our visibility within universities and make the statement that our presence is worth studying, our presence is worth understanding and our contribution to this society, to academic life, to British life and to world life, is worth studying." (Robinson cited in The Guardian Higher Education Network, 25 July 2013, http://www.theguardian.com/higher-education-network/blog/2013/jul/25/race-equality-academia-curriculum). Other commentators disagree and suggest that the capital of Black people in academic settings can only be fully utilised if they "raise the presence and impact" of their academic output through research and publications (Davis, cited in The Guardian Higher Education Network, 25 July 2013, http://www.theguardian.com/higher-education-network/blog/2013/jul/25/race-equality-academia-curriculum).

The call for increasing the number of Black people in further and higher education settings was given impetus after the 1981 uprisings which it was believed stemmed, in part, from the inequities of the educational system (Rex, 1982) which not only prevented Black pupils from achieving their potential but thwarted their access to higher education and satisfying employment. Black Access Courses were one of the measures instituted by Labour-controlled local education authorities in response to the Swann Report (1985), which had concluded that disadvantage among Black children resulted from a failure of the education system (see Chap. 6). Access courses were seen as a means of addressing this disadvantage and aimed towards producing a new generation of Black teachers and other professionals.

This initiative was not without its critics. Those on the right argued that Black Access Courses lowered admission standards while left-wing commentators were concerned about tokenism and institutionalised marginalisation. Some activists also questioned whether such courses simply added another barrier to Black people's entry to higher education and professional careers as some seemed to be an 'access to nowhere'. The Commission for Racial Equality argued that the concept of black access did not address marginalisation but instead sustained it—that it represented no more than 'a gesture of easily forgotten intent to ease any government conscience' (White, 1985, p. 302). The main argument against access courses was that they detracted against demands that institutions should recruit Black people to mainstream courses and remove barriers to Black people's access to the power structures within the education system.

The Manchester Black Access Course aimed to address many of the concerns that had been raised. For a start, it was linked with local Polytechnics and Colleges of Higher Education, which meant that students who were successful on the access programme had automatic entry to a place on a degree programme. Abasindi member Yvonne Hypolite was among the first to gain a qualification in Youth and Community Work through this partnership and went on to gain a degree.

Another difference was that most of the teaching staff and management of the Manchester course were Black and third, the course incorporated an overtly politicised approach within its taught components and included space for the exploration of Black studies alongside other subjects. Abasindi member Paula Jones (Fig. 7.7) was one of the teaching staff who contributed

Fig. 7.7 Paula Jones; Abasindi member and lecturer with the Manchester Black Access Course

towards this ethos, which was a key factor in the programme's appeal to Black students.

Across the educational and political establishment, there was little overall support for black access courses, but at the time, the Manchester course achieved a reputation as 'one of the most effective models available' (White, 1985, p. 301). One of the Black women who taught on the Manchester Black Access course from 1989–1996 and who was closely aligned with the Abasindi Cooperative reflects:

The Manchester Black Access Course came into being after the 1981 uprising. At one level it was an initiative to get the community to police itself – since initially the programme was designed to prepare students for teacher training, social work or youth and community work. It was about progressing people who had been disadvantaged at school onto higher education. One of the admission exercises was to ask people to write about their educational experiences. The stories were amazing and although school hadn't always messed people up, students said they had not been encouraged; some were taken out of class to do sport, while others were told they wouldn't amount to anything. We were trying to address an imbalance. We had a foundation programme for people with no qualifications at all and an access programme for people with GCSEs. In fact the access year was seen as part of the university degree structure and students were able to get a full grant for four or five years of study including the access part of it. Later, links were made with social sciences history, psychology and English. Successful students were guaranteed a place at Manchester Polytechnic (now Manchester Metropolitan University); the university would interview the candidate as part of the access admission process and people were allocated places on one of the respective degree courses. I wanted to encourage and empower our youth but needed to be realistic about a person's ability to manage a university degree. If teachers haven't taken the time to give you the tools you need then you will struggle to do the job. I saw the access course as a way of giving people tools. Our way of teaching was not just talk and chalk. Although we sometimes had formal lectures, most of our teaching was done through seminars and discussions, encouraging debate and critical thinking. Our teaching team was interdisciplinary and our curriculum political. We were very much influenced by the South African struggles and Pan-Africanism, and we wanted to raise political consciousness among the students, empowering them to question everything that was taken for granted. Alongside other subjects like English, Maths and the Social Sciences we incorporated cultural studies, and we integrated African history into almost all our teaching. We explored history from an Africanist perspective and examined pre-slavery, slavery, colonialism, post-colonial periods. I was inspired by Ngugi's call for the decolonization of the mind. The students blossomed intellectually and questioned deeply, and our progression rate was very high. I remember one young woman who had come on the course because she wanted to do something for her kids saying "this is the best educational experience I have ever had". To see her grow through the programme was amazing- she moved on to complete her Masters. The course helped people to find a voice and they were then able to act on that voice – one, for instance, went on to local politics. The students were mainly Black British of African and Caribbean descent; there were some Asian students and at one time the group included an Iranian. In the seven years that I taught on the course, the students were predominantly women. Although most of the feedback was positive, there was one student who had grown up in foster care, in a white environment, for whom the course had a major emotional impact and she left prematurely. Society can be really damaging to Black people's identities and this opened a can of worms for me. I really wondered whether we knew what we were doing when it came to identity issues; I think there was probably a need to build in more support for people who had had negative personal experiences. As for how many students made it through to completion of their degrees, I don't know. From the start there were constant attempts to dismantle the programme and there is nothing documented about our successes. From the outside there was a lot of negativity towards the course. We had to fight to defend it; the major discourse around was that it was rubbish, a Mickey Mouse course – where people just sat around and chatted. Personally I didn't need to defend it, I kept seeing people do incredibly well – this spoke for itself. One important testimony was seeing one of our past students become a University Lecturer. And when it came up for revalidation there were no criticisms of the course except that our assessment requirements were too high. Some students inevitably didn't make it to the completion of their degrees, in some instances they had progressed before they were ready, and I don't mean academically: some students couldn't bridge the gap between intellectual ability and translating ideas onto paper and some students withdrew or failed their university courses. But my recollection is that most of the students did well. Now, when you try to find anything out, all the information about the numbers of Black students we helped is gone, wiped away, like we never existed. The course was dismantled in the 1990s with education reforms and changes to Section 11 funding (Race Relations Act) which had provided much of the financial support. And as for now, so many kids are going to fail and fall out of the system, I can see that we will need a type of Black access course again in the future. This time though the focus should not be on finding a voice but giving a counter voice that interrupts all the negative stuff going on right now with our children. It bothers me about the sexual objectification of girls, how boys are treating them and how girls exploit their own bodies, and it bothers me that when it comes to education, Black children are still being put into boxes and written off. (Anonymous, Abasindi member).

The Manchester Black Access Course illustrates a political agenda aimed at challenging social injustice in education. After the 1981 disturbances, several Labour-controlled Local Education Authorities (LEAs) established initiatives such as this, partly to address the inequalities that provoked the uprisings and also to challenge the New Right policies of the Thatcher government (Weiner, 1997). However, White's 1985 analysis about the marginalising effect of Black access courses was to prove prophetic, since the education reforms of the late '80s and '90s curtailed the powers of LEAs and led to a withdrawal of funding. This resulted in the demise of equality education programmes that were not part of the mainstream of education provision. Nevertheless the success of the Black access courses in Further Education colleges, alongside other equality initiatives such as Community Education Programmes and Literacy

Campaigns, led to a noticeable rise in the number of Black students of African, Asian and Caribbean descent entering further and higher education institutions, from 8.5 per cent in 1991–1992 to 9.8 per cent in 1993–1994 (Avari et al., 1997). As for Abasindi, the organisation benefitted greatly. Not only did we have a positive education programme in which to channel the talent and ambition of the women we worked with, but those of us who had been involved with the course were strengthened personally, professionally and politically.

8

Reflections

Abstract As two Black women academics working in higher education institutions, one with a background in Youth and Community Work and the other in Social Work, the trials of institutional racism and gender discrimination are writ large upon our histories. At the personal level, it is not the being Black or the being female that creates the challenges we face but being at the nexus of the intersection of *both* race and gender discrimination. In the academic setting, although gender clearly matters and has mattered to us at every level of our progression, the injustices we have come across seem mostly to have their roots in racism. This is borne out by evidence discussed in Chap. 6 that shows that while women represent 44 per cent of academics in UK universities, the percentage of Black academics remains disproportionately low at 1.6 per cent. Our immersion in the Abasindi Black Women's Cooperative at a time when our careers were just beginning, emboldened us to stand tall when we were expected to sit, to speak up in engulfing silence and to throw a spanner in the works when acquiescence with injustice was called for. Though we have been enraged at the discrimination we have witnessed, rage is a difficult emotion to sustain and there came a time when it seemed more sensible and more potent to write down the words rather than only speaking them out. Beyond the academic mandate 'publish or peril', writing has therefore become something of a passion of politics for us both—a strategy for the social activist as crucial as any other. But ours is not a calcified approach that assumes cognitive knowledge is enough, and we have been preoccupied equally with the knowledge of experience (situated knowledge), of emotion and of the relevance and application of our writings for activism and for human rights more broadly.

Keywords Black women • Intersectionality • Academic activism • Situated knowledge • Rights

Writing as Political Activism

Separately, as authors, we have researched and written about many different kinds of injustice: gender-based violence, immigration controls, child abuse, Black children in care, racial and gender inequalities, education. And we have written to advance our professional disciplines: Social Work and, Youth and Community Work. Accustomed to the unease caused by our constant clamour against inequality, those around us may have wondered whether we had become quieter. We had not, we had simply become smarter. Replacing the placard with the pen is a political act in itself and documenting the achievements and challenges of the Abasindi Black Women's Cooperative seemed to us to be one of the most important contributions to social justice we could make. This is the first time we have written jointly but so seamless was the process that, together with the other women who contributed to the book, we became but a single historian drawing on multiple perspectives.

> The African Proverb states 'Until the lions have their own historians, the history of the hunt will always glorify the hunter' – in retelling Abasindi's story through the perspectives of its women, the hunter is revealed: the successes were not all his, the lion was strategic, stealthy and brave and but for the hunter's dependence on his weapons of destruction the ending would have been very different, a shallow victory indeed. The book contains valuable information for students and academics in the fields of sociology, gender and, race studies but we hope it will also help to inspire the activists of the future. We conclude by highlighting some of the most valuable lessons that have inspired our own activism.

Self-representation

Abasindi women believed that reclaiming representations of blackness contained the potential to unsettle universalisms about dominant prescriptions of beauty which constrain all women—but also to confront racist ideologies within which these prescriptions are embedded and which constrain the freedom of Black women in particular. This philosophy—the nurturing of self-love and pride in one's African/Caribbean heritage was a gift we passed on to the children we met.

For the Black woman then, it is not only the fields, the workplace, the family, or the institutions that are the site of her struggles but also her skin, her body and her hair. The celebration of skin, body and hair that surfaced within the context of the Abasindi Cooperative suggested an act of insurgency, whether or not this was conscious. The championing of hair left natural and the perfecting of African hair styles, the love of Black skin rather than its grading by shade and the assertion that the Black woman's body, however shaped, is unto itself beautiful but more than this, is hers and hers alone, reveals a reclamation of self that was the starting point for our political activism. Within a context in which beauty is highly commoditised and driven by ethnocentric aesthetic values, the choices a Black woman makes about how to represent her identity, style, desires and realities often carry meanings deep below the surface. A lesson indelibly etched on us by being part of Abasindi was the recognition that a female body that is undisciplinable rather than constrained is more than mere symbol of freedom, it is freedom itself. As the images that are woven throughout this book reveal, we fashioned ourselves in our own likeness and what emerged were diverse, multiple representations of the Black woman—traditional, contemporary, natural and straightened—we wore them all.

Self-expression

In her Nobel Prize Lecture, Toni Morrison argued that language constitutes political action in itself and is not just product or artefact. One of the authors of this book once asked her Sierra Leonean father why it was that he had never taught her any African languages. He replied that as a child growing up in Freetown, he had been beaten if he spoke anything other than 'proper' English. His own indigenous language was quite literally whipped out of him; he recalled being made to recite Victorian poetry at the age of five to aged Aunts on Sunday afternoons so as to perfect his enunciation.

Sierra Leone has long reclaimed its indigenous languages and the descendants of freed slaves who live predominantly in the country's capital and who account for less than 6 per cent of the total population, have elevated their language of Krio (an English-based Creole) crafted out of that discomfiting history to such a status that it is spoken by almost everyone in the country. It is the medium of instruction in many schools, the primary language of television and radio broadcasts, and political speeches are often delivered in Krio. One of the earliest post-independence acts of reclamation of language was the translation of some of Shakespeare's plays into Krio—we think Toni Morrison would nod in appreciation. Films have been made in Krio, academic books written, the Universal Declaration of Human Rights has been translated into Krio, and so has the bible. Within Sierra Leone it now seems a mere irrelevance that the official language of the country is English, a matter more of international expediency than regard for an imposed mother tongue. Language is about consensus, the vernacular that flowers in specific contexts is simply the agreed medium for the transmission of linguistic signifiers and meanings; in Sierra Leone, the people speak Krio and Krio speaks for the people.

Understanding the historical significance of language and the ways in which language can be used as a tool of liberation was an important lesson from the Abasindi Cooperative. Poets SuAndi and Shirley May, whose poems feature in this book, flex their creative muscles against the constraints of formal English to write in ways that speak *for* and *to* Black people. This is not simply poetic licence; these poets are fierce defenders of race and gender equality and their choice of language stands as an opposition to systems of hegemony.

The late Victoria McKenzie, a poet, story teller and author and one of Abasindi's iconic figures, described her proudest achievement: the book she produced in Jamaican Patois. Vicky had become aware that children who spoke Patois were disadvantaged in British schools and she worked to undo the misapprehension that Patois characterized its speakers as unintelligent or uneducated. She had learned this from first-hand experience; Vicky had been one of the workers recruited from Jamaica in the '50s and '60s to shore up the labour needs of the 'Mother Country'. But it was only her labour that was wanted, not her career aspirations or her gifts as an artist, and she found it impossible to gain access to higher education or to find work in the arts. Her Jamaican accent and patois, she believed, were the auditory equivalent of the symbol of intellectual inferiority that was attached to being Black. Vicky spoke of the obstacles she had faced and her frustrations that she had been unable to fulfil her potential. She was determined that subsequent generations would have the opportunities that had been denied to her. Her mission was to get Patois recognized as a language in its own right, not an inferior form of English or simply the language of the streets. As she said, "it's a language that empowers its speakers and gives them the right to their own cultural, social and political identity". Vicky saw all of this in the Jamaican Patois of her homeland, a message she spread among schools and community organisations within Moss Side. Krio, poetry, storytelling, Patois are all forms of self-expression but reclaimed as a political act, self-expression—is also a means of challenging the racial hierarchies of language.

Self-learning

Within the Black community, success is often linked to educational achievements. Parental influence, community education projects and cultural activities were amongst the key factors believed to contribute to the academic success of African-Caribbean children in the UK. However, the thwarting of academic progress through the systemic and institutionalised underdevelopment of Black children's abilities has been a long-standing battle for parents. Abasindi, like many other Black organisations in the '70s and '80s set up a free Saturday Supplementary School to support Black children in gaining the educational skills they needed for success.

Scholars have differentiated between the male strategies of securing social resources and the female strategies of constructing social capital as two versions of community activism—'his and hers'. Abasindi Saturday School was built on the 'hers' model in the sense that it was mainly women that were responsible for its organisation even though both male and female university students volunteered as tutors. In addition to the provision of supplementary teaching, especially in the areas of maths and English, the programme also focused on 'tools to survive racism' in recognition of the fact that in British society, specific attention is needed to help Black children develop a positive sense of identity, pride, and belonging. Many of the Abasindi women did not feel fully at home in Britain, even if they had been born in the UK. One's status as outsider was inferred by skin colour alone and constantly reinforced at both the discursive level and within one's daily reality. "Where are you from", an explicit question that preceded many conversations and buried behind this, the implicit question "why are you here" demanded justification for our presence. This is not the case for our children and grandchildren; they do not often have to carry the burden of justifying their existence in the UK, or so they tell us—this is as much their land as anyone's. Louise Da-Cocodia, who worked alongside Abasindi, stated that the aim of her community work was to "help young Black people understand that this is their home, this is the society they live in, and that they have a part to play in developing it"; an objective we seem to have fulfilled.

The growing number of far-right groups in the UK however, and the persistence of racist ideologies continue to threaten the right of Black young people to live freely and safely within the UK's borders. The racist murder of Stephen Lawrence stands as a key marker to this awful reality. Stephen was murdered in 1993, simply because he was Black. The tireless campaign of his parents, particularly his mother Doreen Lawrence, resulted in two of his killers being imprisoned (three remain at large), and uncovered the extent of racism and the complicity of some police officers within policing practice in London. Her campaign against racial injustice earned her many accolades: she was appointed to the House of Lords as a Labour Peer in 2013 and was named by Radio 4's Woman's Hour as the country's leading 'game changer' of 2014, an award celebrating women who changed the face of power in the UK. In establishing the Stephen Lawrence Charitable Trust in 1993, Stephen's parents' aims were to support young people to achieve their education and career aspirations. This message resonates with the lessons of the Abasindi Cooperative: Black children belong in the UK and we must continue to fight to ensure they have the same access to opportunity as anyone else. Education cannot of itself, prevent our children being exposed to racist attacks, inequality or injustice but their achievements signal a refusal to be constrained by racism and stand as testament to the resilience Abasindi engendered.

Self-care

Self-care requires a commitment to finding places and spaces in which one is able to be one's authentic self. Racism is an ever-present feature of the lives of Black people, as indeed is sexism in the lives of women; we are changed by our encounters with oppression, sometimes we are turned into giants and at others we are diminished. Our children are left confused and distressed by the casual ease with which racist comments are made and Black children who do not have the benefit of a nurturing Black family, such as children in care, are especially vulnerable to the harm this causes. Racism, sexism and classism (and indeed, all the other ways in which discrimination rears its head) may cause us to turn healthy outrage into something more destructive. At times a Black person can be made to feel so unworthy, like Pecola in Toni Morrison's 'The Bluest Eye' that they seek nothing more than to disappear—being invisible seen as a mercy. None of these responses to oppression reflect the authentic self you would be if you cared for yourself, if you felt free to be proud of your heritage, if you learned skills and knowledge that enriched you, if you laughed and loved more and scowled and fought less; if you never wished to be invisible. There is no panacea for racism or sexism and there is no magic trick to finding your authentic self—it is simply a matter of finding people and spaces in which 'victimhood' is nowhere in sight, where your resilience, even in the face of whatever struggles your daily life presents you with is nurtured. For Black women, being around other Black women that accept and affirm you can be often enough. The Abasindi Black Women's Cooperative was such a place (Fig. 8.1).

Fig. 8.1 Shirley Innis, one of the founders of Abasindi ...'a beautiful spirit and a woman who nurtured us all'

Self-care also requires being aware of the emotional impact of being in situations in which one's internal resources are being depleted. For all the benefits we had given and derived from our careers in higher education we, the authors of this book, knew intuitively when it was time to stop and we have both now retired from academia.

Diana Watt can be found at the Louise Da Cocodia Education Trust, where she is a Trustee. The Trust uses community-based research to deliver programmes that support African and Caribbean families, children and young people. As stated in its publicity materials, 'The Trust is passionate about the value of education in transforming lives. We believe in educating our children and young people to make progress aimed at ensuring that they develop into resilient and confident members of society who are leaders in areas of education, employment and enterprise. (https://www.dacocodiatrust.org.uk/). Diana is clearly continuing the Abasindi legacy.

Adele Jones continues to write from her adopted home in Barbados, where she is based. Her writing primarily focuses on violence against women and girls. She states "I've got 40 years of experience of working with women and children to get down on paper – I guess I'll be tied up for the next 40 years". Her retirement reflections can be found here: https://listentomyworld.co.uk/professor-adele-jones/.

Conclusion

Unsung Stories of Black Women's Activism in the UK: Spirits of Resistance and Resilience is a celebration of Black women's activism and provides unique insights into issues that impact Black women and their families including immigration, education, policing, domestic violence and poverty. We have drawn on decades of community activism and scholarly analysis to weave together the story of the Abasindi Cooperative, a woman's organisation famed for its progressive and far-reaching social justice programmes. The book forefronts the experiences and voices of Black women in the UK—'*the Black woman positioned as plot rather than marginalised as plot space*', fundamental to which are identity, language and self-representation. But the book also goes beyond national borders—by exploring links with the trans-Atlantic slave trade, colonialism, the suffragette movement, Pan-Africanism, #Black Lives Matter and the #MeToo movement, its relevance extends to Diasporic communities around the world.

Though this book fills a void in sociological and feminist literature, it is primarily a song in celebration of the unsung voices of Black women activists and the spirits of resistance and resilience that give fire to their bellies (Fig. 8.2).

Fig. 8.2 Spirits of resistance and resilience

References

Abdul-Raheem, T. (Ed.). (1996). *Pan Africanism: Politics, economy and social change in the twenty-first century*. Pluto Press.

Adair, C., & Burt, R. (2013). http://dancehe.org.uk/wp-content/uploads/2014/03/British-Dance-Black-Routes.pdf

Adichie, N. C. (2013). *Americanah: A novel*. Knopf.

Alexander, Z., & Dewjee, A. (Eds.). (1984). *Wonderful adventures of Mrs. Seacole in many lands*. Falling Wall Press.

Alleyne, O. M. (1988). *Roots of Jamaican Culture*. Pluto Press.

Andersen, M., & Collins, P. H. (Eds.). (2001). *Race, class and gender: An anthology* (4th ed., pp. 1–9). Wadsworth.

Andrews, K. (2013). *Resisting racism: Race, inequality, and the Black supplementary school movement*. Trentham Books.

Anonymous. (2003). Letter to a social worker: Reflections on mothering. In A. Douglas & T. Philpot (Eds.), *Adoption: Changing families, changing times*. Routledge.

Ashe, F. (2014). 'All about eve': Mothers, masculinities and the 2011 UK riots. *Political Studies, 62*(3), 652–668.

Associated Press. (May 23, 2022). Olympic champion Caster Semenya says she offered to show track officials her body to prove she was female. https://www.espn.co.uk/olympics/trackandfield/story/_/id/33972416/olympic-champion-caster-semenya-says-offered-show-track-officials-body-prove-was-female

Associated Press. (July 11, 2023). Caster Semenya wins in human rights court, but Paris unlikely. https://www.espn.co.uk/olympics/trackandfield/story/_/id/37993392/caster-semenya-wins-appeal-testosterone-rules-human-rights-court

Association of Women's Rights in Development. (2004). Intersectionality: A tool for gender and economic justice. *Women's Rights and Economic Change, 9*.

Bryan, B., Dadzie, S., & Scafe, S. (2018). *The heart of the race: Black women's lives in Britain*. Verso Books.

Burchill, R. (2009). *Black beauty: aesthetics, stylization, politics*. Ashgate Publishing.

Burman, E., Smailes, S. L., & Chantler, K. (2004). Culture as a barrier to service provision and delivery: domestic violence services for minoritized women. *Critical Social Policy, 2*(3), 332–357.

Campbell, B. (1993). *Goliath: Britain's dangerous places*. Methuen.

Campbell, G. (1990a). History makers. In C. B. Davies & E. S. Fido (Eds.), *Out of the Kumbla*. Africa World Press.

Campbell, M. (1992). Maroons of the Caribbean. Report on the Americas, 25(4), 34–47.

Campbell, M. C. (1990b). *The Maroons of Jamaica 1665-1796*. African World Press, Inc.

Carlton-LaNey, I. B. (2001). *African American Leadership*. NASW Press.

Carrington, B. (1986). Social mobility, ethnicity and sport. *British Journal of Sociology of Education, 7*(1), 4–180.

Carroll, S. (2012). The rights of violence. *Past & Present, 214*(suppl_7), 127–162.

Carter, T. (1986). *Shattering illusions*. Lawrence & Wishart.

Chakrabarti, M., & Hill, M. (2000). *Residential child care: international perspectives on links with families and peers*. Jessica Kingsley.

Cheng, A. A. (2000). Tulsa wounded beauty: an exploratory essay on race, feminism, and the aesthetic question. *Tulsa Studies in Women's Literature, 19*(2), 191–217. University of Tulsa. Retrieved June 11, 2014, from http://www.jstor.org/stable/464426

Chevannes, M., & Reeves, F. (1987). The Black voluntary school movement definition, contexts and prospects. In B. Troyna (Ed.), *Racial inequality in education*. Tavistock.

Clarke, J. (2003). Celebrating struggle: A reflection of Black Women's Stories – The South African Truth and Reconciliation Commission: Conference Report, March 2003.

Clark, K. B., & Clark, M. K. (1939). The development of consciousness of self and the emergence of racial identification in Negro preschool children. *The Journal of Social Psychology, 10*(4), 591–599.

Clark, K. B., & Clark, M. P. (1947). Racial identification and preference in Negro children. In T. M. Newcomb & E. L. Hartley (Eds.), *Readings in social psychology* (pp. 169–178). Holt.

Coard, B. (1971). *How the West Indian child is made educationally sub-normal in the British School System*. New Beacon.

Cohen, S. (2006). *Standing on the shoulders of fascism: from immigration control to the strong state*. Trentham Books.

Collins, M. (1988). Women writers from the Caribbean. *Spare Rib, 94*, 20.

Collins, P. H. (1990). Black feminist thought in the matrix of domination. *Black feminist thought: Knowledge, consciousness, and the politics of empowerment, 138*(1990), 221–238.

Collins, P. H. (1998). The tie that binds: race, gender and U.S. violence. *Ethnic and Racial Studies, 21*, 917–938.

Collins, P. H. (2000). *Black feminist thought: knowledge, consciousness and the politics of empowerment.* Harper Collins.

Collins, S. (1957). *Coloured minorities in Britain.* Lutterworth Press.

Connell, R. W., & Messerschmidt, J. W. (2005). Hegemonic masculinities: rethinking the concept. *Gender and Society, 19*(6), 829–859.

Crenshaw, K. (2023). *On intersectionality: Essential writings.* New Press.

Cross, M. (n.d.). Black unemployment and racial conflict. Evidence submitted to the Scarman Tribunal. *Unpublished.* Available from Research Unit on Ethnic Relations, St Peter's College, Saltley, Birmingham B8 3TE.

Cross, W. E. (1995). In search of blackness and afrocentricity: the psychology of black identity change. In H. W. Harris, H. C. Blue, & E. E. H. Griffith (Eds.), *Racial and ethnic identity psychological development and creative expression.* Routledge.

Cross, W. E., Jr. (1971). *The Negro-to-Black conversion experience* (pp. 13–27). Black World.

Dalphinis, M. (1978). *Approaches to the study of Creole languages – the case for West African language influences.* Black Liberator.

Dargie, D. (1992). *Musical practices of the Xhosa People.* David Phillips.

Davey, A. (1983). *Learning to be prejudiced: Growing up in multi-ethnic Britain.* Edward Arnold.

Davies, C. B., & Ogundipe-Leslie, M. (1995). *International dimensions of Black women's writing.* New York University Press.

Davies, G. (2020). Domestic violence helpline calls surge amid warnings. *The Telegraph* 23 July, https://www.telegraph.co.uk/news/2020/07/23/domestic-violence-helpline-calls-80-june-amid-warnings-surge/

Davis, A. Y. (1981). *Women, race and class.* Random House.

Davis, E., Watt, D., & Packham, C. (2012). *Aspiration and engagement strategies for working with young Black men.* MMU Community Audit and Evaluation Centre.

Day Care Trust. (2011). *Moss Side Ward Report - Central West District.* Day Care Trust. www.manchester.gov.uk/download/downloads/id/.../moss_side_ward.

Day, T. (1994). Sisters under the Skin. *Education Guardian,* 27 September.

Deck, A. (1996). The history of Mary Prince, a West Indian Slave, related by herself. *African American Review, 30*(2), 297–299.

Department of Education and Science. (1985). *Education for all (The Swann Report).* HMSO.

Douglas, J. D. (1985). *'Me Ago England' and 'Culture' Caribbean Man's Blues.* Akira Press.

Dove, N. (1998). *African Mothers.* State University of New York Press.

Dow, G. F. (1927). Slave ships and slavery. In L.A. Fitzpatrick 'African Names and Naming Practices: The impact slavery and European domination had on the African psyche'. *Unpublished dissertation.*

Dumper, H. (2005). *Refugee Council: Making women visible: strategies for a more woman-centred asylum and refugee support system.* Refugee Council.

Edwards-Kerr, D. (2005). Understanding the educational needs of African-Caribbean young men and developing pathways for action. *Unpublished PhD thesis,* Manchester University.

Ekejuiba, A. F. (1995). Gender-responsive agenda for equitable development. In A. O. Pala (Ed.), *Connecting across cultures and continents: Black women speak out on identity, race, and development.* United Nations Development Fund for Woman.

Equality Challenge Unit and Higher Education Academy. (2008). *Ethnicity, gender and degree attainment.* Higher Education Academy.

Fanon, F. (1968). *The wretched of the earth.* Grove Press.

Farrar, M. (1989). 'Better "Mus" Come': rethinking 'community as a radical social imaginary'. *Unpublished essay,* Leeds University.

Felski, R. (2006). "Because it is beautiful": new feminist perspectives on beauty. *Feminist Theory, 7,* 273–282.

Fitzpatrick, L. A. (2012). African names and naming practices: the impact slavery and European domination had on the African psyche. *Unpublished dissertation.*

Flaig, V. (2010). The politics of representation and transmission in the globalization of Guinea's Djembé. (PDF) (Ph.D. thesis), University of Michigan. Retrieved December 10, 2014.

Fook, J., & Askeland, G. A. (2007). Challenges of critical reflection: 'Nothing ventured, nothing gained'. *Social Work Education, 26*(5), 520–533.

Ford Smith, H. (1986). *Lionheart Gal, life stories of Jamaican women.* The Women's Press.

Ford-Smith, H. (1988). *Women and the Garvey Movement in Jamaica. Garvey: his work and impact.* ISER, and UWI Extra Mural Studies Department.

Foster, K., & Francis, A. S. (2020). Black women activists in Britain; Women's histories; British Library. https://www.bl.uk/womens-histories

Frost, D., & Phillips, R. (Eds.). (2011). *Liverpool '81: Remembering the riots.* Liverpool University Press.

Fryer, P. (1984). *Staying power: the history of Black people in Britain.* Pluto Press.

Gewirtz-O'Reilly, E. (2020). The Beginnings of Manchester's Caribbean Carnival – History@Manchester (uomhistory.com).

Gilbert, H. (Ed.). (2001). *Postcolonial plays: An anthology* (1st ed.). Routledge. https://doi.org/10.4324/9781315006147

Gilchrist, E. S., & Thompson, C. (2012). African-American women's perceptions of constitutive meanings of good hair articulated in Black hair magazine advertisements. *Journalism and Mass Communication, 2*(1), 279–293.

Gilchrist, E. S., & Thompson, C. (n.d.). Media effects and Black hair politics. Retrieved July 12, 2014, from http://www.huichawaii.org/assets/gilchrist,-eletra%2D%2D-media-effects-and-black-hair-politics.pdf

Gillborn, D. (2004). Racism, policy and contemporary schooling: Current inequities and future possibilities. *Sage Race Relations Abstracts, 29*(2), 5–33.

Gilman, S. (1992). Black bodies, white bodies: toward an iconography of female sexuality in late nineteenth-century art, medicine and literature. In J. Donald & A. Rattansi (Eds.), *Race, culture and difference*. Sage.

Gilman, S. L. (1985). Black bodies, white bodies: toward an iconography of female sexuality in late nineteenth-century art, medicine, and literature. In H. L. Gates Jr. & K. A. Appiah (Eds.), *"Race", writing, and difference*. University of Chicago Press.

Gilroy, P. (1987). *There Ain't No Black in the Union Jack*. Hutchinson.

Glass, R., & Pollins, H. (1960). *Newcomers: The West Indians in London*. University College London Centre for Urban Studies, and Allen and Unwin.

Gower, M. (2013). *Ending child immigration detention*. House of Commons Library.

Graham, M. (2007). Giving voice to black children: An analysis of social agency. *British Journal of Social Work, 37*(8), 1305–1317.

Graham, M., & Robinson, G. (2004). "The silent catastrophe": Institutional racism and the underachievement of black boys in the British educational system. *Journal of Black Studies, 34*(5), 653–671.

Gramsci, A., & Hoare, Q. (1978). *Selections from political writings (1921-1926): With additional texts by other Italian communist leaders*. Lawrence and Wishart.

Grannum, G. (2011). Researching African-Caribbean Family history. In L.A. Fitzpatrick 'Names and Naming Practices: The impact slavery and European domination had on the African psyche'. *Unpublished dissertation*.

Haaken, J. (2002). Stories of survival: class, race and domestic violence. In N. Holstrom (Ed.), *The socialist feminist project: a contemporary reader in theory and practice*. Monthly Review Press.

Hamnett, C. (1983). The conditions in England's inner cities on the eve of the 1981 riots. *Area*, 7–13.

Hanmer, J., & Itzin, C. (Eds.). (2000). *Home truths about domestic violence*. Routledge.

Haraway, D. (1989a). Teddy bear patriarchy: Taxidermy in the Garden of Eden, New York City, 1908–36. In D. Haraway (Ed.), *Primate visions: Gender, race, and nature in the world of modern science*. Routledge.

Haraway, D. (1992). Ecce homo, ain't (ar'n't) I a woman, and inappropriate/d others: The human in a post-humanist landscape. *Feminists Theorize the Political*, 86–100.

Haraway, D. J. (1989b). *Primate visions: Gender, race, and nature in the world of modern science*. Routledge.

Harker, R. (2012). *Children in care in England: Statistics*. Retrieved July 20, 2014, from www.parliament.uk/briefing-papers/sn04470.pdf

Henrique, F. (1960). *Jamaica, land of wood and water*. MacGibbon & Kee.

Hey, V. (1998). Reading the community: A critique of some post/modern narratives about citizenship and civil society. In P. Baguley & G. Hearn (Eds.), *Transforming the political*. Macmillan.

Hick, P., Arshad, R., & Watt, D. (2011). *Promoting cohesion, challenging expectations: Educating the teachers of tomorrow for race quality and diversity in 21st century schools*. https://www.research.ed.ac.uk/en/publications/promoting-cohesionchallenging-expectations-educating-the-teacher

Hick, P., Arshad, R., Watt, D., & Mitchell, L. (2011). Promoting cohesion, challenging expectations: Educating the teachers of tomorrow for race quality and diversity in 21st century schools. *ESCalate*. http://www.esri.mmu.ac.uk/resstaff/Promoting%20Cohesion%20Challenging%20Expectations.pdf

Higgs, L. (2011). Youth services are slashed in riot-hit areas. *Children & Young People Now*. Retrieved September 14, 2013, from www.cypnow.co.uk/cyp/news/1049494/youth-services-slashed-riot-hit

Higher Education Network. (2013). Race equality in academia: time to establish black studies in the UK? *The Guardian*, Thursday 25 July 2013.

Hill Collins, P. (1998). Intersections of race, class, gender, and nation: some implications for Black family studies. *Journal of Comparative Family Studies, 29*(1), 27–34.

Hill, R. B. (2003). *The strengths of Black families*. University Press of America.

Hinds, D. (2008). Claudia Jones and the 'West Indian Gazette'. Retrieved December 29, 2014, from http://www.irr.org.uk/news/claudia-jones-and-the-west-indian-gazette

HMSO. (1981). West Indian Children in our Schools: Interim report of the Committee on Inquiry into the Education of Children from Minority Groups. Cmd 8273. : Her Majesty's Stationery Office, 1981.

Holmes, R. (2007). *African Queen: The real life of the Hottentot Venus*. Random House.

hooks, b. (1994). *Outlaw culture: Resisting representations*. Routledge.

hooks, b. (1997a). *Killing rage, ending racism*. Holt Paperbacks.

hooks, b. (1997b). Selling hot pussy: Representations of black female sexuality in the cultural marketplace. In K. Conboy, N. Medina, & S. Stanbury (Eds.), *Writing on the body: Female embodiment and feminist theory*. Columbia University Press.

Hooks, B. (2003). *Teaching community: A pedagogy of hope* (Vol. 36). Psychology Press.

http://www.jamaica-gleaner.com/gleaner/20040509/cleisure/cleisure5html. Retrieved March 13, 2015.

http://www.The Telegraph.co.uk/news/worldnews/Nelson Mandela/105/. Retrieved October 14, 2014.

http://www.theguardian.com/higher-education-network/blog/2013/jul/25/race-equality-academia-curriculum. Retrieved October 26, 2014.

Hull, G. T., Scott, P. B., & Smith, B. (Eds.). (1982). *All the women are white and all the blacks are men, but some of us are brave*. Feminist Press.

Hunter, M. (2005). *Race, gender and the politics of skin tone*. Routledge.

Hytner, B. (1981). *Report of the moss side enquiry to the leader of the GMC*. Greater Manchester Council.

IMKAAN. (2017). *Safe pathways? Exploring an intersectional approach to addressing violence against women and girls – Good Practice Briefing.* Ascent (London VAWG Consortium). Available from https://thelondonvawgconsortium.org.uk/wp-content/uploads/2017/03/CORRECT-Good-Practice-BriefingImkaan-Intersectionality.pdf

IMKAAN. (2020). The impact of the dual pandemics: Violence against women & girls and Covid–19 on black and minoritised women & girls.

Impey, A. (1998). Popular music in Africa. In R. Stone (Ed.), *The garland encyclopaedia of world music.* Garland Publishing, Inc.

Institute of Race Relations. (2013). Legal aid cuts: Exclusion from justice – IRR Briefing Paper No.7. Retrieved November 10, 2014, from http://www.irr.org.uk/pdf2/IRR_Briefing_No.7.pdf

International Rescue Committee. (2012). *Let me not die before my time: domestic violence in West Africa.* IRC.

Jackson, R. L. (2006). *Scripting the Black masculine body: Identity, discourse, and racial politics in popular media.* State University of New York Press.

Jacobs, M. (25 April 2022). *The causes and consequences of the 1981 Moss Side Riots.* Manchester Historian; The Causes and Conclusions of the 1981 Moss Side Riots, by Millie Jacobs – Manchester Historian.

Jacques Garvey, A. (1972). The role of women in liberation struggles. *The Massachusetts Review, 13*(1/2), 109–112.

Jarrett-MacCauley, D. (1998). *The life of Una Marson, 1905-65.* Manchester University Press.

Javed, H. M. (2012). *What does it mean to move from magical consciousness to critical consciousness?* Unpublished diss., Manchester Metropolitan University.

Jenkinson, J. (2009). *Black 1919: Riots, racism and resistance in imperial Britain.* Liverpool University Press.

Jones, A., & Waul, D. (2005). Residential care for black children. In D. Crimmens & I. Milligan (Eds.), *Facing forward: Residential care in the 21st century.* Russell House Publishing.

Jones, A. D., & Jemmott, E. T. (2014). Status, privilege and gender inequality: Cultures of male impunity and entitlement in the sexual abuse of children: Perspectives from a Caribbean study. *International Social Work,* 0020872814537853.

Joseph Rowntree Foundation. (2017). *Patterns of poverty in Greater Manchester's neighbourhoods.* https://hummedia.manchester.ac.uk/institutes/mui/igau/growth-monitor/GM-MSOA-poverty-briefing-note-2017.pdf

Kankpeyeng, B. W. (2009). The slave trade in northern Ghana: Landmarks, legacies and connections. *Slavery and Abolition, 30*(2), 209–221.

Kara, M., & Figen Özgür, F. (2023). Perception of beauty in different cultures. In İ. Vargel & F. F. Özgür (Eds.), *Beauty, aging, and anti-aging* (pp. 11–19. ISBN 9780323988049). Academic Press. https://doi.org/10.1016/B978-0-323-98804-9.00018-9

Karn, V. (1983). Race and housing in Britain: the role of major institutions. In N. Glazer & K. Young (Eds.), *Ethnic pluralism and public policy*. Heinemann.

Kasturirangan, A., Krishnan, S., & Riger, S. (2004). The impact of culture and minority status on women's experience of domestic violence. *Trauma, Violence, & Abuse, 5*(4), 318–332.

King, M. (1973). The politics of sexual stereotypes. *Black Scholar, 4*, 6–7.

King, M. C. (1973). The politics of sexual stereotypes. *The Black Scholar, 4*(6–7), 12–23.

King, J. E. (Ed.). (2006). *Black education: A transformative research and action agenda for the new century*. Routledge.

Kirwen, M. C. (2008). *African cultural domains, Book 1*. MIAS Books.

Kundnani, A. (2007a). *Echoes of empire: racism, migration and the war on terror*. Pluto Press. Retrieved October 10, 2014, from http://www.ebrary.com

Kundnani, A. (2007b). *The end of tolerance: racism in 21st century Britain*. Pluto Press.

La Rose, J., John, G., & Johnson, L. K. (2011). *The New Cross Massacre Story: Interviews with John La Rose*. New Beacon Books.

Larrabee, M. J. (2006). "I know what a slave knows": Mary Prince's epistemology of resistance. *Women's Studies: An inter-disciplinary journal, 35*, 453–473.

Lawrence, D. (1974). *Black migrants: White natives: a study of race relations in Nottingham*. Cambridge University Press.

Lea, J., & Hallsworth, S. (2012). Understanding the riots. *Criminal Justice Matters, 87*(1), 30–31.

Lea, J., & Young, J. (1982). The riots in Britain 1981: Urban violence and political marginalisation. In D. Cowell, D. Jones, & J. Young (Eds.), *Policing the riots*. Junction Books.

Lee, J. A. B. (2001). *The empowerment approach to social work practice: building the beloved community* (2nd ed.). Columbia University Press.

Lewis, D. (2011). Claudia Jones: Beyond Containment Autobiographical Reflections, Essays and Poems, edited by Carole Boyce Davies [Review of *Claudia Jones: Beyond Containment Autobiographical Reflections, Essays and Poems*, by C. B. Davies]. *Agenda: Empowering Women for Gender Equity, 25*(4(90)), 118–120. http://www.jstor.org/stable/23287210

Lewis, G. (1994). Black women's employment and the British economy. In W. James & C. Harris (Eds.), *Inside Babylon: the Caribbean diaspora in Britain* (pp. 73–96). Verso.

Lewis, G. (2005). Situated voices: 'Black women's experience' and social work. In *Feminist review* (pp. 24–56). Routledge.

Lewis, G., & Cohen, R. (2011). *Gail Lewis interviewed by Rachel Cohen* (Sisterhood and After: The Women's Liberation Oral History Project). https://www.bl.uk/collection-items/gail-lewis-black-feminist-texts

Li, S. (2006). Motherhood as resistance in Harriet Jacobs's incidents in the life of a slave girl. *Legacy, 23*(1), 14–29. University of Nebraska Press. Retrieved January 2, 2015, from Project MUSE database.

Limb, M. (2023). Black women in England are at greater risk of late cancer diagnosis than white women. *BMJ, 380*, 211. https://doi.org/10.1136/bmj.p211

Lorde, A. (1995). *The Black Unicorn: Poems*. Norton and Company.

Lovejoy, P. (2007). Review of African Queen: The real life of the Hottentot Venus, by Rachel Holmes. *Journal of Historical Biography, 2*, 97–99. Retrieved June 13, 2014, from www.ufv.ca/jhb

Loveys, K. (2011). School that banned 11-year-old boy for having 'cornrow' hairstyle was 'racist', High Court judge rules. 18 June 2011, Daily Mail On-line. Retrieved July 15, 2014, from http://www.dailymail.co.uk/news/article-2004693/School-banned-11-year-old-boy-having-cornrow-hairstyle-racist-High-Court-judge-rules.html#ixzz37qoJnJtJ

Maathai, W. (2007). *Unbowed – One woman's story*. William Heinemann.

Mama, A., & London Race and Housing Research Unit. (1989). *The hidden struggle: Statutory and voluntary sector responses to violence against black women in the home*. London Race and Housing Research Unit.

Manchester Evening News. (July 6, 2011a). Moss Side riots: Doctor who had to help despite the risks. http://menmedia.co.uk/manchestereveningnews/news/s/1425816_moss-side-riots-doctor-who-had-to-help-despite-the-risks

Manchester Evening News. (July 9, 2011b). Special Report: Moss Side Riots, 30 years on http://www.manchestereveningnews.co.uk/news/greater-manchester-news/moss-side-riots-the-night-years-864536

Mann, S. A., & Grimes, M. D. (2001). Common and contested ground: Marxism and race, gender & class analysis. *Race, Gender & Class*, 3–22.

Marco, J. L. (2012). *Hair representations among Black South African women: Exploring identity and notions of beauty*. Doctoral dissertation, University of South Africa.

Matthews, M. D. (1979). "Our women and what they think": Amy Jacques Garvey and the Negro World. *Black Scholar: Journal of Black Studies and Research, 10*, 8–9.

Maxime, A. J. (1986). Some psychological models of black self-concept. In S. Ahmed, J. Cheetham, & J. Small (Eds.), *Social work with children and their families*. Batsford.

Mcilwaine, C., Granada, L., & Valenzuela-Oblitas, I. (2019). *The right to be believed: Migrant women facing Violence Against Women and Girls (VAWG) in the 'hostile immigration environment'* in London. https://doi.org/10.13140/RG.2.2.31107.35367

Mercer, K. (1994). *Welcome to the jungle: New positions in black cultural studies*. Routledge.

Mercer, K. (2000). Black hair/style politics. In K. Owusu (Ed.), *Black British culture & society*. Routledge.

Messerschmidt, J. W. (2000). *Nine lives: Adolescent masculinities, the body, and violence*. Westview.

Milburn, K. (2012). The August riots, shock and the prohibition of thought. *Capital & Class, 36*(3), 401–409.

Minh-ha, T. T. (1989). *Postcoloniality and feminism*. Indiana University Press.

Minshall, P. (2000). "To Play Mas"; Towards 2000 – Models for multi-cultural arts education. *Caribbean Quarterly, 45*(2/3), 30–35.

Mirza, H. S. (2009). Plotting a history: Black and postcolonial feminisms in 'new times'. *Race, Ethnicity and Education, 12*(1), 1–10.

Morokvasic, M. (1983). Women in migration: beyond the reductionist outlook. In A. Phizacklea (Ed.), *One way ticket, migration and female labour*. Routledge & Kegan Paul.

Morrison, T. (1994). *The Bluest Eye*. Plume.

Muir, H., & Adegoke, Y. (2011). Were the riots about race. In *The Manchester guardian*, Thursday 8 Dec 2011. https://www.theguardian.com/uk/2011/dec/08/were-the-riots-about-race

Naples, N. A. (1998). *Grassroots warriors*. Routledge.

National Union of Students. (2010). *Race for Equality, A report on the experiences of Black students in further and higher education,* National Union of Students. Retrieved October 26, 2014, from www.nus.org.uk/PageFiles/12350/NUS_Race_for_Equality_web.pdf

NCB. (n.d.). Good outcomes working with black and minority ethnic children. Retrieved July 20, 2014, from www.ncb.org.uk/media/.../ncercc_goodoutcomeswithbmechildreninrcc

Ndlovu, C. (1991). *Transcription of African Music*. Unpublished paper presented at the African Music conference at the University of Venda, South Africa.

Nettleford, R. M., & LaYacona, M. (1985). *Dance Jamaica: Cultural definition and artistic discovery: The National Dance Theatre Company of Jamaica, 1962-1983*. Grove Press.

New York Times. (July 22, 1981). Reports of Police Abuse Studied in Manchester. http://www.nytimes.com/1981/07/22/world/reports-of-police-abuse-studied-in-manchester.html

Newburn, T. (2012). 30 years after Brixton, what would Lord Scarman have made of the 2011 riots? *The Guardian*. Retrieved November 2, 2014, from www.theguardian.com/uk/2012/jul/01/brixton-lord-scarman-2011-riots

Newburn, T., Lewis, P., & Metcalf, J. (2011). A new kind of riot? From Brixton 1981 to Tottenham 2011. *The Guardian*. Retrieved October 20, 2013, from www.guardian.co.uk/uk/2011/dec/09/riots-1981-2011-differences

Nixon, J., & Humphreys, C. (2010). Marshalling the evidence: Using intersectionality in the domestic violence frame. *Social Politics: International Studies in Gender, State & Society, 17*(2), 137–158.

Nnaemeka, O. (1997). *The politics of (M) mothering*. Routledge.

North, A. (May 3, 2019). "I am a woman and I am fast": what Caster Semenya's story says about gender and race in sports, https://www.vox.com/identities/2019/5/3/18526723/caster-semenya-800-gender-race-intersex-athletes

Nuttall, S. (2006). Rethinking beauty. In S. Nuttall (Ed.), *Beautiful ugly: African and diaspora aesthetics*. Duke University Press.

Nyamnjoh, F. B., Durham, D., & Fokwang, J. D. (2002). The domestication of hair and modernised consciousness in Cameroon: A critique in the context of globalisation. *Identity, Culture and Politics, 3*(2), 98–124.

Obadina, T. (1997). *Pan Africanism: Politics, economy and social change in the twenty-first Century.* Oxfam.

Olusoga, D. (2023). The ties that bind us. In *The cotton capital – How slavery shaped the guardian.* Britain and the Rest of the World. https://www.theguardian.com/news/ng-interactive/2023/mar/28/slavery-and-the-guardian-the-ties-that-bind-us

Omalade, B. (1994). *The rising song of African-American women.* Routledge.

Owen, C., & Statham, J. (2009). *Disproportionality in child welfare* (The prevalence of Black and minority ethnic children within the 'looked after' and 'children in need' populations and on child protection registers in England). UK Department for Children, Schools and Families.

Palmer, G., & Kenway, P. (2007). *Poverty rates among ethnic groups in Great Britain.* Joseph Rowntree Foundation. Retrieved November 10, 2014, from http://www.jrf.org.uk/publications/poverty-rates-among-ethnic-groups-great-britain

Pan African Development Education and Advocacy Programme. http://www.padeap.net/the-history-of-pan-africanism

Pankhurst, E. (2015). *My Own Story (1914) Vintage Classics.* Penguin Books. ISBN: 9781784871253.

Parham, T. A. (1989). Cycles of psychological nigrecense. *The Counseling Pyschologist, 17*(2), 187–226.

Pedraza, S. (1991). Women and migration: The social consequences of gender. *Annual Review of Sociology, 17*(1), 303–325.

Patterson, S. (1965). *Dark strangers: A study of West Indians in London.* Penguin.

Phillips, J., Ray, K., & Barnes, H. (2007). *Social cohesion in diverse communities.* Joseph Rowntree Foundation.

Phillips, M., & Phillips, T. (1998). *Windrush.* Harper Collins.

Phillips, M., & Phillips, T. (1998). *Windrush: The irresistible rise of multi-racial Britain.* Harper Collins.

Phillips, R. (1975). The Black Masses and the political economy of Manchester – Introduction. *The Black Liberator, 3*(3), 290–300.

Phinney, J. S. (1990). Ethnic identity in adolescents. *Psychological Bulletin, 108*(3), 499–514.

Phizacklea, A. (Ed.). One way ticket, migration and female labour. Routledge & Kegan Paul.

Pilkington, A. (2003). *Racial disadvantage and ethnic diversity in Britain.* Palgrave Macmillan.

Platts-Fowler, D. (2013). "Beyond the loot": Social disorder and urban unrest. *The British Society of Criminology, 13*, 17–32. University of Leeds www.brit-soccrim.org

Plowden Report. (1967). *Children and their primary school.* HMSO.

Politics.Co.UK. (n.d.). 'Unemployment'. Retrieved October 25, 2014, from http://www.politics.co.uk/reference/unemployment

Pollard, T. F. (2011). *The Black British Boy: "Expressions of Masculine Cultural Identity".* Routledge.

Pool, H. (2009). I'll tell you why a small doll causes such a big fuss. *The Guardian,* 6 Feb. https://www.theguardian.com/media/2009/feb/06/bbc-race-golliwog

Prasad, R. (2011). Rebels with a cause: Rioters Claim Payback against the Police. *The Guardian,* 5 December.

Prince, M. (1831). The history of Mary Prince a West Indian Slave. *Project Gutenberg.* Retrieved December 12, 2014, from http://www.gutenberg.org/ebooks/17851

Pryce, K. (1979). *Endless pressure: A study of West Indian lifestyles in Bristol.* Penguin.

Ramdhanie, B. (2005). African dance in England: spirituality and continuity. *Doctoral dissertation,* University of Warwick. Retrieved December 10, 2014, from http://webcat.warwick.ac.uk/record=b2072944~S9

Ramdin, R. (1987). *The making of the black working class in Britain.* Gower.

Rampton, A. (1981). *West Indian children in our schools; Interim Report of the Committee of Inquiry into the Education of Children from Ethnic Minority Groups.* Her Majesty's Stationery Office. http://www.educationengland.org.uk/documents/rampton/rampton1981.html

REACH. (2007). *An independent report to government on raising aspiration and attainment of black boys and young black men.* Department for Communities and Local Government. Retrieved August 8, 2014, from dera.101.ac.uk/7609/1reach-report.pdf.

Reay, D., & Mirza, H. S. (1997). Uncovering genealogies of the margin: Black supplementary schooling. *British Journal of Sociology of Education, 18*(4), 477–499.

Rex, J. (1982). The 1981 urban riots in Britain. *International Journal of Urban and Regional Research, 6*(1), 99–113.

Rhamie, J., & Hallam, S. (2002). An investigation into African-Caribbean academic success in the UK. *Race, Ethnicity and Education, 5*(2), 151–170.

Richardson, J. T. E. (2008). The attainment of ethnic minority students in UK higher education. *Studies in Higher Education, 33*–48.

Richie, B. E. (2000). A black feminist reflection on the antiviolence movement. *Signs, 25*(4), 1133–1137.

Riley, D. W. (2002). *The complete Kwanzaa.* Castle Books.

Ristock, J. L. (2002). *No more secrets: violence in Lesbian relationships.* Routledge.

Rollock, N. (2019). *Staying power: The career experiences and strategies of UK Black female professors*; ucu_rollock_february_2019.pdf

Rooks, N. M. (2000). *Hair raising: beauty, culture and African American women.* Rutgers University Press.

Roots Oral History. (1992). *Rude awakening: African Caribbean settlers in Manchester – An account.* Roots Oral History Project.

Rowe, J. A. (2023). *Jomo Kenyatta. Encyclopedia Britannica.* https://www.britannica.com/biography/Jomo-Kenyatta

Russo, N. F., & Pirlott, A. (2006). Gender-based violence. *Annals of the New York Academy of Sciences, 1087*(1), 178–205.

Safety4Sisters. (2010). *Working towards securing greater protection, safety and support for women who have experienced gender violence and who have no recourse to public funds or state benefits.* Retrieved October 27, 2014, from www.wast.org.uk/new/.../plugin-A-Practitioners-Guide-Feb-2010.pdf

Safety4Sisters. (2021). *Locked in abuse, locked out of safety; The pandemic experiences of migrant women.* https://www.safety4sisters.org/

Sallah, M., & Howson, C. (2007). *Working with Black young people.* Russell House Publishing.

Scarman, L. (1981). *The Brixton Disorders, 10th-12th April, 1981.* HMSO.

Schaffe, T. (2009). *Abasindi.* MA Television Documentary, University of Salford.

Schramm, K. (2009). Negotiating race: Blackness and Whiteness in the context of homecoming to Ghana. *African Diaspora, 2*(1), 3–24.

Segal, L. (1995). A feminist look at the family. In J. Muncie, M. Wetherell, R. Dallos, & A. Cochrane (Eds.), *Understanding the family.* Sage.

Selvon, S. (1956). *The Lonely Londoners.* Wingate.

Senoga-Zake, G. W. (1986). *Folk music in Kenya.* Act Printing Ltd.

Sewell, T. (1997). *Black masculinities and schooling: How black boys survive modern schooling.* Trentham Books.

Sheperd, V. A. (1999). *Women in Caribbean history.* Ian Randle.

Shepherd, V. (2006). Knowledge production and the construction of 'Africa(ns)' in the Caribbean. *International Journal of African Renaissance Studies, 1*(1), 129–146.

Shepherd, V., Brereton, B., & Bailey, R. (1995). *Engendering history.* Ian Randle.

Sherwood, M. (1999). *Claudia Jones.* Lawrence & Wishart.

Shiloah, A. (1995). *Music in the World of Islam: A socio-cultural study.* Wayne State University Press.

Short, G. (1985). Teacher expectation and West Indian underachievement. *Educational Research, 27*(2), 95–101. https://doi.org/10.1080/0013188850270202

Sissay, L. (2019). *My name is why.* Canongate Books.

Sistren Theatre Collective and Ford-Smith, H. (1986). *Lionheart gal: Life stories of Jamaican women.* The Women's Press.

Small, J. (1984). The crisis in adoption. *International Journal of Social Psychiatry, 30*(1/2), 129–142.

Smith, M. (2020). *5 Essential Black Figures In The Women's Suffrage Movement,* GBH, 5 Essential Black Figures In The Women's Suffrage Movement (wgbh.org).

Sokoloff, N. J., & Dupont, I. (2005). Domestic violence at the intersections of race, class, and gender: Challenges and contributions to understanding violence against marginalized women in diverse communities. *Violence Against Women, 11*(1), 38–64.

Solomos, J. (1993). *Race and racism in Britain.* Macmillan.

Solomos, J. (2011). Race, rumours and riots: past, present and future. *Sociological Research Online, 16,* 4.

Spellers, R., & Moffitt, K. (2010). *Blackberries and redbones: Critical articulations of black hair/body politics in Africana communities*. Hampton Press.

Stallard, M. (2023). Cotton, slavery & the rise of modern Manchester, *The Cotton Capital – How Slavery Shaped the Guardian, Britain and the Rest of the World*, The Manchester Guardian Special Issue, pp. 17–18.

Sterling, L. (1995). Partners: The social organisations of rotating savings and credit societies among exilic Jamaicans. *Sociology, 29*(4), 653–666.

Stirling, S. (2009). Manchester Conference for Black Parents, Children and Young People - Public Engagement Fellowship Conference Report.

Stone, M. (1981). *The education of the black child: the myth of multi-cultural education*. Fontana Press.

Stone, R. (1998). *Africa, the garland encyclopaedia of world music*. Garland Publishing Inc.

Strand, S. (2010). Do some schools narrow the gap? Differential school effectiveness by ethnicity, gender, poverty and prior attainment. *School Effectiveness and School Improvement, 21*(3), 289–314.

Sudbury, J. (1998). *'Other Kinds of Dreams': Black women's organisations and the politics of transformation*. Routledge.

Swaby, N. (2010). Amy Ashwood Garvey: A Revolutionary Pan African Feminist. Retrieved December 23, 2024, from http.//revisionist.com

Tannenbaum, C., & Bekker, S. (2019). Sex, gender, and sports. *BMJ, 364*, l1120. https://doi.org/10.1136/bmj.l1120

Tate, S. (2005). *Black Skins, Black Masks: Hybridity, dialogism, performativity*. Ashgate.

Tate, S. (2007). What's shade got to do with it? Anti-racist aesthetics and Black Beauty. *Ethnic and Racial Studies, 30*(2), 300–319.

Taylor, S. (1984). The Scarman Report and explanations of riots. In J. Benyon (Ed.), *Scarman and after: Essays reflecting on Lord Scarman's Report, the riots and their aftermath*. Pergamon Press.

The Guardian. (9 March 2014). (Ed Pilkington), Caribbean nations prepare demand for slavery reparations. http://www.theguardian.com/world/2014/mar/09/caribbean-nations-demand-slavery-reparations

The Guardian. (7 May 2023). Home office accused of being 'unashamedly racist' towards Sudanese. https://www.theguardian.com/world/2023/may/07/home-office-accused-of-being-unashamedly-racist-towards-sudanese

The Guardian Higher Education Network. (25 July 2013). http://www.theguardian.com/higher-education-network/blog/2013/jul/25/race-equality-academia-curriculum

The Guardian/London School of Economics. (2011). Reading the Riots: Investigating England's Summer of Disorder. Retrieved September 30, 2014, from http://www.guardian.co.uk/uk/interactive/2011/dec/14/reading-the-riots-investigating-england-s-summer-of-disorder-full-report

The Runnymede Trust. (1997). *Black and ethnic minority young people and educational disadvantage*. Runnymede Trust.

The Runnymede Trust. (n.d.). *The struggle for racial equality: an oral history of the Runnymede Trust, 1966-1988*. Retrieved October 4, 2014, from http://www.runnymedetrust.org/histories/race-equality/83/repatriation-demand.html

Thiam, A. (1978). *Black sisters: speak out, feminism and oppression in Black Africa*. Pluto Press.

Thompson, C. (2009). Black women, beauty, and hair as a matter of being. *Women's Studies, 38*, 831–856.

Thomson, R., Bell, R., Holland, J., Henderson, S., McGrellis, S., & Sharpe, S. (2002). Critical moments: Choice, chance and opportunity in young people's narratives of transition. *Sociology, 36*(2), 335–354.

Times Higher Education 6.4.14. *'Race discrimination in universities still a problem, reports survey'* www.timeshighereducation.co.uk/news/race...in...a.../2012474. article

Topping, A., Diski, R., & Clifton, H. (2011). Women and the riots. In D. Roberts (Ed.), *Reading the riots: Investigating England's summer of disorder (guardian shorts)*. The Guardian.

Ung, T., O'Connor, S. H., & Pillidge, R. (2012). The development of racial identity in transracially adopted people: an ecological approach. *Adoption & Fostering, 36*, 73.

United Nations Convention on the Rights of the Child. (1989). www.unicef.org.crc/

Venner, M. (1981). The disturbances in Moss Side, Manchester. *New Community, 9*(3), 374–377.

Voice for the Child in Care. (2004). *The care experience: through black eyes*. Voice for the Child in Care.

W.I.O.C.C. (1995). Report of a Conference on 'Black Values Versus State Education', Manchester.

Wain, N., & Joyce, P. (2012). Disaffected communities, riots and policing: Manchester 1981 and 2011. *Safer Communities, 1*(3), 125–134.

Walker, A. (1983). *In search of our mothers' garden, womanist prose*. The Women's Press.

Watt, D. (1994). The effectiveness of the Strategy to Elevate People (STEP) project in raising the self-esteem of inner city pupils. *Unpublished dissertation*, University of Manchester.

Watt, D. (2002). Motherhood and mothering – The experience of three generations of Jamaican-heritage women. *Unpublished dissertation*, Manchester Metropolitan University. Retrieved March 3, 2014, from www.wearethebelovedcommunity.org/bcquotes.html

Webster, W. (1998). *Imagining home: Gender, 'race' and national identity, 1945-64*. UCL Press.

Weekes, D. (1997). Shades of blackness: Young black female constructions of beauty. In *Black British feminism: A reader* (pp. 113–126). Routledge.

Weiler, K. (2009). The history of women's education and the construction of the modern subject. *Journal of Women's History, 21*(2), 177–184.

Weiner, G. (1997). 'New Era or Old Times: Class, Gender and Education', South Bank University, Paper Presented at The British Educational Research Association Annual Conference: University of York. Retrieved October 27, 2014, from www. Leeds.Ac.Uk/Educol/Documents/000000357.Htm

Welsh, K. (2004). *African Dance*. Chelsea House Publishers.

White, G. (1985). Black access to higher education. In P. D. Pumfrey & G. K. Verma (Eds.), *Race relations and urban education: contexts and promising practices*. Psychology Press. Retrieved October 4, 2014, from www.leeds.ac.uk/educol/documents/000000200.htm

White, S. B. (2005). Releasing the pursuit of bouncin' and behavin' hair: natural hair as an Afrocentric feminist aesthetic for beauty. *International Journal of Media & Cultural Politics, 1*(3), 295–308.

Williams, F. (1997). Women and community. In J. Barnett *Community Care, A Reader*. Retrieved December 1, 2014, from www.usatoday.com/story/news/nation.now.mandela.../388469

Willis, D. (Ed.). (2010). *Black Venus 2010: they called her 'Hottentot'*. Temple University Press.

Wolfe-Robinson, M. (Ed.). (2023). The cotton capital – How slavery shaped the guardian. In *Britain and the rest of the world*. The Manchester Guardian Special Issue. https://www.theguardian.com/news/series/cotton-capital

Women's Aid. (2019). *The Domestic Abuse Report 2019: The economics of abuse*. Women's Aid.

Woodward, K. (1997). Introduction. In K. Woodward (Ed.), *Identity and difference*. Sage in Association with the Open University.

Wright, C., Standen, P., & Patel, T. (2010). *Black youth matters – Transitions from school to success*. Routledge.

Zephaniah, B. (2005). Over and out. In B. Richardson (Ed.), *Tell It like it is: How our schools fail Black children*. Bookmarks Publications, Trentham Books.

Printed in the USA
CPSIA information can be obtained
at www.ICGtesting.com
CBHW060917101024
15650CB00005B/59

9 783031 642005